"Tried as by Fire"

Tried as by Fire

Southern Baptists and the Religious Controversies of the 1920s

James J. Thompson, Jr.

Mercer University Press

All books published by Mercer University Press are produced
on acid-free paper which exceeds the minimum standards set by the
National Historical Publications and Records Commission.

Library of Congress Cataloging in Publication Data

Thompson, James J., 1944-
    Tried as by fire.

    Bibliography: p. 217
    Includes index.
    1. Theology, Baptist—History—20th century.
2. Southern Baptist Convention—History—20th century.   I. title.
BX6207.S68T47   1982   286'.132   82-8056
ISBN   0-86554-032-2   AACR2

124178

To
My Mother
Mildred Thompson
and
to the Memory of My Grandmother
Mildred Holland

Table of Contents

Preface

I began this study as a way of combining my interest in three topics: religion, the South, and the 1920s. I then decided to put one Southern denomination in the spotlight and examine how this particular segment of Protestantism fought out the issues raised in a decade rife with religious controversy. None of these issues was unique to the 1920s; since the late nineteenth century, debates over evolution, biblical criticism, social action, Roman Catholicism, and the decline of rural America had sundered American Protestantism into quarreling factions. But during the 1920s these debates reached a level of intensity and bitterness that had not existed before, and in most cases would not exist again after the decade had passed.

I especially wanted to analyze the controversies of the decade as they involved Southern Baptists, for though these people comprise one of the most important denominations in the history of American religious development, they have often been shunted off to the margins of serious historical study. That hardly seems justified, when today the Southern Baptist Convention boasts the largest membership of any Protestant group in the world. Given this fact, the study of Southern Baptist history attracted me as an opportunity to understand better some of the forces that have shaped the religious configuration of present-day America.

Intellectually, then, my chosen topic offered considerable attraction, but the scholar works with his heart as well as his head. In my case, personal reasons added to my scholarly interest in Southern Baptists. As one raised by the canons of what has often disparagingly been called that "old-time religion," I sought in the study of the South's Baptists answers to questions that had vexed me for many years. With my labors now at an end I realize that I have found some of these elusive answers, but I have also discovered new questions; old religious dilemmas have given way to new ones. Still, I continue to believe that by examining the sources from which we spring we can come at least a bit closer to understanding ourselves. As William Faulkner, a man not untouched by the old-time religion, once wrote: "The past is never dead. It's not even past."

Acknowledgments

This book began as a doctoral dissertation in the Department of History of the University of Virginia. I am indebted to two professors there: Paul Gaston started me on the study of Southern history and directed me toward Southern religion; and Joseph Kett led me patiently through the field of American intellectual and cultural history. Ferenc Szasz of New Mexico State University, Richard M. Brown of the University of Oregon, and William Ellis of Eastern Kentucky University offered advice and encouragement and shared with me their knowledge of the 1920s; I am especially grateful to Professor Ellis for guiding me through the manuscript collections at Southern Seminary.

I could not have completed this study without the help and kindness shown me by librarians and archivists at the following institutions: the University of Virginia, the University of Richmond, the University of North Carolina, Wake Forest University, Southern Baptist Theological Seminary, the Dargan-Carver Library of the Southern Baptist Sunday School Board, Southwestern Baptist Theological Seminary, and Baylor University.

I wish to thank *The Mississippi Quarterly* and *Foundations* for permitting me to use parts of this book that originally were published in those journals. Chapter one appeared in slightly altered form as "Southern Baptists and Postwar Disillusionment, 1918-1919," in *Foundations* 21 (April-June 1978): 113-22; part of chapter eight appeared as "A Free-and-Easy Democracy: Southern Baptists and Denominational

Structure in the 1920s," in *Foundations* 22 (January-March 1979): 43-50; part of chapter nine, as "Southern Baptist City and Country Churches in the Twenties,"in *Foundations* 17 (October-December 1974): 351-63; part of chapter seven, as "Southern Baptists and the Antievolution Controversy of the 1920s," in *Mississippi Quarterly* 29 (Winter 1975-1976): 65-81; part of chapter nine, as "Southern Baptists and Anti-Catholicism in the 1920s," in *Mississippi Quarterly* 32 (Fall 1979): 611-25.

My greatest debt is to Professor Samuel S. Hill, Jr., of the University of Florida. He read the manuscript twice, offered valuable suggestions, and convinced me to pursue the painful task of turning a dissertation into a book. For me, he stands as a worthy model of the gentleman as scholar.

James J. Thompson, Jr.
Rockford, Illinois, 1982

Foreword

To the general public, the Southern Baptist denomination is known for two features. First, it is the nation's largest Protestant body, with membership now approaching fourteen million. Second, it exercises a profound influence over the culture of the Southern region, in politics, moral values, and outlook and manner of living. Far less is known about the internal life of the Southern Baptist Convention and how it came to be the ways it is. James Thompson's study of the denomination in the years between the end of World War I and the Great Depression sheds light on these whats and hows.

Interpreters of historical development as it impinges on a contemporary institution are fond of fingering a set period of time as decisive for the shape it has taken. Doing so is risky business, of course. Many periods of time and myriad other factors contribute to the personality of old and complex organizations. Nevertheless, the 1920s may be pinpointed as an uncommonly important era for making the Southern Baptist Convention what it has become in "modern history."

The central issue in Thompson's frame—and, I would say, generally—is the response of Southern Baptists to change and new challenges. We may learn a great deal about institutions and/or persons by noting their responses to change and challenges. Down to the 1920s, to be sure, the region and its predominantly white Baptist body had lived in constant interaction with the rest of the world and what was happening in it. That set its agenda; that provided its problem. Its very settlement by people from Europe, and its having Africans delivered to its doorstep began the process. In turn, it was molded by participation alongside other Americans in a war for independence from that European state; the defense of slavery as a social institution; the bloody conflict with those other Americans; and most recently its attitudinal isolation from the nation at large. All these staples of regional life reflected the intensity of its interaction with new or alien forces, prompting change and presenting challenges.

Still, the 1920s were exceptional. Economic recovery was occurring and its eventual achievement predictable. Developments located in New England or the Middle East or Europe or Asia were on their way to becoming part and parcel of Southern experience. The Great War itself involved America, not some part of America, in military confrontation, in fashioning a common patriotism, and in the build-up of war-related industries. The South was in America in those years, psychologically and commercially, as it had not been for a half century. And there was to be an intensification of that condition, hardly any turning back.

The Southern Baptist people found themselves face to face with circumstances that required them to act. Some of those circumstances pertained to the internal organization of the Southern Baptist Convention, others to new developments initiated mostly outside the South. Internally, Southern Baptists had to come to terms with theological differences—the Convention never has been a monolith— on issues such as premillennialism and biblical criticism. Also staring Southern Baptists in the face was a financial overextension resulting from a proliferation of boards and agencies created to provide Christian services and ministries of many kinds, at home and abroad. Owing to their resourcefulness and spirited dedication, the Southern Baptist leadership and people overcame those challenges of doctrinal conflict and financial deficiency. They were to come out of the 1920s unified (if not united) and solvent (if not yet a wealthy organization).

A longer list of graver threats emanated from the larger world. British biological research refined and popularized by American scientists (hardly any from the South) led to disputation over the text of Genesis. Copious achievements in the ranks of scholarship generated harsh debate over biblical hermeneutics. The arrival of several million immigrants from Central, Southern, and Eastern Europe posed the spectre—never the reality—of a sullied Southern stock. Northern Protestantism's vision of the Christian mission in an urbanizing, industrial, heterogeneous, and interdependent society introduced Southern Protestants to an alternative idea of their task, the "Social Gospel." Many of these same instincts moved Northern Christians toward ecumenical notions of the church. But all of these were merely options, or threats, none of them taking root in Southern soil.

James Thompson serves us well by demonstrating how far the collapse of Southern regional isolation had advanced. What was affecting the rest of America was having more effect than ever on its Southern region. There is no better example than Black Monday on Wall Street in Manhattan's Lower East Side in October 1929.

Yet we must not slight the developments within Southern society that made possible a maturing and muscle-flexing Southern Baptist Convention: transportation—highways and autos, trains; communication—newspapers, periodicals, and radio; population—enlarging and more concentrated in cities and towns. The twentieth century, especially from its twenties, afforded the Southern Baptist Convention and its people ideas and capacities for contending with the changes and challenges it thrust upon them.

The result was the denomination as we have known it in bold relief for a third, maybe a half, century by now. It became self-aware, starting to think of its people as "children of destiny," the new Rome or, more pallatably, the new Puritan New England, looming large as the hub of a planet needing to be Christianized, the hope of the South, the nation, indeed the entire world. The sense of a unique mission arose. Vigorous denominational loyalty emerged. A kind of religious-cultural ethnocentrism emanated from the 1920s in which success, centralization, and confidence were evident traits.

Personally I am grateful to Jim Thompson for illuminating life in the decade in which I was born (late, of course) and the religious community that nurtured me. The Southern Baptist Convention is a marvel, a wonder, a spectacle, a mighty force, a home for millions and a *cause celebre* for tens of thousands. Southern Baptists need to know more about the "modern" origins of their convention, and America at large needs to learn more about its syle and dynamic. *Tried as by Fire* should well meet both those needs.

Samuel S. Hill, Jr.
Gainesville, Florida
Eastertide, 1982

PART ONE

Southern Baptists and the Postwar World, 1919-1920

CHAPTER 1

Postwar Attitudes Take Shape

In early 1919, Southern Baptists joined other Americans in pondering the meaning of the world war that had ended on 11 November 1918. William L. Poteat, president of Wake Forest College, put into words the attitude of many Baptists when he wrote: "We thank God that night has past [sic] and the day has dawned at length. We have achieved a signal victory which promises to be permanent for civilization against barbarism."[1] The Home Mission Board suggested that 1918 would be recorded as the second greatest year in history, surpassed only by the year of Christ's birth.[2]

With the war over, Southern Baptists proudly recalled their support of the United States government. The Southern Baptist Convention and the various state organizations had proclaimed Baptist patriotism and loyalty. Church members had poured money into the nation's war effort, and more important, they had sent their sons to Europe, some of whom had never returned. Southern Baptist clergymen had made it easier for their congregations to sacrifice in the national interest: few of the denom-

---

[1]William L. Poteat, "The German Demonstration," p. 4: typescript of an address delivered to the Southern Baptist Education Association, Nashville, Tennessee, 24 January 1919, William L. Poteat Papers, Baptist Historical Collection, Wake Forest University, Winston-Salem, North Carolina.

[2]Southern Baptist Convention, *Annual*, 1919, p. 364.

ination's ministers had advocated pacifism, and those who had, had wielded scant influence.[3]

The war had provoked intense feelings among Southern Baptists for, as Poteat commented, "the German menace outraged us."[4] This outrage did not fade with the German surrender, but lingered on into 1919, explaining why Southern Baptists continued to discuss the war. To the denomination's intellectuals, Germany had presented a philosophical challenge that had to be met. Germany's alleged combination of atheism and militarism, best personified for Baptists in the "godless ravings" of Friedrich Nietzsche, had to be crushed. The choice, Professor A. T. Robertson of the Southern Baptist Seminary in Louisville wrote, had been between "Kaiser or Christ, Napoleon or Jesus, Corsica or Galilee."[5] Exalting brute force, Germany had scorned Christian love, kindness, and compassion. This had left Christ's followers with no choice but to fight for their faith. Most Southern Baptists had not pursued their thoughts this far; for them, the words of Robert H. Pitt, editor of the Virginia Baptists' *Religious Herald*, were sufficient: "The German government in nearly all it did represented the spirit of anti-Christ."[6] The Prince of Peace against the Powers of Darkness; right versus wrong—it had been simple for the Baptist folk of the South.

Valuing political and religious democracy as they did, Southern Baptists had denounced Germany's autocracy as vehemently as they had decried her atheism and militarism. "Overlords, either in religion or civil government, have to Baptists an ill favor," James B. Gambrell, president of the Southern Baptist Convention, said in May of 1919.[7] As much as anything this devotion to democracy had compelled Southern Baptists to join the crusade against the "Central Powers."* William O. Carver,

---

[3]George W. McDaniel, *The People Called Baptists* (Nashville: Sunday School Board, 1919), pp. 21-22.

[4]William L. Poteat, "Culture and the Unfinished War," in his *Youth and Culture* (Wake Forest, North Carolina: Wake Forest College Press, 1938), p. 100. Poteat delivered this address in 1919.

[5]A. T. Robertson, *The New Citizenship: The Christian Facing a New World Order* (New York: Fleming H. Revell, 1919), p. 25.

[6]*Religious Herald* (Richmond, Virginia), 2 January 1919, p. 17.

[7]SBC, *Annual*, 1919, p. 17.

*In World War I, "Central Powers" designated Germany and Austria-Hungary, with their allies Turkey and Bulgaria, as opposed to the "Allies" (Great Britain, France, Russia, and their allies).—Ed.

professor of missions at Southern Baptist Theological Seminary, had developed this position in an article written in the summer of 1918, but not published until 1920. America had been chosen by God as the repository of "democratic freedom," Carver wrote. The Lord had sheltered the nation for centuries, he went on to say, keeping her isolated from international politics so that democracy could develop unhindered. World War I and the coming of age of the American political system had coincided, he continued. God had commanded America to destroy German autocracy and to carry civil and religious democracy to the world. "And we had to accept this stewardship of democratic freedom or prove ourselves recreant cowards and condemn democracy as unfit for the organized life of a great people," Carver concluded.[8]

It seemed part of this divine plan that Woodrow Wilson— Southerner, Protestant, and Democrat—had been elected President of the United States just as American democracy had reached maturity. Baptists believed that Wilson had accepted God's guidance in matters of state; indeed, he had made the deity a ranking member of his Cabinet. As proof of Wilson's alliance with God, Baptists noted that his statement of war aims had meshed perfectly with their own principles. He had called for observance of the rights of small nations, prompting Baptists to point out that within their ranks the smallest church possessed the same prerogatives as the largest. Baptists had matched Wilson's advocacy of the self-determination of peoples with their belief in a democratic church polity. Finally, Wilson's call for a crusade to make the world safe for democracy had impressed Southern Baptists as an extension of their own efforts to universalize religious democracy.[9]

World War I had been satisfying for Southern Baptists, and as they viewed the past few years from the perspective of early 1919, the experience loomed as an auspicious beginning for the postwar era. Southern Baptist Convention President James Gambrell expressed this attitude well when he remarked that "the triumph of the rights of humanity by the defeat of the Central Powers in the war, brings the world to the dawn of a new era in civilization."[10]

---

[8]William O. Carver, "Some Aspects of Education in the Light of the War's Revelations," *Review and Expositor* 17 (January 1920): 78-79.

[9]Robertson, *The New Citizenship*, pp. 27-28; McDaniel, *The People Called Baptists*, pp. 166-67.

[10]SBC, *Annual*, 1919, p. 17.

During 1919 and on into 1920, Southern Baptists watched this "new era" take shape, looking expectantly toward the decade ahead. But whatever the future held, Baptists believed that World War 1 had disrupted the flow of history. "The old world passed away when Belgium took her stand in front of the Kaiser's hosts," A. T. Robertson wrote. "Modern history began on that date."[11] Florida Baptists observed that in one stroke changes had occurred that ordinarily would have taken centuries.[12] Other Baptists mined their vocabularies for images to describe postwar conditions. The *Religious Herald* characterized the world as soft plastic, ready to be reshaped,[13] and James F. Love of the Foreign Mission Board portrayed the period as a crucible in which "religion will be *tried as by fire*."[14] However they phrased it, Southern Baptists sensed that they lived in an unstable and amorphous age that awaited an ordering hand. As Southerners they knew what accompanied the aftermath of war, for their fathers and grandfathers had lived through an earlier reconstruction. More than other Americans they had been forced to grapple with the turmoil of war. Now, in 1919, as victor and not vanquished, they moved to cope with forces unleashed by another great conflict.

Southern Baptists' patriotism and religious fervor encouraged them to believe that the war would facilitate the triumph of righteousness. This view was ably expressed by Edgar Y. Mullins, president of Southern Seminary, who had said in 1917 that the European conflict would "prepare for new fulfil[l]ments of God's purpose in Christ."[15] This attitude remained with Southern Baptists, and at the war's conclusion led them to argue that the increased opportunity to spread the gospel had been the "one greatly intended object and end" of World War I.[16] The war had shown the folly of human wisdom and had proved conclusively that man was evil and needed salvation. Further, it had dramatized the fate of nations that tried to escape God's sovereignty.[17] The ravages of war

---

[11]Robertson, *The New Citizenship*, p. 8.

[12]Florida Baptist Convention, *Annual*, 1919, p. 31.

[13]*Herald*, 10 July 1919, p. 7.

[14]James F. Love, "Baptist Missions in the New World Order," *Review and Expositor* 17 (July 1920): 258; italics added.

[15]E. Y. Mullins, *The Christian Religion in Its Doctrinal Expression* (Philadelphia: Judson Press, 1917), p. 352

[16]*Herald*, 9 January 1919, p. 4.

[17]William O. Carver, "Baptists and the Problem of World Missions," *Review and Expositor* 17 (July 1920): 319.

would redound to the credit of God's cause, for as Louisiana Baptists pointed out,

> Only the Cross of Christ stands untouched and unscratched, "towering o'er the wrecks of time." Human folly and rage have dashed themselves in vain against its immeasurable truth and goodness. Humanity wearied and worn at trying everything else now stands ready to find its bearings and steer its course by the eternal lights of faith, hope, and love.[18]

Equally important to this exposure of "human folly," the struggle against the Central Powers had awakened America from ease and complacency. A new militancy and revived fervor, originally stimulated by the demands of national emergency, now waited to be employed in the battle for Christ. Accompanying this was a spirit of self-sacrifice that prompted Baptists to ask: if Americans could pour out money and sons for Woodrow Wilson, could they not do even more for Christ? Finally, the war had forced Americans to lay aside petty divisions and unite to meet a common danger. Baptists assumed that this solidarity could be transformed into peacetime unity for Christ and then be extended to the entire world: Americans and Europeans who had fought side by side could evangelize together.[19]

For Southern Baptists the war's greatest significance was in the way God had used it to promote democracy. The suzerainty of Pope, Sultan, and Kaiser had suffered irreparable damage, and the idea that the common people could not govern themselves had been rejected in favor of Wilson's principle of self-determination. Neither church nor state could dictate any longer to the masses.[20] America had heralded a new day by promoting democracy and weakening autocracy. When democracy gained international ascendancy men would be free to choose for themselves in fields other than politics. Religious self-determination would result, and, given such an opportunity, Southern Baptists reasoned, most people would opt for the Baptist version of Christianity.

---

[18]Louisiana Baptist Convention, *Annual*, 1920, pp. 76-77.

[19]James B. Gambrell, *Baptists and Their Business* (Nashville: Sunday School Board, 1919), p. 136.

[20]Ibid., p. 16; Robertson, *New Citizenship*, p. 49.

Such logic might lead to the conclusion that Baptists saw only what they wished to see: a suffering world, cleansed of autocracy, turning gratefully to the Baptist God, and a united America ready to aid repentant mankind in its quest for salvation. But just when their rhetoric seemed about to lure Baptists into a fantasy land, reality snapped them back, forcing them to recognize the less desirable results of the war. As Louisiana Baptists pointed out, an age of opportunity could also be a time of "chaos and confusion":

> The condition of the world since the great war, is that of a patient who has undergone a serious surgical operation. The incision has been made. The excision of deceased parts has been effected and abnormal conditions corrected. But the wound has not been dressed. It has been left open, exposed to all the death-dealing germs afloat in a contaminated atmosphere. Many of these germs have already entered the social body and a complicated case of infection has set up.[21]

"Death-dealing germs" abounded in the world, making it impossible for Southern Baptists to ignore the war's harmful by-products. Although the "external restraints" of autocracy had been struck off the world's multitudes, the "internal constraint" provided by the gospel had not yet taken hold, and anarchy threatened to step into the breach.[22] The pendulum had swung from German autocracy to Russian "anarchy," or "Bolshevism," as Americans identified this outburst of revolutionary fervor. "The shadow of Bolshevism stalks behind the vanishing ghost of pan-Germanism," A. T. Robertson cautioned.[23] Baptists heeded his warning, for though most of them had never seen a Bolshevik or an anarchist, they joined their countrymen, who were caught up in the "Red Scare" of 1919, in sounding the alarm against the undermining of American ideals.

Prosperity ranked close behind anarchy on the list of "death-dealing germs." This may seem strange in view of the poverty that had plagued the South since the Civil War, but the idea of a "New South" of prosperity

---

[21]Louisiana, *Annual*, 1920, p. 83.

[22]SBC, *Annual*, 1919, pp. 196-97.

[23]Archibald T. Robertson, "The Cry for Christ Today," in *The Christ of the Logia* (Nashville: Sunday School Board, 1924), p. 233. This article originally appeared in the January 1920 issue of *Biblical World*.

and plenty had won adherents among Baptists, especially in the person of Richard H. Edmonds, active Baptist layman and editor of the *Manufacturers' Record* of Baltimore. Many Southerners had begun to see their region as prosperous, even though this proved to be little more than an ephemeral wish.[24] Moreover, the war had bolstered the nation's economy, and the South had not gone untouched by national gains. But whether illusion or reality, prosperity presented difficulties. J. Frank Norris, pastor of Fort Worth's First Baptist Church, remarked: "The most dangerous thing under the sun is prosperity. People do right more often under adversity than they do under prosperity. Very few people can stand success."[25] The South labored under this burden also, for, as Victor I. Masters of the Home Mission Board warned, "dollar-lust" threatened to subvert spiritual values that had been developed over long periods of adversity. The South must somehow tame its advancing affluence and show that this new prosperity could exist harmoniously with spirituality.[26]

An Arkansas pastor recognized a third problem when he wrote in March 1919: "We are having a wave of worldliness and many forms of evil."[27] The addition of "worldliness" completed the Southern Baptist catalog of the war's adverse effects. "Worldliness" never received a careful definition; indeed, its vagueness was its beauty, for it could be used to damn everything from short dresses to dope addiction. The condition thrived on postwar "commercialism" and "materialism," Baptists said, because more money meant more to spend on evil pursuits. Most Baptists settled the issue by equating worldliness with immorality and relegating whatever they found distasteful about the modern world to this all-purpose category.[28]

By listing the war's adverse effects, Southern Baptists realized that the postwar world's promise of success would go unfulfilled if they did

---

[24]Paul M. Gaston, *The New South Creed: A Study in Southern Myth-making* (New York: Alfred A. Knopf, 1970), pp. 190-207.

[25]*Searchlight* (Fort Worth, Texas), 10 July 1919, p. 3.

[26]Victor I. Masters, *The Call of the South: A Presentation of the Home Principle in Missions, Especially as It Applies to the South* (Atlanta: Home Mission Board, 1920; original publication, 1918), pp. 29-30.

[27]C. S. Wales to George W. Truett, 21 March 1919, George W. Truett Papers, Southwestern Baptist Theological Seminary, Fort Worth, Texas.

[28]SBC, *Annual,* 1920, p. 369; Louisiana, *Annual,* 1919, p. 38.

not act quickly. An unprecedented opportunity for evangelization existed, one that might never reoccur, but the South's Baptists must move swiftly if they expected to win the unconverted masses to Jesus Christ.

Baptist strategy for converting the unchurched multitudes may be pictured as a set of stairsteps. The top step bore the notation "The World," for the task of preaching the gospel to all men beckoned to Baptists as their ultimate goal. The next step was labeled "America" because Baptists concluded that this nation had been granted a unique opportunity. Never in history had a people been offered such auspicious circumstances in which to Christianize the world. With mankind wallowing in despair, God had elevated the United States, the world's preeminent Christian and democratic nation, to a position of leadership.[29] Contending that God had directed their country to this juncture in history, Baptists concluded that "America is in fact God's new Israel for the race of men. It is a land divinely chosen, preserved with providential purpose, prospered now with world power, and pledged to a divine mission."[30] Although Baptists believed that God had chosen America to fulfill His plan of salvation, they realized that the nation was not as righteous as it should be. Social and intellectual restlessness, materialism, worldliness, and a pervading air of irreverence threatened to crumble the foundations of this great Christian nation. Baptists saw that the conversion of mankind depended upon the salvation of the United States; Georgia's Baptists, for example, advised that "we must save America to save the world."[31] America must become the Christian standard for mankind. In terms originally employed by the Puritan founders of Massachusetts Bay Colony, A. T. Robertson said: "America is a city set on a hill these days seen of all men. The eyes of the world are turned upon us. We must clean up our house and keep it clean if we are to lead the nations of the earth in the paths of peace to God and righteousness."[32]

Never forgetting their regional ties, Southern Baptists marked their next strategic step "The South." Here lay the hope of America, for only the South could convert the nation to God. Baptists need not be ashamed

---

[29]Masters, *The Call of the South*, p. 34; *Herald*, 27 February 1919, p. 7.

[30]SBC, *Annual*, 1919, p. 79.

[31]Baptist Convention of Georgia, *Minutes*, 1919, p. 16.

[32]Robertson, *The New Citizenship*, p. 9.

of their sectional consciousness, Victor Masters counseled; their awareness of regional differences benefited the United States immensely. The
anguish experienced by Southerners after the Civil War had given them
"a certain depth of soul" and an acute sense of history. Masters contended
that through its suffering the region had reached the limits of despair and
there had rededicated itself to God. Southerners, unlike other Americans,
Masters wrote, knew how badly the postwar world needed God, for the
South had experienced a similar soul-sickness in the aftermath of an
earlier war. Southerners must use this sensitivity to the past to build "a
great Christian civilization in America." Because it held the key to
continued American greatness, the region could return to its once-proud
position of dominance within the nation. All America now looked southward, not to berate and condemn as in the past, but to seek aid in time of
trouble, Masters concluded.[33]

At the base of the strategic steps, supporting the others, lay the step
labeled "Southern Baptist." Southern Baptists must save the South; the
South would convert America; and America would evangelize the world.
"As goes America, so goes the world. Largely as goes the South, so goes
America. And in the South is the Baptist center of gravity of the world."[34]
This belief fired Baptists with a sense of destiny, a note sounded by M. E.
Dodd in the annual Southern Baptist Convention sermon preached at
Atlanta, Georgia, in May 1919. "We have arrived at that moment in our
history for which our forefathers toiled and sacrificed and prayed; for
which they suffered and bled and died. The Baptist hour of all the
centuries has sounded," Dodd exulted.[35] President James Gambrell
agreed with Dodd, adding that Baptists had been divinely appointed to
carry the gospel to all men.[36] God had provided the opportunity for
evangelization and had called Southern Baptists to take advantage of the
situation; the rest was up to them. "The Baptists of the world should
come into close alliance, and put on a worthy program, a world program
of evangelization," a Louisiana pastor wrote. "This is our day and our
opportunity; will we meet and be equal to the opportunity?"[37]

---

[33]Masters, *The Call of the South*, pp. 17-18, 209.

[34]Victor I. Masters, "Baptists and the Christianizing of America in the New Order,"
Review and Expositor 17 (July 1920): 297.

[35]*Herald*, 29 May 1919, p. 4.

[36]Gambrell, *Baptists and Their Business*, pp. 5-6.

[37]D. C. Freeman to A. T. Robertson, 14 February 1919, A. T. Robertson Papers,

If Baptists doubted that their time had come, they forgot their fears when they surveyed their surroundings. Conditions within and without the denomination pointed specifically to Southern Baptists as God's chosen people. For one thing, they found themselves sharing in the prosperity that had accompanied the war. Although prosperity could be dangerous, Baptists had not hoarded their newfound wealth; they had contributed unprecedented amounts of money for both home and foreign missions. Baptists who had faltered before World War I now shouldered their share of the financial burden.[38] In the second place, Baptists believed that these resources had been granted to a people especially given to missionary work, for by definition Baptists were missionary-minded. "Baptists are born with a love for evangelism. They are as surely evangelistic as they are born of the spirit, and they cannot be laborers together with God unless they love those who are perishing, nor can they follow in the footsteps of Jesus unless they are seeking the lost," the Southern Baptist Convention asserted in 1920.[39] With wealth and ability at their command Southern Baptists offered the "missionary enterprise" as their answer to William James's call for a "moral equivalent of war."[40]

External conditions also summoned Baptists. A world in disarray awaited the order and stability the gospel could supply. Although mankind would profit from general Christian principles, it particularly needed the Christianity proffered by Baptists, the denomination urged. E. Y. Mullins, one of the denomination's senior statesmen, pointed out the "defects of the culture and civilization which brought on the world war" and suggested that they could be corrected through adoption of Baptist principles.

• To begin with, human degradation would be rectified through emphasis on the sanctity of the individual, Mullins said.

• Political and religious autocracy formed a second defect of the Old World, but Baptist democracy would usher in a new era.

• Third, regenerate adult membership would be substituted for the "unspiritual church membership" that came from infant baptism.

• The priestly, sacramental nature of Old World religion—the

Southern Baptist Theological Seminary, Louisville, Kentucky, Folder 1919A.

[38]SBC, *Annual*, 1919, pp. 197-98.

[39]Ibid., 1920, p. 413.

[40]*Herald*, 13 February 1919, p. 5.

fourth defect—had blinded men to the beauty of Christianity. This "evil" would be replaced by the priesthood of all believers and the doctrine that the sacraments were simply symbols with no saving power in themselves.

• Fifth, Baptists would sunder the church-state ties of the Old World.

• Finally, Mullins said, "the cardinal defect of the older civilization has been the substitution of culture salvation" for repentance from sin. Baptists would downgrade cultural growth and return repentance to its rightful preeminence.

• Mullins concluded: "The Baptist conception of the Christian religion contains elements which in the highest degree are adapted to meet the needs of the modern world."[41]

Their sense of destiny and awareness of limitless opportunity gave Southern Baptists a feeling of well-being and optimism. Expressions of this mood abounded in the books, articles, and resolutions authored by Baptists in the immediate postwar period. Relief at an end to the killing, and anticipation of the future, prompted the *Religious Herald* to proclaim on 2 January 1919: "Surely this is the greatest Christmas since Christ was born in Bethlehem."[42] Baptist missionaries contributed to the mood, for the Lord was blessing their efforts as never before.[43] Perhaps the greatest witness to this optimism, however, appeared in the testimony of those who recognized the existence of grave difficulties but still believed in the ultimate triumph of righteousness. An Oklahoman, writing in the state's Baptist newspaper, remarked that although strife continued to sweep the world in the war's wake, Christians knew that "the end will be light and right." Pessimism among God's people, he concluded, constituted heresy "in the worst sense."[44]

This optimism furnished the final characteristic of the Southern Baptist denomination in the postwar period. The denomination did not bestride the South in unbroken uniformity, for it contained considerable diversity. Socially, it varied from Tidewater aristocrats to Texas cowboys;

---

[41]E. Y. Mullins, "Baptist Theology in the New World Order," *Review and Expositor* 17 (October 1920): 405-407.

[42]*Herald*, 2 January 1919, p. 18.

[43]Pearl Caldwell to A. T. Robertson, 4 March 1919, Robertson Papers, Folder 1919A.

[44]*Baptist Messenger* (Oklahoma City, Oklahoma), 15 January 1919, p. 1.

intellectually, it ran the gamut from A. T. Robertson, world-renowned New Testament scholar, to the least-educated Baptist layman. But beneath these differences lay a similarity too obvious to be denied. Whether illiterate laborer or seminary professor, all Southern Baptists held certain beliefs in common. They read the same Bible and went to churches that preached essentially the same message. Equally important, they were Southerners, bound together by time and place into a distinct group that defied the pull of national conformity. The experience of World War I, working on minds molded by a common doctrine and regional consciousness, produced the attitudes that were the common possession of Southern Baptists. Armed with these attitudes and gripped by a sense of their unique circumstance and opportunity, Baptists entered the decade of the 1920s.

CHAPTER 2

Triumph and Warning

In retrospect, two episodes from the years 1919 and 1920 appear especially significant for the following decade. The Seventy-Five Million Campaign, begun in May 1919 to raise $75,000,000 in five years, was the first event. The initial success of this program, obvious by the end of 1919, reaffirmed the "children-of-destiny" role of Southern Baptists and convinced them that they had correctly interpreted the meaning of the First World War. The fund drive's favorable beginning validated the optimism, unity, sacrifice, and spiritual vitality stimulated by the war. God had now provided the financial means to evangelize the world, and, Baptists contended, had given them a sign that He would ultimately bestow victory upon the denomination.

The financial campaign, with its immediate results and promises of vast riches to come, continued to hold center stage; at the same time, another movement, equally laden with meaning, forced its way on the scene. Few Southern Baptists understood its significance or recognized the warning it offered, for in 1919 Baptists believed that the Seventy-Five Million Campaign foreshadowed the future. Had Baptists been blessed with foresight they would have seen that a more accurate portrait of the future could be found in the controversy over interdenominationalism that disturbed the denomination in 1919 and 1920. Baptist rejoicing over the first fruits of the Seventy-Five Million Campaign overshadowed the warning embedded in the flurry over the ecumenical movement. Division, strife, and self-doubt—all foretold by this controversy—would be more typically the lot of Southern Baptists in the 1920s than the unity and confidence inspired by the fund-raising drive. But Baptists failed to recognize this until too late; in the immediate postwar era the bright glow of optimism obscured the black clouds on the horizon.

Exuberant and deeply conscious of their duty to mankind, Southern Baptists met in Atlanta, Georgia, 14-18 May 1919, to give concrete expression to the emotions that had swept the denomination in the wake of World War I. In Atlanta, capital of the "New South," Southern Baptists initiated an unparalleled drive to raise $75,000,000 in five years. They intended to create a "New South"—somewhat different from the one conceived by Henry Grady in the 1880s—but nonetheless, a new South. But far beyond what Grady and other New South spokesmen had dreamed of, Southern Baptists sought to establish a "new America" and a "new world" as well. Baptists predicted that the spontaneous outpouring of millions of dollars would enable them to realize their vision of a world dedicated to Christ.

No plans for establishing the campaign had been developed before the Atlanta meeting. Convention delegates maintained that God's spirit moved upon the assembled Baptists, awakening them to the need for a dramatic effort to advance the Lord's work. As Lee R. Scarborough, president of Southwestern Baptist Seminary in Fort Worth, Texas, commented: "It was God's Convention and God's program. The Divine Spirit manifested Himself everywhere." Although this belief in the workings of Providence gave Baptists a special sense of security, even Scarborough recognized the multitude of forces that had laid the foundation for the Seventy-Five Million Campaign. He pointed out that the First World War had decisively altered Baptists' conception of evangelism by forcing them to reconsider traditional methods of soul winning in light of the magnitude and efficiency of the American war effort.[1] This led the denomination to emphasize the importance of "utilizing on behalf of our Kingdom enterprises the altruistic spirit, the enlarged vision, and the thorough methods of organization that have come from our experiences with the World War."[2]

---

[1]Lee R. Scarborough, *Marvels of Divine Leadership or the Story of the Southern Baptist 75 Million Campaign* (Nashville: Sunday School Board, 1920), pp. 7, 13, 16-17.

[2]SBC, *Annual*, 1919, p. 32.

The war had also encouraged Baptists to revise their financial methods. Wartime taxes and the staggering amounts spent on the military convinced them that they had to provide more funds for the war against evil. Among Baptists the energy and emotion of patriotism transcended the confines of national pride, spilled over into religious life, and made "giving" one of the many passions aroused by the war.[3] Finally, the Seventy-Five Million Campaign owed much to previous denominational fund drives. The Foreign Mission Board had recently established the Judson Fund to obtain money for education in mission fields, and the Home Mission Board had raised over a million dollars for construction of new churches. Various state conventions, not waiting for the Southern Baptist Convention to act, had already expanded their work for missions and education. Georgia Baptists had established a five-year program to raise six-and-one-half million dollars, and Alabama, Arkansas, Texas, and Tennessee had similiar campaigns in progress. Perhaps the most important precedent lay in the Education Commission's efforts to raise $15,000,000. These programs furnished the Southern Baptist Convention with a strong base upon which to build.[4]

With these developments as a backdrop, 4,200 Baptist "messengers"* in Atlanta in May 1919 determined to set new goals for the Lord's work. President Gambrell addressed the assembly, warning of grave perils facing Southern Baptists, but at the same time forecasting a brilliant future for the denomination. He closed his speech with a stirring call to action: "It is my deep conviction that this Convention ought to adopt a program for work commensurate with the reasonable demands on us and summon ourselves and our people to a new demonstration of the value of orthodoxy in free action." The messengers appointed a committee to discuss the issues raised by Gambrell, and this committee in turn selected another committee instructed to plan for the future. This study committee reported back to the Convention with a number of suggestions; most important, the committee advised that "in view of the

---

[3]*Baptist Record* (Jackson, Mississippi), 16 January 1919, p. 4; Benjamin F. Riley, *A Memorial History of the Baptists of Alabama* (Philadelphia: Judson Press, 1923), p. 372.

[4]Scarborough, *Marvels of Divine Leadership*, pp. 12-13.

*Since every local church affiliated with the Southern Baptist Convention is autonomous, and the authority of the local church is never delegated, representatives of the local churches at sessions of the Southern Baptist Convention (as also at association and state convention sessions) are designated as "messengers."—Ed.

needs of the world at this hour, in view of the numbers and ability of
Southern Baptists, we suggest . . . that in the organized work of this
Convention we undertake to raise not less than $75,000,000 in five
years." The messengers responded by appointing a Campaign Commission to set up the program.[5]

Two weeks after the delegates had left Atlanta the fifteen members of
this commission met in the city's First Baptist Church where they
selected Lee Scarborough as director of the campaign and set quotas for
each state.[6] The plans called for workers to gather pledges for the full
$75,000,000, along with as much cash as possible, until 7 December 1919.
A certain proportion of a pledge would be due each year until the end of
1924, when the full $75,000,000 would be in hand.

Scarborough and his staff covered the South with literature and
solicitors, but the workers confronted severe difficulties. First of all, there
were only six months to complete the first phase of the campaign as
planned, and during this brief period postwar unrest kept people's minds
occupied with national and international events. Many Southern Baptists, though willing to aid in the Lord's work, had grown weary of
wartime money drives, of "wheatless" and "meatless" days, and the other
trappings of the crusading spirit. The Seventy-Five Million Campaign
resembled a Red Cross or YMCA drive to them. Moreover, many Baptists
disliked the five-year commitment attached to their pledges. Even those
willing to contribute lived across a wide swath of territory in areas
difficult for the solicitors to reach. As an added handicap, it rained
frequently in eight Southern states from the beginning of September
until the end of November.[7]

Scarborough and his workers kept at their task in spite of these
obstacles. The cooperation that had characterized Baptists during the
early months of 1919 gradually prevailed over the problems that arose.
From across the South came renewed expressions of optimism and good
will. "The brethren say that things were never in better condition," a
Baptist pastor wrote from Chattanooga, Tennessee.[8] Southwestern

---

[5]SBC, *Annual*, 1919, pp. 22-23, 74; Scarborough, *Marvels of Divine Leadership*, 17.

[6]Scarborough, *Marvels of Divine Leadership*, pp. 22-23.

[7]Ibid., pp. 90-91.

[8]Harold Major to A. T. Robertson, 30 September 1919, Robertson Papers, Folder
1919A.

Seminary reported high spirits among students and faculty,[9] and Virginia Baptists noted that the fund drive had seized "the minds and hearts of our people from the mountains to the sea."[10] On the eve of the campaign's conclusion, a Mississippi pastor wrote that "we expect next Sunday afternoon to raise our quota to the 75 million campaign. The building movement and the 75 million campaign put us under a $100,000 proposition, but by the Lord's help, we hope to do our part in the right way."[11] Even Frank Norris, later arch-critic of the Southern Baptist Convention, exhorted his church members to raise money.[12]

The Campaign Commission designated the week of 30 November to 7 December 1919, as Victory Week, the time when all pledges and as much cash as possible were to be reported. The week's results did nothing to dampen Baptist optimism. The pledges far exceeded the goal, totaling over ninety-two million dollars, while cash receipts amounted to more than twelve million dollars. "The most momentous period in Baptist history since the Day of Pentecost" had ended.[13]

Baptists hailed the results of Victory Week as a magnificent triumph for the denomination, the South, America, and the world. "The overwhelming success of the 75 Million Campaign is the greatest achievement ever made by any denomination in the world's history," Richard Edmonds wrote.[14] Most Southern Baptists viewed this "overwhelming success" in financial terms. As the Home Mission Board announced: "The reign of the penny for the support of the Gospel has been superseded by the dollar."[15] The Campaign Commission agreed that money represented the primary tangible gain, but in a larger sense, finances came second to the spiritual blessings. The benefits discerned by the commission resembled those produced by World War I. Both the war and the Seventy-Five Million Campaign had encouraged unity, sacrifice,

[9]Walter T. Conner to Lee R. Scarborough, 10 October 1919, Walter T. Conner Papers, Southwestern Baptist Theological Seminary.

[10]Baptist General Association of Virginia, *Minutes*, 1919, p. 34.

[11]Zeno Wall to A. T. Robertson, 25 November 1919, Robertson Papers, Folder 1919A.

[12]*Searchlight*, 25 September 1919, p. 1.

[13]SBC, *Annual*, 1920, p. 50.

[14]*Herald* , 8 January 1920, p. 11.

[15]SBC, *Annual*, 1920, p. 421.

enlarged vision, organization, and fervor. The Campaign Commission
left no doubt that the two events were related, writing that:

> The impartation and implantation of the conquering,
> heroic, martial spirit is one of the chief results of the Cam-
> paign. The religious life of the people has been simplified and
> the heroic element in religion has been magnified and a
> mighty impelling, conquering power has been given to their
> faith. Never again will Southern Baptists halt at difficulties
> nor falter at overwhelming odds. They have learned to be
> crusaders and conquerors. The Campaign put into every fiber
> of our denominational life the challenge and appeal of the
> heroic, and has given to our souls the adventurous, conquering
> spirit of the apostolic times; and this is a great asset.[16]

The Seventy-Five Million Campaign proved to be both beginning and
end for Southern Baptists, both prologue to the 1920s and epilogue to a
brief era of optimism and cooperation. When the drive ended Southern
Baptists interpreted it as confirmation of what they had expected in the
postwar period. The war had ushered in a new spiritual vitality, an increased solidarity, and a heightened desire to sacrifice for the good of
the gospel. From war's end until well into 1920, these feelings held sway
among the South's Baptists. Regional, personal, and intellectual differences retreated in the face of this spirit, while the problems that
existed—mainly those of postwar readjustment—appeared manageable.

But the Seventy-Five Million Campaign was more an epilogue than a
prologue, for though it witnessed the high point of postwar optimism, it
marked the last time this spirit would prevail among Southern Baptists
for at least a decade. Issues that split the denomination, nagged at its
leaders, and drew attention away from evangelism soon arose. Many
Southern Baptists, especially denominational leaders, tried to keep their
fellow churchmen away from the byways that seductively beckoned. But
one by one the complex issues of the 1920s snared Southern Baptists in
theological dispute and personal recrimination. Already in 1919 the first
issue—interdenominationalism—had arisen. Although it often got lost
amidst visions of the future, it served as a harbinger of the unsettling
problems that would beset Southern Baptists in the decade ahead.

---

[16]Ibid., pp. 54-56.

Anxiety over the church union movement did not suddenly emerge at the end of World War I. It had been troubling Baptists for several decades, and especially since the organization of the Federal Council of Churches in 1908. A new context, not a new issue, confronted Baptists after the war. World conditions convinced them that they had a unique mission, and this realization stimulated a desire to delimit denominational lines and to bind church members more closely to the denomination. This made Southern Baptists acutely aware of the threat posed by the church union movement. Interdenominationalism remained an issue throughout the 1920s; indeed, it still disturbs Southern Baptists. But it never again reached the intensity it had in 1919 and 1920. Since most Southern Baptists refused to tamper with denominational ties, the ideal means of dealing with the problem would have been to ignore it. In declining this course, Baptists injected a note of controversy into an atmosphere suffused with good will, hope, and unity.

James Gambrell set the tone for discussion of relations with other churches. Upon his election to the presidency of the Southern Baptist Convention in 1917, Gambrell tried to sever the ties individual Southern Baptists held with interdenominational groups. After discovering that William O. Carver of Southern Seminary remained the only prominent Southern Baptist serving with an interdenominational agency, he asked Carver to resign from the Foreign Missions Conference. Carver refused, and Gambrell pursued the matter no further, but the dispute had been opened.[17]

Carver proved to be a minor irritant, for what really rankled Gambrell and his fellow churchmen was the interdenominational policy of the United States government during World War I. Gambrell charged that Dr. John R. Mott, secretary of the Young Men's Christian Association, had secretly worked out a plan with the government that had forced representatives of Protestant denominations to work under the auspices of the YMCA. To implement this plan the government had established a commission which, Gambrell charged, had included a Catholic, a Jew, and four Protestants of the "unionizing persuasion." Gambrell further stated that he had heard the Assistant Secretary of War admit that "the whole trend and the whole desire of the [war] department is in the interest of

---

[17]William O. Carver, *Out of His Treasure: Unfinished Memoirs* (Nashville: Broadman Press, 1956), pp. 72-73.

breaking down rather than emphasizing denominational distinctions."[18] In Gambrell's opinion the government had deliberately trampled on Baptist rights.

Baptists could have forgiven the government had nothing more than a few misguided bureaucratic policies been involved, but government favors, they charged, had nurtured and emboldened Protestant unionists. Gambrell discerned a vast unionizing conspiracy, led by Mott and Dr. Robert E. Speer of the Presbyterian Church, intent on sweeping Protestants into one religious body. The Federal Council of Churches, the YMCA, the Edinburgh Conference, the Foreign Missions Conference, and the Inter-Church World Movement, tied to one another in the person of Mott, comprised an insidious threat to denominational integrity. To Gambrell, the movement seemed to be an "enveloping, penetrating, enervating" creature that thrived on innocent Protestants who spoke naively of brotherhood and fellowship. Backed by money, prestige, and organizational talent, Mott and Speer stealthily worked out their plot. Nothing remained beyond their grasp, Gambrell said, for YMCA men had even begun to subvert Southern Baptist missions in China.[19]

Other Baptists took up Gambrell's crusade in the early months of 1919. An Oklahoman demanded that Southern Baptist preachers who favored church union resign their pastorates and leave the denomination, for men of halfhearted convictions would not be tolerated.[20] A Mississippian, writing in the state's Baptist journal, advised his brethren to fight the unionizing threat "with the most vigorous denominationalism that we have ever exhibited."[21] Even George Truett, a Texan who believed in good fellowship with all Christians, advised that "the sacrifice of convictions for the securement of Union in church work is disloyal to Christ, cannot be defended and results only in a camouflage union."[22]

This concern peaked at the Atlanta convention in May 1919. In the president's address, the same speech that fired its listeners to launch the Seventy-Five Million Campaign, Gambrell assailed the United States

---

[18]James G. Gambrell, *Baptists and Their Business* (Nashville: Sunday School Board, 1919), pp. 95-97.

[19]Ibid., pp. 86-87, 98-100.

[20]*Messenger*, 23 April 1919, p. 4.

[21]*Record*, 13 March 1919, p. 3.

[22]Truett to C. S. Wales, 13 April 1919, Truett Papers.

government for promoting the church union movement. The Home Mission Board chimed in with an attack on the nondenominational "Liberty Churches" that the War Department had established on its munitions reservations. And in his emotional sermon, M. E. Dodd asked: "Shall we go with the federated throngs of the day by compromising our spiritual message and adopting a half materialistic philosophy, or shall we stand alone in the sustaining truth that Christ is fulfilling his promise, 'Lo I am with you alway'[?]" Dodd answered his own question in words inspired by William Jennings Bryan's famous speech of 1896. "For my part," Dodd said, "I choose the latter alternative and hereby declare that the world shall not crucify our convictions upon a cross of unionism nor will we sell our principles for thirty pieces of popular praise."[23] Small wonder, then, that when J. Campbell White, representing the Inter-Church World Movement, addressed the gathering he made no discernible impact; Southern Baptists had made up their minds.[24]

Lest anyone harbor doubts about Southern Baptist attitudes toward church union, the committee appointed to discuss Gambrell's address devoted an important part of its report to the subject. The committee urged Southern Baptists to resist the call for union for two reasons: one, the movement advocated an autocratic organization in place of democratic autonomy; and two, a vast conglomerate of Protestants would be inefficient. Baptists could best bear their message by maintaining their distinctive principles and separate existence. The committee further asserted that Baptists welcomed union so long as it rested upon the dictates of the New Testament.[25] Some interpreted this to mean that, since Baptists claimed to be the only correct interpreters of the Scriptures, church union would occur when all Protestants became Baptists.

While Southern Baptists turned their attention to the Seventy-Five Million Campaign, men of the "unionizing persuasion," especially those affiliated with the Inter-Church World Movement, sought to convert Southern Baptists. Baptist leaders, hard at work heightening denominational awareness in order to raise money, resented the efforts of Inter-Church agents. Lee Scarborough warned against the encroachment of interdenominationalism, writing to Gambrell that representatives of the

---

[23]SBC, *Annual*, 1919, pp. 19, 75, 369-70.

[24]*Herald*, 29 May 1919, pp. 5-6.

[25]SBC, *Annual*, 1919, pp. 111-13.

Inter-Church World Movement "have a complete, well worked out system and are going to do their best to get Baptists in."[26] Scarborough asked Gambrell to write to the various state conventions, requesting them to pass resolutions against interdenominationalism. Whether Gambrell followed Scarborough's urging remains uncertain, but for whatever reason, when the state conventions met in November 1919 they demonstrated their awareness of the problem. Baptists in Georgia, Kentucky, Mississippi, North Carolina, and Virginia condemned the undermining of denominationalism.[27]

Most Southern Baptists applauded counterattacks on the church union movement, agreeing with Gambrell that it must be struck down before it gained a foothold within the denomination. But this antagonism toward other churches saddened some Southern Baptists and led them to ask if evangelism had not suffered from militant denominationalism. Robert Pitt of the *Religious Herald* commented early in 1920 that "in recent weeks our leaders and editors have seemed almost panic-stricken lest we should lose our denominational identity. It seems to us that they have put the whole business in a false perspective." Two weeks later he again voiced his concern, urging Baptists to spend more time on their own programs instead of worrying about the activities of others. If the agitation over church union continued, Pitt said, Southern Baptists would become so mired in the dispute that evangelism would slacken.[28]

For Pitt the solution lay in halting discussion of the matter. He closed the columns of the *Religious Herald* to arguments over interdenominationalism and encouraged his readers to cease further agitation.[29] But the issue could not be shut off so easily, for men such as Victor Masters and P. I. Lipsey, editor of the Mississippi *Baptist Record*, continued to stir Baptist emotions. Masters's book *The Call of the South*, widely used by Baptist study groups, attributed every imaginable evil to the union movement and

---

[26]Scarborough to Gambrell, 23 October 1919, James B. Gambrell Papers, Southwestern Baptist Theological Seminary.

[27]Georgia, *Minutes*, 1919, pp. 37-38; General Association of Baptists in Kentucky, *Proceedings*, 1919, pp. 54-55; Mississippi Baptist Convention, *Proceedings*, 1919, p. 96; North Carolina Baptist State Convention, *Annual*, 1919, p. 30; Baptist General Association of Virginia, *Minutes*, 1919, pp. 126-27.

[28]*Herald*, 12 February 1920, p. 2; 26 February 1920, p. 11.

[29]Ibid., March 4, 1920, p. 3.

blasted interdenominationalism for its subversion of Baptist principles.[30]
Even Pitt could not resist the clamor, and the *Religious Herald* broke its
silence with a fresh attack on the church union movement written by
Richmond pastor William W. Weeks.[31]

Although the controversy never completely died out, the demise of the
Inter-Church World Movement in the late 1920s and the failure of other
ecumenical bodies to attract Baptist support led to a tapering off of Baptist
fears. But the dispute broke out again during the fundamentalist controversy, this time as an internal threat from arch-conservative Baptists who
looked longingly at those of similar views in other Protestant churches.
But the real significance of the agitation over interdenominationalism lay
in the form it took in 1919 and 1920. Amidst the optimism and sense of
purpose that swept Southern Baptists after World War I, it served as a
harbinger of the difficulties of the 1920s. Leaders of the fight against
interdenominationalism argued that the furor was necessary to preserve
Baptist unity in the face of outside threats. Robert Pitt saw the dangers in
this policy. For Pitt denominational unity served one purpose: to facilitate
the preaching of the gospel and the salvation of mankind. He believed that
the controversy over church union hindered this by distracting people's
attention. The course of the 1920s vindicated Pitt, but for then, Southern
Baptists wanted no part of such an attitude.

---

[30]Masters, *The Call of the South* (Atlanta: Home Mission Board, 1920), pp. 21-22.
[31]*Herald*, 21 October 1920, pp. 4-5.

PART TWO

Southern Baptists and the Religious Issues of the 1920s

CHAPTER 3

Combating the Social Gospel

The problem of the church's relationship to society began clamoring for attention even before the denomination had pushed the church union issue aside. Southern Baptist ranks, largely unbroken by the fight over interdenominationalism, wavered when confronted by the question of the gospel's social content. The South's Baptists recognized the problem's existence, took differing positions on it, and thus opened the door a bit farther to the dissension and querulousness originally sparked by the church union controversy.

Southern Baptists had become increasingly aware of the debate over the church's position in society ever since the Social Gospel had emerged in the late nineteenth century. This movement, a response to the America spawned by industrialism and the growth of cities, had forced Protestants to ponder the church's role in raising wages, fighting political corruption, housing the homeless, and feeding the hungry.[1]

---

[1]Standard works on the rise of social Christianity include Aaron I. Abell, *The Urban Impact on American Protestantism* (Cambridge: Harvard University Press, 1953); Charles H. Hopkins, *The Rise of the Social Gospel in American Protestantism, 1865-1915* (New Haven: Yale University Press, 1967; original publication, 1940); and Henry F. May, *Protestant Churches and Industrial America* (New York: Harper & Row, 1967; original publication, 1949). The course of the Social Gospel after World War I may be traced in Paul A. Carter, *The Decline and Revival of the Social Gospel: Social and Political Liberalism in American Protestant Churches, 1920-1940* (Ithaca: Cornell University Press, 1956).

A theological reinterpretation, growing out of the application of biblical scholarship and the findings of evolutionary science to orthodox belief, undergirded this attention to concrete problems. Leading Social Gospelers, notably the Northern Baptist Walter Rauschenbusch, called for the Christianizing of society and urged their fellow churchmen to concentrate less on the promise of eternal life and to assume the task of earthly reconstruction. Rauschenbusch and his colleagues rejected the doctrine of human depravity, replacing it with the idea of man's benign nature. They emphasized instead the belief that "sin" arose from a bad environment. Individual salvation, the Social Gospel argued, should no longer be conceived in otherworldly terms, but should be considered a by-product of the struggle for the betterment of mankind.[2]

In a broader sense, Christian awareness of the temporal priorities of religion lay rooted in a tradition far older than the Social Gospel. From the time of Christ until the present, men have debated the nature of the Christian religion. Christ's contemporaries had argued over whether the Master should devote His time to addressing man's spiritual needs or to ministering to the social ills of the day. Throughout Christianity's history these conflicting impulses have warred within believers' minds, compelling some to translate the gospel into a program of social action, while directing others to ignore society in their quest for eternal life. Christians since the time of Christ have sought a comfortable position between these extremes.

The South's Baptists thus turned to an historic issue in the 1920s, seeking an answer to the question that had troubled men for centuries: what attitude does Christianity demand toward the problems of society? Faced with the need to understand the relationship between religion and society, some Southern Baptists tried to explain the different arguments advanced by Christian thinkers. John M. Price, director of Southwestern Seminary's School of Religious Education, undertook this task in the 1920s. Though published in 1928, Price's book *Christianity and Social Problems* presented ideas he had been teaching since 1918 in a course on Christian sociology. Price discerned three major groupings in Christianity. The "Ultra-Radicals" comprised those who replaced personal regeneration and individual salvation with a theology of "group life" and "social

---

[2]Walter Rauschenbusch's *A Theology for the Social Gospel* (New York: Macmillan Co., 1917) offers a clear statement of the new theology.

reform." On the other extreme stood the "Ultra-Conservatives" who believed that "the world is inevitably and inescapably bad and that it is none of our business to try to make it better." Between these positions lay a third approach, of which Price wrote approvingly:

> It is a mediating view. It believes both in personal regeneration and in social reform. It says that while people are being regenerated within, the environment without should be so transformed that it may be as nearly as possible conducive to the new life within. In other words, internal and external conditions should be made harmonious. So we should work both on the individual and his environment if the best results are to follow.[3]

Although Price perceptively analyzed these contrasting views, one must be careful in applying his classifications to Southern Baptists. Price's Ultra-Radicals found few allies among the South's Baptists. Because of Southern Baptist conservatism those who advocated the "mediating view" often found themselves on the denomination's left wing, though on the spectrum of Protestant thought they occupied a moderate position. The Ultra-Conservatives, "premillennial despairers" as Texas pastor Joseph M. Dawson called them, formed a potent contingent among Southern Baptists; they rejected social activism and looked longingly to Christ's Second Coming as the solution to society's ills.[4]

Despite the paucity of genuine Social Gospelers in their denomination, Southern Baptists spent much time discussing the threat of social Christianity. At the same time, Baptist moderates labored to establish a middle position that combined personal regeneration with social betterment. Premillennialists rejected both the Social Gospel and the moderate compromise. Finally, large numbers of Southern Baptists not mentioned in Price's scheme showed little concern for the Social Gospel, premillennialism, or a compromise between the two. These people, unknown and ignored as they were, played an important role, for their apathy aided premillennialists and hindered the moderate program. These elements

---

[3]John M. Price, *Christianity and Social Problems* (Nashville: Sunday School Board, 1928), pp. 41-43.

[4]Joseph M. Dawson, *The Light that Grows: Sermons to College Students* (New York: George H. Doran Co., 1923), p. 125.

wove in and out of Baptist thought in the 1920s. The ensuing debate over the relationship between religion and society formed an indispensable stage for the development of the denomination's social consciousness; but, viewed within the context of the 1920s, the debate siphoned energy away from the task of world evangelization for which the decade seemed so favorable.

The Southern Baptist reaction to the Social Gospel has received considerable attention in recent years. Although the denomination's conservatism would seem to hold little attraction for scholars interested in social Christianity, a number of historians have pictured the South's Baptists as becoming increasingly friendly to the Social Gospel in the first few decades of the twentieth century. Kenneth Bailey, in his *Southern White Protestantism in the Twentieth Century*, maintained that Southern Baptists, along with their Methodist and Presbyterian counterparts, emerged as "advocates of social justice" between 1900 and 1915.[5] Wayne Flynt has argued more recently that an important segment of Alabama's Baptists advocated social solutions similar to those of Protestant activists in the North.[6] Both these studies reaffirm ideas originally advanced by John Eighmy in his 1959 doctoral dissertation on the Southern Baptist social conscience, a work published in expanded form in 1972 as *Churches in Cultural Captivity: A History of the Social Attitudes of Southern Baptists*. Eighmy contended that social Christianity had first penetrated Baptist ranks around 1900, and "by 1920 the social gospel ideology had made definite inroads into the thought and practice of Southern Baptists."[7]

Evidence exists to support this position. Eighmy pointed to the seminaries as seedbeds of the new thinking, and the statements of a number of professors lend substance to his thesis. Walter T. Conner of Southwestern Seminary remarked that his views had been broadened by his studies under Walter Rauschenbusch at Rochester Theological

---

[5]Kenneth K. Bailey, *Southern White Protestantism in the Twentieth Century* (New York: Harper & Row, 1964), pp. 42-43.

[6]Wayne Flynt, "Dissent in Zion: Alabama Baptists and Social Issues, 1900-1919," *Journal of Southern History* 35 (November 1969): 524.

[7]John L. Eighmy, "The Social Conscience of Southern Baptists from 1900 to the Present as Reflected in Their Organized Life" (Ph.D. dissertation, University of Missouri, 1959), pp. 14-15, 42.

Seminary from 1908 to 1910.[8] A. T. Robertson praised Rauschenbusch as a "brave spirit" who had helped Americans "see that Christianity had a great part to play in the task of national regeneration."[9]

A few Baptist editors, notably L. L. Gwaltney of the *Alabama Baptist*, took stances similar to those of Northern Social Gospelers. Reflecting on the clash between advocates of social Christianity and those who clung to the idea of individual salvation, Gwaltney labeled the dispute a pointless fight over a confusion of terms. He argued that only one gospel existed, "the Gospel of Jesus Christ," which required Christians both to reform society and to bring lost sinners to Christ.[10] Other editors found themselves caught up, if only temporarily, in the search for Christianity's social consequences. Even P. I. Lipsey of the conservative Mississippi *Baptist Record* urged Mississippians "to welcome anything . . . that enables us to understand the implications and applications of his [Christ's] teaching to modern conditions in society and business and government, in labor and capital."[11]

William L. Poteat, president of Wake Forest College from 1905 to 1927, furnishes the most important proof of a Social Gospel tradition within the Southern Baptist denomination. At times Poteat's words were indistinguishable from those of the most ardent proponents of social Christianity:

> Religion must impose its ennobling restraints upon private greed and class antagonisms, erect the Christian standard in the market place and mill, insist that industries were made for man, not man for industries, and demand, as it does now demand, that the industrial system in all its manifold sections outlaw the enlightened selfishness of the orthodox political economy, recognize equality of opportunity and privilege for all men, give assurance of employment and tomorrow's bread, care for the incapacitated worker, provide a

---

[8]Walter T. Conner, "My Religious Experiences," undated manuscript in the Conner Papers.

[9]Archibald T. Robertson, *The New Citizenship* (New York: Fleming H. Revell, 1919), p. 149.

[10]Leslie L. Gwaltney, *Forty of the Twentieth or the First Forty Years of the Twentieth Century* (Birmingham: published by the author, 1940), pp. 124-28.

[11]*Record*, 12 June 1919, p. 4.

minimum of necessary working hours under a maximum of
wholesome life conditions, and allow the workers
representation in directing the enterprise and a fair share in
the profits and losses for which they are responsible.[12]

In view of this statement it cannot be denied that social Christianity
received a hearing among Southern Baptists around the time of World
War I. But the case must not be overstated, for the Southern Baptist
masses remained hostile to demands for social activism regardless of
what a few professors or editors might say. As social activist Joseph
Dawson recalled in his autobiography: "For a quarter of a century I was
only a voice crying in the wilderness."[13]

Although Dawson exaggerated his plight, Baptist scholars, in a
number of studies from the 1940s to the present, have proven the
underlying truth in Dawson's cry, while drawing a more realistic picture
of the impact of the Social Gospel on their denomination. During World
War II, Hugh Brimm pointed out that from 1910 to 1935 social
Christianity had virtually no influence on Baptist attitudes toward
minority races, mill hands, tenant farmers and migrant workers.[14] In a
thesis written at Southwestern Seminary in 1948, Charles P. Johnson
explored the Southern Baptist rejection of the Social Gospel.[15] Patrick
Hill, a doctoral student at Southern Seminary, concluded a year later that
from 1915 to 1940 Southern Baptist editors had failed "to make the
ethical insights of Jesus socially effective."[16] More recently, Samuel S.
Hill, Jr. has noted the absence of a reform ethic inspired by the South's
churches.[17] As these studies show, one must speak of the Social Gospel

---

[12]William L. Poteat, *The Way of Victory* (Chapel Hill: University of North Carolina Press, 1929), pp. 61-62.

[13]Joseph M. Dawson, *A Thousand Months to Remember* (Waco: Baylor University Press, 1964), pp. 170-71.

[14]Hugh A. Brimm, "The Social Consciousness of Southern Baptists in Relation to Some Regional Problems, 1910-1935" (Th.D. thesis, Southern Baptist Theological Seminary, 1944).

[15]Charles P. Johnson, "Southern Baptists and the Social Gospel Movement" (Th.D. thesis, Southwestern Baptist Theological Seminary, 1948).

[16]Patrick H. Hill, "The Ethical Emphases of the Baptist Editors in the Southeastern Region of the United States, 1915-1940" (Th.D. thesis, Southern Baptist Theological Seminary, 1949), p. 295.

[17]Samuel S. Hill, Jr., *Southern Churches in Crisis* (New York: Holt, Rinehart, and Winston, 1966), pp. 113-14.

among Southern Baptists with the understanding that the views of a small minority are being considered. The overwhelming majority of Southern Baptists repudiated anything resembling social Christianity; for them it represented a threat that had to be combated.

In the 1920s four issues accounted for Southern Baptist concern over the Social Gospel.

• First, the movement's origins and goals made it difficult for most Southern Baptists to enter its ranks.

• Second, World War I cast new light on social Christianity and strengthened Baptist opposition.

• Third, when the fundamentalist controversy flared up after the war Baptists became more aware of the liberal tone of social Christianity's recasting of traditional theology.

• Finally, Baptists feared that social concern would destroy the spiritual core of their religion and hasten the church toward secularism.

Given the circumstances which produced the Social Gospel, it is small wonder that so few Southern Baptists were attracted to it. As Aaron Abell, Charles Hopkins, and Henry May have pointed out, the movement arose in response to a rapidly industrializing and urbanizing America. Smoke-belching factories, poverty-stricken urban masses, and bloody strife between workers and their bosses undergirded the urge to Christianize the social order. In Hopkins's words, "the social gospel . . . may be regarded as American Protestantism's response to the challenge of modern industrial society."[18]

As late as the 1920s the South lacked many prerequisites of social Christianity. Except for Birmingham, Alabama, the South had none of the massive industrial centers that did so much to prod the Social Gospelers into action in the North. Manufacturing remained limited, and the textile mills so proudly acclaimed by Southern chambers of commerce employed people with strong rural ties, workers inhospitable to socialism, or even to the mild blandishments of organized labor. Not until the end of the decade did Southern laborers begin to awaken. Moreover, the immigrant masses that had stirred reformers in the North had largely bypassed the South's cities.[19]

---

[18]Hopkins, *The Rise of the Social Gospel*, p. 318.

[19]George B. Tindall, *The Emergence of the New South, 1913-1945* (Baton Rouge: Louisiana State University Press, 1967), pp. 318-53.

The urban, industrial life that did exist in the South went unsampled by most of the region's Baptists. In the 1920s ninety-two percent of the denomination's churches existed in open country or in towns of less than 2500 population, and these congregations accounted for over seventy percent of the South's Baptists.[20] Many Baptists residing in cities had recently lived in the country, and ordinarily they belonged to urban churches that encouraged them to revere their rural origins. Moreover, during the twenties two events—the fundamentalist controversy and the presidential election of 1928—made Southern Baptists fiercely conscious of their rural roots and heightened their hostility to political, social, and religious ideas emanating from Northern cities. In part, then, the nature of Southern society made Baptists unreceptive to social Christianity.

As with many problems, the Social Gospel took on new coloration in light of World War I. A heightened sensitivity to the menace of social Christianity appeared in M. E. Dodd's sermon at the first postwar gathering of Southern Baptists in 1919. Dodd charged that "sickly, enervating sentimentalism" and a "no heart and all head humanitarianism" threatened to undermine the spread of the gospel. Virginia Baptists, warning that "social service is the fad and dissipation of the present," criticized those who professed to be their "brother's keeper," a label which fit everyone from "soft, slobbering sentimentalists who squander other people's money" to the "downright dishonest."[21]

Baptists drew many lessons from the war, but none more important than its exposure of the rough underside of human nature. Georgia Baptists charged that before 1914 proponents of a socially conscious Christianity had held a "rosy, genial belief that human nature under proper conditions could recreate itself." This shallow optimism had been dispelled by the evil unleashed by the war, for the Social Gospel's belief in progress through human enlightenment had encountered appalling acts perpetrated by a supposedly advanced German nation. "They [the Germans] were perhaps the most highly trained minds of the world yet committed deeds of horror and acted like untamed animals," Georgia's Baptists concluded.[22] Social Christianity's confidence in reform,

---

[20]U.S. Bureau of the Census, *Religious Bodies* (1926), 2:103.

[21]*Herald*, 29 May 1919, p. 6; Virginia, *Minutes*, 1919, pp. 86-87.

[22]Georgia, *Minutes*, 1919, pp. 31-33.

education, and scientific progress seemed unfounded to many Baptists. As Victor Masters noted: "It is written so plainly that all may read that the titanic struggle, foisted on the world by Germany, was a confession that a nation may lead in science, sanitation, cooperative industry, and human learning, and yet the inner sources of its power may be brutal, godless, and unspeakably corrupt."[23] In the eyes of Southern Baptists, the war, by exposing man's inherent evil, had weakened the case for social Christianity.

Before World War I the theological liberalism of the Social Gospel had served as one of many reasons for Southern Baptist unease, but with the war's end and the renewal of the controversy between liberal and conservative Protestants, the ties between the Social Gospel and liberalism received new emphasis. This indictment of social Christianity appeared most strikingly in the writings of Victor Masters, highly respected author, editor, and publicist. Initially, with his books and articles written while publicity secretary of the Home Mission Board and after 1921 through the editorial pages of the influential Kentucky *Western Recorder*, Masters waged war on the Social Gospel. He charged that "pantheism and evolution" had been popularized by those preaching social salvation, lumped social Christianity with church unionism as "among the most significant means of rationalistic propaganda for tearing down the Christian bodies," and accused "those who follow this cult of humanitarian service" of doubting Christ's divinity.[24] Despite Masters's stridency, his words did not represent the isolated voice of extremism, for even the prominent moderate A. T. Robertson cautioned against the "naturalistic social gospel" that had ceased to stress salvation for sinful men.[25]

Baptists felt that Social Gospelers, with their emphasis on improving society, had neglected the inner transformation required of sinners. Addressing this problem, Virginia Baptists admitted that material circumstances should not be scorned; after all, God had placed Adam and Eve in the Garden of Eden, amidst perfect surroundings, with all their

---

[23]Masters, *The Call of the South*, p. 28.

[24]*Herald*, 16 January 1919, p. 8; Victor I. Masters, *Making America Christian* (Atlanta: Home Mission Board, 1921), p. 112; Masters, *The Call of the South*, p. 25.

[25]Archibald T. Robertson, *The Mother of Jesus* (Grand Rapids: Baker Book House, 1963; original publication, 1925), p. 30.

physical needs supplied. But the lesson of Eden was clear: a perfect environment, even one fashioned by God, could not preserve the purity of a man inclined to sin.[26] George Truett, pastor of the First Baptist Church in Dallas, complained that social Christianity had reduced "religion to a mere ethic," in which the command to do good had replaced the necessity of inward spiritual change.[27] Other Baptists discerned an effort to preach salvation through imitation of Christ's life, while ignoring the significance of His death and resurrection. Such "an attempt to save people by the life of Christ alone," A. C. Dixon, pastor of the University Baptist Church in Baltimore, wrote, "is like trying to cross a river on a bridge, built half way across and on the other side of the river."[28] Orthodoxy's transcendent God appeared about to be toppled by a weak, spiritually wan deity who asked only that man live a good life and grow gradually into salvation. Social Christianity thus endangered the "sense of the divine," the dependence on God, and the belief in a dramatic alteration in man so essential to Baptists.[29] To Southern Baptists, this movement foreshadowed a day when an ethic of brotherhood and social reform would supplant individual regeneration.

Some of the time and energy spent worrying about social Christianity could have been used more profitably by Southern Baptists, for the movement had scarcely gained a foothold within their denomination. On the other hand, the Social Gospel's proclivity for diluting spirituality with temporal concerns presented a real problem. In recognition of this, the South's Baptists sought to show that man's ultimate purpose lay in preaching the gospel of salvation to a lost world, and not, as Social Gospelers claimed, in ending war, fighting poverty, and promoting better labor relations. Baptists presented their case simply and explicitly. A malignant nature, which could be exorcised only through the miracle of conversion and spiritual rebirth, dwelled within the heart of every individual. After experiencing the new birth, the sinner dedicated himself to helping others find God; thus, evangelism—the preaching of

---

[26]Virginia, *Minutes*, 1925, pp. 120-21.

[27]George W. Truett, *Follow Thou Me* (New York: Ray Long and Richard, 1932), pp. 61-62.

[28]Amzi C. Dixon, "A Mossback's Reply to Modernism," pp. 16-17, ca. early 1920s typescript, Amzi C. Dixon Papers, Dargan-Carver Library, Nashville, Tennessee, Box 12.

[29]*Messenger*, 15 June 1921, p. 8; *Herald* 26 June 1919, pp. 8-9.

the gospel—not social melioration, constituted man's assigned task on earth. The beauty of this argument lay in the unanimity it commanded, for no one calling himself a Southern Baptist could easily disagree with it, and, indeed, few did. In a decade of dissension, Southern Baptists gladly welcomed such unanimity.

In opposition to the Social Gospel's admiring view of human nature, Southern Baptists stressed man's inherent evil. Human beings possessed an "evil spirit" that controlled their thoughts and actions, producing a being hateful in the eyes of God. In his natural state man stood naked in the darkness, alienated from God, bereft of hope, alone in the world of evil and despair. Human beings shared the common fate of being passengers in the "sinking boat of depravity," and sin, the curse inherited from Adam by all men at birth, dominated their lives. "Total depravity" best described the human condition. This did not mean that man possessed no benevolent impulses or that he acted evilly at all times, but rather that all men labored under the dictatorial rule of sin.[30]

Baptists discerned a growing tendency among others to disregard this human condition. North Carolinian Richard T. Vann, noting that contemporary Protestant ministers seldom mentioned the dreadfulness of sin, pointed to this omission as one of the central problems of the age.

> We have come to think and speak lightly, even jestingly, of sin. To some, it is nothing more than a mental disease or a physical disorder, inherited, or produced by unfavorable environment, in no case involving any moral responsibility nor any guilt.[31]

Vann condemned psychologists for promoting this attitude, but obviously social Christianity, with its concern for material conditions and its cavalier treatment of sin, shared the blame. Baptists could not forgive Social Gospelers for neglecting sinfulness, a central concern of the Christian tradition, and thereby throwing their influence to the forces of

---

[30]William W. Weeks, *The Face of Christ* (Nashville: Sunday School Board, 1927), pp. 52-53; Lee R. Scarborough, *Christ's Militant Kingdom* (New York: George H. Doran Co., 1924), p. 47; Scarborough, *A Search for Souls* (Nashville: Sunday School Board, 1925), p. 34; Edgar Y. Mullins, *The Christian Religion in Its Doctrinal Expression* (Philadelphia: Judson Press, 1917), p. 294.

[31]Richard T. Vann, *The Things Not Seen* (Nashville: Sunday School Board, 1931), pp. 141-42.

modernity. To the South's Baptists, sin formed the mother lode from which all man's problems could be extracted. George Truett remarked: "The primary tragedy of the world is not ignorance, bad as ignorance is, nor is it poverty and poor wages. The primary tragedy of this world is sin, and man's fundamental need is the need of a Saviour and Redeemer from sin."[32]

Although Southern Baptists bandied about such terms as "total depravity" and "sinful nature," most of them, except for the chronically misanthropic, advanced beyond this condemnation. They recognized a second dimension, often buried amidst the debris of sin, but nonetheless another side of human nature. "There is in a real sense, a very beautiful personality lying latent within the animal life of every man," Ashby Jones of Atlanta observed.[33] Baptists contended that in the centuries following Adam and Eve's expulsion from Eden the human race had degenerated. But God had preserved a vision of perfection, a memory of a man and woman created in His image. He had sent His Son to this earth to die in order to rekindle the flame of divine beauty that centuries of wickedness had reduced to a smoldering ember. Because God realized that "man's greatness consists, not in what he is, but in what he may become," Baptists held hope for mankind.[34]

This guarded optimism depended on the miracle of the new birth rather than on prospects for cultural growth or social reform. Recognizing the futility of man's efforts at self-development in the face of heredity and environment, God enabled mortals to escape the clutches of determinism through spiritual rebirth. With the blood of His Son God regenerated man's "psychic nature," cleansed him of sin, and snatched him from the bonds of eternal death.[35] For his part, the sinner had to repent and, struck by his own evil, turn to God for help. After the sinner's repentance, God began to remold him in the divine image. A "new ideal," a "new call" to righteousness, and a "new hope" for eternal life unfolded within the individual, and through the grace of God he conquered his evil

---

[32]Truett, *Follow Thou Me*, p. 62.

[33]Ashby Jones, "The Human Harvest," in Joseph Fort Newton, ed., *Best Sermons 1925* (New York: Harcourt, Brace, and Co., 1925), p. 122.

[34]Vann, *The Things Not Seen*, p. 100; Weeks, *The Face of Christ*, p. 150.

[35]William O. Carver, *The Self-Interpretation of Jesus* (Nashville: Broadman Press, n. d.; original publication, 1926), p. 171; Scarborough, *Christ's Militant Kingdom*, p. 31.

nature. Born into a new life, he emerged as a being in whom "egoism" and selfishness, the essence of sin, had been slain.[36]

A miracle indeed: a creature filled with hatred, envy, and selfishness was transformed into a "lily among thorns" and a "light shining in a dark place."[37] But none of the accounts of conversion and rebirth mentioned external conditions. Whether a sinner lived in squalor in a Mississippi tenant shack, or dwelled in the middle-class comfort of Atlanta, he stood equal with his fellows before God. All men, rich and poor alike, had to experience the new birth. This change remained purely spiritual; increasing a man's wages or improving his housing brought him no closer to God. Southern Baptists accused social Christianity of impeding this process by grafting secular concerns onto a spiritual occurrence. Social reform, Baptists said, must never be allowed to interfere with the internal change of the new birth. Moreover, the dramatic, miraculous nature of this event must be preserved. There could be no tolerance of social Christianity's belief in man's ability to win favor with God through a life of good deeds.

Following this logic, Southern Baptists concluded that evangelism, not social reform, furnished the reason for the Christian's existence. The Christian must work with God in spreading the gospel and aid the Master in saving men from sin's deadly embrace. The desire to preach the message of salvation inevitably followed the new birth, for God established a "dynamic for the conquest of the world" in the heart of each saved man.[38] This new person of beautiful soul and pure heart then took his place in the ranks of God's army. "Soul winning" became his "primal Christian duty," and he eagerly spread "the good news of the gospel of Jesus Christ and. . . persuade[d] men to accept Him as Saviour and Lord and King."[39] Baptists did not speak of soul winning in theoretical terms, for they meant for each Christian to hurl himself into the face of evil and wrest men away from sinfulness. They believed that the Social Gospel, by preaching social reform, directed Christian energies away from this

---

[36]Vann, *The Things Not Seen*, pp. 172-73; Dawson, *The Light That Grows*, pp. 146-47; Weeks, *The Face of Christ*, p. 59; Edwin M. Poteat, "Stewardship and Redemption," *Missionary Review of the World* 43 (February 1920): 115.

[37]Weeks, *The Face of Christ*, p. 45.

[38]Scarborough, *Christ's Militant Kingdom*, 33.

[39]Scarborough, *A Search for Souls*, p. 7; SBC, *Annual*, 1921, p. 71.

"primal" duty into perplexing secular concerns.

Throughout the 1920s Southern Baptists gave clear evidence of their support of evangelism. Evangelists such as Mordecai Ham and Baxter McLendon stumped the South, blazing trails of righteousness through the morass of evil. Frank Norris, George Truett, and other prominent pastors periodically forsook their pulpits for whirlwind campaigns. Non-Baptist soul winners, notably Billy Sunday, found eager audiences in the South.[40] Even a liberal Baptist such as McNeill Poteat, who referred to Sunday and his colleagues as "peripatetic exhorters,"[41] saw the need for evangelistic meetings. Lee Scarborough, one of the most influential Baptists in the 1920s, boosted evangelism enormously in his teaching, preaching, and writing. And finally, in 1920 the Southern Baptist Convention, stirred by the Seventy-Five Million Campaign, called for "One Hundred Evangelists and 100,000 converts each year for the next five years,"[42] and at the next session laid elaborate plans for every Baptist to take as his motto "Every One Win One."[43] This activity showed that Southern Baptists meant to maintain the process of repentance, conversion, and rebirth threatened by the secularizing tendencies of social Christianity.

By stressing these time-honored doctrines, Southern Baptists found some unity in a decade of disagreement. In this sense, concern over social Christianity produced beneficial results. But equally important, the battle against the Social Gospel set Baptists on edge and heightened their awareness of a hostile world seeking to undermine their principles. Whether the denomination gained more from the struggle than it lost remains a moot point.

---

[40]William G. McLoughlin, Jr., *Billy Sunday Was His Real Name* (Chicago, 1955), 272.

[41]McNeill Poteat to Gordon Poteat, 12 April 1929, Edwin McNeill Poteat, Jr. Papers, Southern Historical Collection, University of North Carolina, Chapel Hill, North Carolina, Box 1.

[42]SBC, *Annual*, 1920, p. 371.

[43]SBC, *Annual*, 1921, pp. 72-73.

CHAPTER 4

Moderates, Premillennialists, and the Southern Baptist Social Conscience

In the 1920s most Southern Baptists rejected the Social Gospel because it symbolized the secularism and groundless optimism of an alien urban-industrial culture. Some historians, notably Paul Carter in *The Decline and Revival of the Social Gospel,* have played down this hostility by stressing the importance of Prohibition as a unifying force in Protestant circles. Carter contends that in the twenties Social Gospelers shunted aside many cherished causes and made Prohibition a "surrogate" for the Social Gospel.[1] This enabled conservatives to unite with their former enemies to crush the liquor interests. Kenneth Bailey agrees with Carter, asserting that "with equal fervor, conservative, moderate, and liberal churchmen rallied behind prohibition as the great social cause of the ages."[2]

Carter and Bailey create a false impression by implying that unity over the liquor issue measurably weakened conservative animus toward

---

[1]Paul A. Carter, *The Decline and Revival of the Social Gospel: Social and Political Liberalism in American Protestant Churches, 1920-1940* (Ithaca: Cornell University Press, 1956), p. 42.

[2]Kenneth K. Bailey, *Southern White Protestantism in the Twentieth Century* (New York: Harper & Row, 1964), p. 68.

social Christianity. At the same time, it cannot be denied that the fight against alcohol commanded the attention of most Protestants during the twenties. Southern Baptists of varying social and theological persuasions agreed that Prohibition had to be enforced. On the denomination's left wing stood William Poteat, evolutionist and advocate of social justice, but also president of the North Carolina Anti-Saloon League and crusader against John Barleycorn. On the other extreme was Frank Norris, premillennial opponent of social Christianity, but at the same time an ardent supporter of Prohibition. Between these two positions rested the mass of Southern Baptists, some willing to push into the realm of social action, a larger number totally apathetic to the preoccupations of social Christianity, but all willing to battle the "satanic" forces of alcohol.

This unity prompted Bailey to write that "prohibition served to calm and moderate internal dissensions and to draw warring factions into a common cause and purpose."[3] Although Bailey's statement contains a good deal of truth, it fails to recognize the discord that lay behind the united front against alcohol. Socially conscious moderates, who wished to involve the denomination in society's problems, sought more than a crusade against beer, wine, and whiskey. Although they wanted only to attune Baptists to secular ills without transforming them into Social Gospelers, the denomination's conservatism forced them to the left of most of their fellow churchmen. At the opposite end of the spectrum, premillennialists, preaching cataclysm and destruction, rejected any program that suggested coping with the world; to them the earth was a cesspool, a place one hurried through on his way to the promised land. Proponents of these opposing views sought the support of the vast group of Baptists in the center. The ensuing contest conformed to the pattern of the 1920s: the denomination turned from the work at hand—spreading the gospel—to deal with a competing issue.

Moderates formed a small but vocal minority within the denomination. The exact size and characteristics of the group cannot easily be determined, for it included a loosely knit company of men, scattered across the South and bound together by a desire to prick the denomination's social conscience. Moderates came from the educated and articulate segment of the denomination and from important positions, though generally not from the highest echelons of leadership. College

---

[3]Ibid., p. 95.

and seminary professors, editors, and ministers furnished most of the recruits for the moderate cause.

Southern Seminary in Louisville, Kentucky, harbored several of the most influential member of the group. Professors A. T. Robertson, William Carver, and Charles S. Gardner called for social awareness, while President E. Y. Mullins entreated Baptists to become involved in the world. Fort Worth's Southwestern Seminary claimed fewer moderates, understandably so in light of Baptist conservatism west of the Mississippi River. But even here, two prominent professors—John Price and Walter Conner—called for sensitivity to temporal ills.

Baptist colleges and universities contained the greatest number of moderates. Although many of these men remained unknown, they labored tirelessly to enlighten the youth who passed through their classrooms. In the Southeast, Rolvix Harlan of the University of Richmond, William Poteat of Wake Forest College, and Rufus Weaver of Mercer University urged their students to dedicate themselves to aiding mankind. Farther west, moderates became more scarce, but they existed in such schools as Baylor University.

Among Baptist editors, L. L. Gwaltney of the *Alabama Baptist* spoke most forthrightly in defense of the church's social role. A number of Gwaltney's colleagues, notably Robert Pitt of the Virginia *Religious Herald*, Livingston Johnson of the North Carolina *Biblical Recorder*, Z. T. Cody of the South Carolina *Baptist Courier*, and Louie D. Newton of the Georgia *Christian Index*, if not as aggressive and outspoken as Gwaltney, at least aided and encouraged the moderate cause. Finally, P. I. Lipsey, editor of the Mississippi *Baptist Record*, occasionally issued statements surprisingly liberal in view of his own premillennialism and the conservatism of Mississippi Baptists.

The most courageous moderates stood in Southern Baptist pulpits urging their congregations to remember the plight of their fellowman. These pastors balanced precariously on the edge of ruin, always at the mercy of their church members, but refusing to shrink from preaching the whole gospel and not a version stripped of its ethical content. As with their academic allies, many of these men remained nameless, their acts of courage unknown. But a number of them left their imprint upon the denomination. Sparks W. Melton of Norfolk, Virginia, published a book in 1934 entitled *Will He Find Faith?*, in which he echoed many of social Christianity's themes. McNeill Poteat, missionary to China and after 1929 pastor of a Raleigh, North Carolina, church, spoke continually of the social demands of Christianity. In Georgia, Ashby Jones preached the message of social righteousness. As in the case of teachers and editors, few ministers could be found outside the Southeast who were willing to expound their moderate beliefs from the pulpit. A notable exception appeared in Texas, where Joseph Dawson reminded Baptists of the social demands of their faith.

A final group of moderates belonged to the southwide and state committees on social service. These bodies drew most of their members from teachers, editors, and ministers seeking outlets for their views, but they also contained laymen who fitted none of these categories. Whether from conservative influence, timidity, or a desire for unity, annual reports submitted by these groups generally avoided controversy by concentrating on Prohibition, dancing, divorce, gambling, and other matters of personal morality. Still, through their recognition of the need for Christian solutions to secular problems, these committees encouraged Baptists to expand their view of society. Arthur J. Barton, chairman of the Southern Baptist Convention's Social Service Commission from 1910 to 1942, exemplified this approach, for though he spent much time dealing with Prohibition, he helped to prod the denomination into a new era of social sensitivity.

Moderates used a number of approaches to engage their denomination in reform activity. In the first place, they slipped carefully worded appeals into southwide, state, and local social service reports. In books, articles, and resolutions they tried to awaken their brethren to the need for social commitment. Moderates acknowledged the existence of apathy and outright hostility to their program, but they kept at their labors. To ease this opposition, they spent much time allaying the widespread suspicion that Baptist activists formed a seditious minority intent on foisting alien ideas on God's people. These assurances generally emerged as finely wrought appeals to biblical tradition as precedent for earthly reform. More important, moderates tried to forge a reform ethic within the confines of Baptist doctrine, attempting to prove that social concern complemented spiritual rebirth, personal salvation, and soul winning. The final step involved preaching a modified version of the doctrine of the kingdom of God on earth, through which moderates hoped to show that God intended Christians to feel compassion for man's material plight as well as anguish for his soul.

Baptist moderates endeavored to spark their fellow churchmen to action with constant reminders of their social obligation. Nowhere could this be seen more clearly than in the annual reports of the Social Service Commission under the chairmanship of Arthur Barton. The report of 1921 summed up the moderate position:

> We, as Southern Baptists, have scarcely begun to enter the great and ever widening field of social service. It is the serious judgment of your Commission that this phase of our work should be materially strengthened and enlarged. Baptists must bear their full share of responsibility and discharge their full obligation in this field. They must make the largest and best contribution possible to the promotion of social service, and to the saving of social service from the purely humanitarian and somewhat materialistic basis to which, in many instances, it has been brought.[4]

This statement was more than an isolated example of pious rhetoric. Similar advice in the 1924 and 1927 reports demonstrated Barton's determination to keep the topic alive.[5]

The moderate program received equally important boosts from other sources as well. In 1925 a committee chaired by E. Y. Mullins drew up a confession of faith that called for Baptists to aid and comfort God's less fortunate children.[6] State conventions also promoted the moderate cause, as evidenced by the Alabama Committee on Social Service's suggestion in 1927 that the state's Baptists should inject "into our community life all the principles of benevolence and justice which we profess in our pulpits and Bible classes on the First Day of the Week."[7] The writings of individual Baptists provided equally fruitful outlets for moderate sentiment. Numerous examples of this exist, but to cite a representative case, W. T. Conner, in his widely read book *Gospel Doctrines*, argued that Christians could improve their characters by "striving against sin in the social order."[8]

Despite the importance of such calls for recognition of the church's responsibility, moderates realized that they must push beyond these mild

---

[4]SBC, *Annual*, 1921, p. 85.

[5]Ibid., 1924, p. 118; 1927, p. 113.

[6]Ibid., 1925, p. 74.

[7]Alabama Baptist State Convention, *Annual*, 1927, pp. 135-36.

[8]Walter T. Conner, *Gospel Doctrines* (Nashville: Sunday School Board, 1925), p. 106.

pleas if they hoped to stimulate action. They attempted to give substance to their summons by building a strong case for social action. Wisely, Baptist moderates realized that this case must be firmly based on the Bible; consequently, for a Baptist people nurtured on the Good Book, moderates hastened to show that adherence to God's word undergirded their program.

John Price, a Baptist keenly aware of his denomination's social shortcomings, never failed to reassure his readers. In *Christianity and Social Problems* Price argued that the Bible contained the perfect formula for relations between society and the individual: the Scriptures hew to a moderate line, advocating neither "extreme individualism" nor "extreme socialism." The sacred book called for "socialized individualism," or as Price explained, "it recognizes the individual as the ultimate unit, but also identifies his interests with those of others."[9] Price felt that the Bible's "socialized individualism" offered ample room in which to forge a Southern Baptist social ethic.

In their efforts to claim biblical support for their program Southern Baptist moderates invoked the activism of the Old Testament prophets. Price, for example, combed the Bible from Genesis to Malachi for precedents, singling out Elijah, Isaiah, and Nehemiah for special praise.[10] But more often, those in search of biblical prototypes turned to the New Testament. In typical fashion Louisiana Baptists remarked that "the story of the Good Samaritan is the social gospel dramatized; Paul's collection among the believers in Macedonia, Achaia and Galatia for the poor, hungry Jewish Christians and unbelieving Jews at Jerusalem is the social gospel in sacrificial action."[11] Moderates delighted in the New Testament's account of Christ's ministry. In the Master they saw one who had urged ethical conduct as a test of Christian life and who had suffered the agonies of those who care for the poor, sick, and hungry. Jesus had set the pattern for Christians to follow, for He had attacked corruption, healed the sick, engaged in philanthropy, and laid down far-reaching principles of reform.[12] Rolvix Harlan, a professor of sociology, contended that Jesus had

---

[9]John M. Price, *Christianity and Social Problems* (Nashville: Sunday School Board, 1928), p. 73.

[10]Ibid., pp. 56-72.

[11]Louisiana Baptist State Convention, *Annual*, 1921, p. 63.

[12]Archibald T. Robertson, *Paul and the Intellectuals: The Epistle to the Colossians*

established the model for organized social work in his celebrated feeding of the five thousand. Christ had also set forth the principles of individual worth and dignity and had promulgated the "law of cooperation or mutuality," Harlan said.[13] To Harlan and like-minded Southern Baptists Christ's life spoke eloquently of the need to aid the earth's unfortunates.

Reform-minded Baptists also gathered support from the revered doctrines of the Baptist faith. They argued that belief in conversion, rebirth, and individual salvation meshed perfectly with their program, for the restructuring of society must be accompanied by the conversion of individual souls. These saved souls, imbued with righteousness, bore the "fruits" of salvation, among them the desire to alleviate the world's suffering and injustice. Christ's death on the Cross, His suffering so that sinners could have new life, obligated man to labor for others.[14] E. Y. Mullins summed up the relationship between individual salvation and social service in an article in the *Religious Herald* in 1919, remarking that:

> The very essence of the new life in Christ is regard for the welfare of others. And regard for the welfare of others finds normal expression in social service. So also the conversion of the individual is a necessary condition of the most effective social service.[15]

Baptists reluctant to commit their denomination to social reform needed only to turn to William Poteat for reassurance of the doctrinal purity of social activists. Poteat, one of the few Southern Baptists close to the Social Gospel movement, frequently drew conservative wrath for his acceptance of biological evolution. But cries of heresy to the contrary, he maintained an orthodox view of the relationship between individual regeneration and social reform. "What we require is not a new system of government, a new scheme for the distribution of wealth, a new social organization," Poteat commented, but "what we require is new people."[16]

(Garden City: Doubleday, Doran, and Co., 1928; original publication, 1926), p. 171; Price, *Christianity and Social Problems*, pp. 68-69.

[13]*Herald*, 18 January 1923, pp. 2, 6-7.

[14]State Convention of the Baptist Denomination in South Carolina, *Minutes*, 1929, p. 153; *Herald*, 3 July 1919, p. 4; SBC, *Annual* 1922, p. 96.

[15]*Herald*, 14 August 1919, p. 4.

[16]William L. Poteat, *Christianity and Enlightenment* (N. p., n. d.), p. 9.

Although redemption of the individual promised the social order's salvation, the process would not work in reverse, Poteat asserted.[17] For a left-wing Baptist such as Poteat, as well as for his more moderate colleagues, personal salvation must precede any dramatic alteration in temporal institutions.

Southern Baptist moderates recognized the need to relate social serivce to their denomination's passion for evangelism. Feeling the attraction toward preaching the gospel as much as anyone, moderates attempted to show that evangelism and service to the needy complemented each other. Evangelism produced saved souls ready to reconstruct their environment, while social service simplified the task of evangelism by demonstrating the power of Christian love.[18] In this vein, P. I. Lipsey discerned three reasons for combining social service and evangelism. In the first place, social work would falter without soul saving, for only a regenerate individual would stick to the job of earthly reform. Second, the two went together because only a callous person could minister to spiritual needs and ignore material poverty. Finally, Lipsey concluded, social work in foreign lands would facilitate the conversion of the heathen.[19] The Southern Baptist Convention's 1923 report on social service captured the essence of the moderate position, asserting that "a good soul winner ought to be earnest and efficient in social service, and certainly an intelligent social worker ought to be an earnest and efficient soul winner."[20]

Moderates received little criticism for their use of biblical examples and traditional Baptist doctrines. After all, who could argue too vehemently with a man who studied his Bible, revered the doctrines of repentance, conversion, and redemption, and called for the preaching of the gospel? But when moderates unveiled the final part of their brief for social commitment—the idea of the kingdom of God on earth—they risked the ire of their brethren by promoting a concept dangerously close to one advanced by advocates of social Christianity. Social Gospelers maintained that the reign of the kingdom of God, an era free from strife, hatred,

---

[17]William L. Poteat, *The Way of Victory* (Chapel Hill: University of North Carolina Press, 1929), p. 29.

[18]Baptist State Convention of North Carolina, *Annual*, 1921, p. 112; Mississippi Baptist Convention, *Proceedings*, 1923, p. 76.

[19]*Baptist Record*, 29 November 1923 p. 4.

[20]SBC, *Annual*, 1923, p. 101.

and greed, would be established on this earth a thousand years before Christ's Second Coming. They accepted postmillennialism, the belief that Christ's return to earth comes *after* the thousand-year period of peace and righteousness. God's people could advance the coming reign by joining the antiwar movement, promoting industrial justice, performing urban social work, and engaging in any activity that encouraged harmony and brotherhood. In the minds of Social Gospelers, all such work would help to Christianize the social order and usher in the millennium.[21]

Few Southern Baptists pursued the kingdom idea to its logical conclusion. Of major Baptist thinkers in the 1920s only William Poteat accepted the doctrine in its entirety, or at least, only he spoke so openly of his adoption of it. In the fashion of Walter Rauschenbusch, Poteat believed that in the early days of Christianity, soon after the death of Christ, the promise of earthly hope contained in the Messiah's ministry had been shunted aside by men preaching an otherworldly gospel. To Poteat, conditions seemed ripe in twentieth-century America to reestablish the goal of social salvation: "democracy, the evolutionary philosophy, the unity of the world under the applications of science, and the economic expansion" had paved the way for a recovery of the idea of the kingdom of God on earth. God would ultimately reign in all human relations, His kingdom would be established on this earth, and a "New Republic of Man" would supplant the existing order of strife, greed, and evil.[22]

Though lacking Poteat's faith in science and his belief in evolution, most moderates agreed with him on certain aspects of the kingdom doctrine. They stopped short of his proclamation of a "New Republic of Man," but they foresaw improvement in earthly conditions as the gospel permeated the world. In the optimistic aftermath of World War I the *Religious Herald* promised that "the principles that Jesus taught will yet be supreme in human society," and A. T. Robertson exulted that "there will be a new social order."[23] Even after postwar hopefulness had faded, in fact throughout the 1920s, a few Southern Baptists continued to envision a

---

[21]H. Richard Niebuhr, *The Kingdom of God in America* (New York: Harper & Row, 1959; original publication, 1937), pp. 164-98.

[22]Poteat, *The Way of Victory*, pp. 40-41, 43-44; Poteat, "The Coming Kingdom," *Biblical Recorder* (Raleigh, North Carolina), 12 November 1930, p. 3, clipping in the W. L. Poteat Papers.

[23]*Herald*, 2 January 1919, p. 17; Archibald T. Robertson, *The New Citizenship* (New York: Fleming H. Revell, 1919), 145.

future reasonably close to that prophesied by Social Gospelers. W. T. Conner, for example, forecast a time on earth when disease would be conquered and natural catastrophes banished,[24] and in 1932 George Truett spoke of a coming day when war would cease and money spent on instruments of death would be used "to enrich and gladden life."[25]

Despite these efforts to convince Southern Baptists of the social demands of their religion, moderates faced apathy and opposition. Admitting that "widespread skepticism" existed toward the mere mention of secular problems, much less toward any attempt to solve them, the author of Georgia's 1922 social service report concluded that Georgia Baptists saw no social implications in the gospel message.[26]

John Price attempted to explain this problem in *Christianity and Social Problems*. (1) First, Price said, Baptists stressed religious emotionalism at the expense of practical application of the gospel. (2) Coupled with this went an "otherworldism" that contrasted heavenly beauty with worldly iniquity. (3) Third, Baptists spent too much time haggling over such doctrines as the Lord's Supper and baptism, while ignoring the Bible's social principles. (4) Fourth, an appalling "ignorance of social conditions" existed among Southern Baptists. "The average citizen has little conception of social evils eating like a cancer on the body politic," Price said. (5) The fifth reason for Baptist opposition to social service lay in the belief that preaching the undefiled gospel comprised the sole duty of the believer. (6) Finally, Price concluded, "self-centeredness and indifference" caused people to turn their backs on the problems of others.[27]

Price's analysis furnishes an important basis for understanding the problems faced by moderates. Although all the reasons singled out by him played a role, the moderates' difficulties sprang mainly from three sources.

(1) First, opposition to the Social Gospel encouraged hostility toward all social service on the church's part. Baptist attacks on social Christianity often appeared to reject any conception of a religiously based reform ethic. Along with moderate calls for commitment to reform, Southern Baptists

---

[24]W. T. Conner, *A System of Christian Doctrine* (Nashville: Sunday School Board, 1924), p. 292.

[25]George W. Truett, *Follow Thou Me* (New York: Ray Long and Richard, Inc., 1932), p. 66.

[26]Georgia Baptist Convention, *Minutes*, 1922, p. 22.

[27]Price, *Christianity and Social Problems*, pp. 97-99.

had been bombarded, especially in books and articles by Victor Masters, with denunciations of any activity that might be construed as an endorse-ment of social Christianity. After 1921 Masters edited the Kentucky *Western Recorder*, one of the most influential Baptist weeklies published in the twenties, and used its pages as a platform from which to denounce the secularization of the gospel. Those who had not read Masters's diatribes had probably heard J. Frank Norris, A. C. Dixon, "Cyclone Mack" McLendon, Mordecai Ham, or one of the other evangelists who criss-crossed the South condemning social Christianity and related "evils." The intensity of this attack aroused Baptist suspicions over the mild program of social betterment advocated by moderates who, because they sometimes sounded like Social Gospelers, suffered from guilt by association.

(2) The second major problem faced by moderates arose from the Southern Baptist refusal to adulterate the gospel by mixing it with worldly concerns. W. O. Carver, reflecting in the 1950s on his long years as a moderate, complained that Baptist evangelism had failed to persuade converts to live a life "to begin here and now to be tested and expressed by ethical living in the midst of earthly conditions."[28] Conflict with evange-lism arose because moderates, in their efforts to awaken the denomination, interfered with the main concern of Southern Baptists in the 1920s. Baptists considered the preaching of the gospel to be the main reason for their existence; moderates agreed, but wanted to form a partnership between evangelism and social service. Most Baptists rejected the plea for a balance between the two and reasserted their belief in the primacy of preaching the gospel.

(3) The third source of moderate difficulty came from the denomina-tion's extreme right wing of premillennialists. Most Baptists distrusted moderates either out of opposition to the Social Gospel, or because they feared that involvement in secular affairs would blunt the drive to evangelize mankind. Militant premillennialists, concentrated in the Southwest and led by J. Frank Norris, castigated moderates for their doctrine of the kingdom of God on earth and vehemently disagreed with them over the time of Christ's Second Coming. In their embrace of the premillennial system Norris and his followers placed themselves in a tradition stretching back to the messianic Jewish sects that had flourished

---

[28]William O. Carver, *Out of His Treasure: Unfinished Memoirs* (Nashville: Broadman Press, 1956), pp. 55-56.

in Palestine before the time of Christ. Premillennial cries of mounting world evil and cataclysmic destruction could be traced most directly to the apocalyptic visions recorded by the Apostle John in the Revelation. From raw materials contained in this mystical and very figurative book, millenarians from the Middle Ages to the twentieth century had woven a fabric of prophecies and signs concerning the end of time. In America premillennialism had periodically ebbed and crested, reaching a high point in the Millerite movement in the 1840s. The 1920s, a period bounded by world war and economic collapse, presented another opportunity for rekindling the theory.[29]

Premillennialists assailed the moderate belief that world conditions, under the benign influence of Christianity, had been improving for the last nineteen hundred years. Though most moderates rejected the rosy prognostications of the Social Gospel, they believed that Christianity had improved the spiritual and physical lot of mankind.[30] In a 1923 report on temperance and public morals Kentucky Baptists objected to this view of progress, perceiving as they did "monstrous forms of evil" in a world "worse than it has ever been." The report's author added:

> The world today is drunk with pleasure, with passion and with pride and with prosperity. It is on a constant debauch. It sits always at Belshazzer's feast. It is money and movie mad and drunk with the strong wine thereof. It is the strong wine of indulgence and inebriety. It staggers and reels, fawns and spawns and vomits like an overfed gormand. Its reason is dethroned and its steps unsteady and its tongue is loose and glib. It quaffs the brew of hell and drinks from the still of Satan.[31]

Continued world crises enabled premillennialists to say with Norris: "We are living in the last days, not a shadow of doubt in my mind about it."[32] To premillennialists the world brimmed with evil, already past the point at which God had destroyed Sodom and Gomorrah. T. T. Martin,

---

[29]A brief survey of premillennialism in American history appears in Ira V. Brown, "Watchers for the Second Coming: The Millenarian Tradition in America," *Mississippi Valley Historical Review* 39 (December 1952): 441-58.

[30]Conner, *A System of Christian Doctrine*, p. 52.

[31]Kentucky Baptist Convention, *Proceedings*, 1923, p. 74.

[32]Norris to Joe H. Hankins, 16 January 1931, J. Frank Norris Papers, Dargan-Carver Library, Box 19.

famed Mississippi evangelist, reminded Baptists that Jesus had promised He would return to earth when such conditions existed.[33] From 1919 to 1931, right-wing Baptists discerned sign after sign announcing the impending doom of the world. In the wake of World War I, Norris warned that gorefilled trenches in France, rampant prosperity in America, famine and anarchy in Russia, and disease throughout the world foretold the start of the "tribulation period." As the decade waned and the economic depression deepened, premillennialists increased their cries of doom, one evangelist predicting another world war that would kill 600,000,000 people.[34]

Premillennial fascination with Christ's return as the solution to society's ills led them into conflict with moderates. A few premillennialists, notably James Gambrell, denied that they rejected social reform and insisted they could labor to improve man's earthly lot without endangering their belief in the imminence of the Second Coming.[35] But despite such assertions, most premillennialists showed little concern for social issues other than Prohibition. Norris's *Searchlight* and the books, articles, and sermons of other leading premillennialists exhibited virtually no social consciousness. When industrial strife or poverty intruded into the premillennial system they generally appeared as signs of the end of time. Perhaps most significant, as the Depression worsened in 1930 and 1931 premillennialists spoke mainly of the world's end and said little about ministering to the needy. Norris's weekly, for example, largely ignored the dislocation and poverty imposed on millions of Americans, a group that included many Baptist farmers and laborers.

This neglect came from a carefully reasoned conception of the role of God's people and not from insensitivity to human suffering. Exploring the church's mission in an article published just before his death in 1925, A.C. Dixon saw no social role for the church. God's people should call a handful of righteous men and women out of the world's iniquity, who would then welcome Christ back to earth. Not social work nor universal regeneration, but rather the gathering of the little flock concerned the Lord's messengers. As Dixon explained: "The mission of the Spirit and the gospel is

---

[33]Thomas T. Martin, *The Second Coming of Christ* (N. p., n. d., but ca., 1922), p. 13.

[34]*Searchlight* (Fort Worth, Texas), 17 April 1919, p. 3; clipping dated 18 November 1931, Norris Papers, Box 36.

[35]Oklahoma Baptist *Messenger*, 4 August 1920, p. 4.

to gather out a people . . . as the Bride of Christ who shall return as the Bridegroom for the great wedding day."[36]

Among premillennialists this view of the church's role produced an attitude "psychologically allied to the Messianism of later Judaism, that saw no hope for society except in a cataclysm."[37] A. C. Dixon furnishes a good example of how this conclusion influenced the thinking of premillennialists. Dixon seldom missed an opportunity to point out the hopelessness of contemporery conditions. Society had degenerated to the point that the only humane act would be for God to snuff out "such a monstrous condition of affairs," Dixon suggested.[38] In a sermon delivered at the University Baptist Church in Baltimore, he expressed a longing for an end to the earth's travail, admitting that "I am willing that all my plans should be smashed to pieces by the return of the Lord."[39] Given this attitude, premillennialists had no time for earthly concerns, for "the coming of our Lord is the only hope of this 'Groaning creation.' "[40] But no matter how bleak their prophecies, premillennialists possessed a fortitude that could not be easily shaken by life's trials and disappointments. Grasping the hope of a cataclysmic end of time and a fresh beginning in a new life, they discerned "the day star in the darkness before dawn."[41]

Southern Baptists of varying social and theological opinions were alarmed at premillennialism. Many Baptists accused the militants of causing discord at a time when the denomination needed to stand together. Moderates had an additional worry: they realized that premillennialism threatened to undercut their attempt to promote more liberal social attitudes. W. T. Conner, in his theological treatise *A System of Christian Doctrine*, devoted considerable space to a refutation of premillennialism. He denied its contention that the Bible predicted an ever-rising level of evil in the world, arguing that New Testament admonitions of worsening

---

[36]Amzi C. Dixon, "Why I Am a Premillennialist," *Moody Bible Institute Monthly* (August 1925): 535-37, clipping in the Dixon Papers, Box 12.

[37]Edwin McNeill Poteat, Jr., "Religion in the South," in William T. Couch, ed., *Culture in the South* (Chapel Hill: University of North Carolina Press, 1934), p. 254.

[38]Amzi C. Dixon, "A Mossback's Reply to Modernism," 20, undated typescript, Dixon Papers, Box 12.

[39]Amzi C. Dixon, "My Church," 6 January 1924, copy in the Dixon Papers, Box 5.

[40]S. J. Betts to Frank Norris, 31 August 1928, Norris Papers, Box 2.

[41]Norris to Isaac E. Gates, 3 November 1927, Box 16.

conditions referred to the writers' own day and not to the future. Concentration on the imminence of Christ's Second Coming promoted fanaticism, Conner warned, and led to an unhealthy elevation of evangelism above other forms of Christian activity.[42] A. T. Robertson urged Baptists to ignore the foreboding prophecies of the denomination's right wing and to exude the joy of a people working with God to establish a better life. His study of the Gospel of Luke led him to conclude that the parables of Jesus emphasized the ethical rather than the apocalyptic side of the Master's teaching.[43] For Robertson, "the test of life lies here, in the willingness to go on with the world program of Christ."[44] Robertson's colleague W. O. Carver opposed premillennialism as adamantly as anyone during the 1920s. In his memoirs he recalled the threat posed by the doctrine after World War I.

> Its worst effect was—and is—the denaturing of the gospel of its ethical content and passion. Its delusive dividing of the Christian gospel into a gospel of personal salvation and a social gospel and its utter detestation of the social gospel contribute to the sinful tendency of man to seek personal security for the future world while evading the demand for righteousness in the present world.[45]

Carver fought this "denaturing of the gospel," seeking, along with other moderates, to rescue Baptists from the simplicities of premillennialism and to develop in them a sense of the Christian's duties in this life.

Although Carver and his allies did not win a decisive victory over their premillennial opponents, they could still point to a number of accomplishments. If Prohibition consumed much of their energy during the 1920s, they still saw their work pay off in other areas. Particularly as the decade closed some Baptists seemed to be gaining a new realization of the church's duty to speak to society's problems. From a number of states came enlightened pronouncements on war, race relations, unemployment, and

---

[42]Conner, *A System of Christian Doctrine*, pp. 520-22, 537.

[43]Archibald T. Robertson, *Luke the Historian in the Light of Research* (New York: Charles Scribner's Sons, 1920), pp. 149, 165.

[44]*Herald*, 26 February 1920, p. 5.

[45]Carver, *Out of His Treasure*, pp. 76-77.

collective bargaining.[46] Moreover, two conservative states, Texas and Oklahoma, showed a willingness to enlarge the scope of their social concerns. In 1927 the Texas Baptist Committee on Civic Righteousness added "and Social Welfare" to its title,[47] and three years later Oklahoma Baptists scrapped their Temperance Committee for a newly designated Temperance and Social Service Committee.[48] Compared with advances made by Northern denominations these were small achievements, but Southern Baptist moderates had expected no miracles.

Premillennialists won few converts to their theological position through their fight against the moderates. Their arguments simply reinforced the distaste most Baptists already felt toward social activism for other reasons. Realization of this left premillennialists undisturbed, for they found their reward in gathering out the flock of true believers and not in persuading everyone to accept their views. They consoled themselves by reveling in self-rectitude, certain that Christ's soon return would validate their teachings. The controversy further alienated premillennialists from their moderate fellow churchmen; Norris and his followers, convinced that pleas for greater involvement in society formed part of a liberal plot to subvert old-time religion, accused their opponents of heresy. Whether one embraced a moderate scheme for betterment or a radical version of social Christianity made little difference to militant right wingers; both sullied the gospel's purity.

The contest between moderates and premillennialists confused the Baptist masses. While they heard some leaders calling for attention to problems of war, race, and industry, they also listened to denunciations of secular involvement as a diversion spawned by Satan. In the long run, most Baptists probably remained unmoved by the furor, although they must have wondered at times what social attitudes their religion did demand. The controversy wreaked greatest havoc in the denomination's higher ranks. Editors, teachers, ministers, and laymen, mustering their forces in opposing camps, aired their views on the relationship between religion and society and thus weakened the unity needed for conquest of the world for God. Many Baptists realized that though they agreed on a common

---

[46]Kentucky, *Proceedings*, 1929, p. 82; North Carolina, *Annual*, 1929, pp. 42-43; Georgia, *Minutes*, 1931, p. 32; Alabama, *Annual*, 1930, p. 29.

[47]Baptist General Convention of Texas, *Annual*, 1927, p. 97.

[48]Baptist General Convention of Oklahoma, *Minutes*, 1930, p. 104.

goal—spreading the good news of salvation—they divided sharply on means. In this atmosphere the preaching of the gospel lagged, and the South's Baptists fell behind their timetable for world evangelization.

CHAPTER 5

The Challenge of
Modernism and Fundamentalism

Disputes over interdenominationalism and social Christianity troubled Southern Baptists in the 1920s, disrupting the single-mindedness needed to evangelize the world. But these difficulties caused little harm in comparison to the destruction wrought by the denomination's involvement in the fundamentalist-modernist controversy. Although Baptists and Presbyterians in the North experienced the greatest strife, few Protestants escaped reverberations from the clash. Southern Baptists suffered less than their Northern brethren, but the controversy hit them at a time when they could ill afford to be sidetracked from spreading the gospel.

In broadest perspective the feuding of the 1920s represented another episode in the recurring conflict between religion and science. In this sense, the fundamentalist-modernist controversy began when the first priest expounded truths revealed to him by the gods and drew a skeptical response from the first "scientist." "Fundamentalists" and "modernists" have always been engaged in combat, one side struggling to preserve the old verities, the other attempting to harmonize religion with science and scholarship. Only a short step, after all, separates Galileo from the 1920s.[1]

---

[1]Two standard works on fundamentalism are Stewart G. Cole, *The History of Fundamentalism* (New York: Richard R. Smith, Inc., 1931); and Norman F. Furniss, *The*

In the United States conflict between liberals and conservatives resulted from a number of intellectual and social developments in the second half of the nineteenth century. "Modernism" or "liberalism," as defined by conservative Protestants, included the theories of biological evolution and scholarly criticism of the Bible, neither of which theory reached the United States on a significant scale until after the Civil War. The evolutionary theory, its shadowy existence given concrete form in Charles Darwin's *Origin of Species* published in 1859, forced churchmen to reexamine the Genesis account of creation. Rational treatment of the Bible, like the doctrine of evolution, had roots embedded deeply in Western thought. The higher criticism of the nineteenth century prompted scholars to subject the Scriptures to searching analyses to establish the date, authorship, and authenticity of the books of the Bible. This sent waves of anxiety sweeping over conservatives, for critics questioned the Mosaic authorship of the Pentateuch, established new dates for Old Testament prophetic writings, and cast doubt on the authority of many New Testament teachings.[2]

Darwinism and higher criticism reached the United States at a time of unsettling economic and social change. Although the simple America of the past (a land of farms and small towns peopled by Northern European Protestants) had begun to deteriorate before the Civil War, the real crisis struck in the decades after Appomattox. Industrialization rapidly challenged agriculture's dominance, and cities burgeoned, stimulating new values that perplexed rural and small-town folk. Immigrants poured into the cities, transforming them into "un-American" masses of humanity. Even more distressing, these people came from the Roman Catholic lands

Fundamentalist Controversy, 1918-1931 (New Haven: Yale University Press, 1954). Ernest R. Sandeen has challenged the interpretations of Cole and Furniss in a provocative book entitled *The Roots of Fundamentalism: British and American Millenarianism, 1800-1930* (Chicago: University of Chicago Press, 1970).

[2]Loren Eiseley, *Darwin's Century: Evolution and the Men Who Discovered It* (Garden City: Doubleday, 1961; original publication 1958) discusses the development of evolutionary theory, and Bert James Loewenberg, "Darwinism Comes to America, 1859-1900," *Mississippi Valley Historical Review* 28 (December 1941): 339-68, deals with its arrival in the United States. A short survey of the rise of higher criticism appears in Andrew W. White, *A History of the Warfare of Science with Theology in Christendom,* 2 vols. (New York: D. Appleton and Co., 1925; original publication, 1896), 2:288-396. William R. Hutchison has brilliantly traced the rise of modernism in *The Modernist Impulse in American Protestantism* (Cambridge, Massachusetts: Harvard University Press, 1976).

of Southern and Eastern Europe, bringing to America's shores reinforcements for the "papal hordes" already in the United States. The nation had changed too fast for small-town and rural Americans who formed the backbone of conservative Protestantism. They faced a bewildering array of social and economic developments that resisted adaptation to their world view, created uneasiness, and compelled them to seek stability in religion.

In the years after the Civil War conservatives struck back at the liberal menace. Popular evangelists, inspired by the successful preaching of Dwight L. Moody, inaugurated what some historians have considered a third Great Awakening. Not to be outdone by their peripatetic colleagues, resident pastors, especially Presbyterians and Baptists, denounced modernism from their pulpits. Princeton Theological Seminary and other conservative institutions continually replenished the supply of anti-modernist clergymen, and through their professors provided intellectual respectability for the campaign against liberalism. Conservatives kept academic wellsprings pure by dealing harshly with liberal professors, some of the most controversial cases involving Vanderbilt University's banishment of Dr. Alexander Winchell in 1878; Professor James Woodrow's ejection from the Presbyterian seminary in Columbia, South Carolina, in 1886; and the indictment of Union Theological Seminary's Professor Charles A. Briggs for heresy in 1892. Annual Bible conferences sprang up in the 1870s to promote interdenominational solidarity among conservatives. Finally, evangelical journals in both the North and South denounced Darwinism and higher criticism.[3]

This warfare between conservatives and liberals continued throughout the late nineteenth and early twentieth centuries, but the most heated phase of the controversy occurred after World War I. A change in terminology accompanied the intensification of the debate. Adopting the name "fundamentalist" for themselves and "modernist" for their opponents, premillennial conservatives transformed the dispute into the "fundamentalist-modernist" controversy. Unfortunately for nonpremil-

---

[3]William G. McLoughlin, *Modern Revivalism: Charles Grandison Finney to Billy Graham* (New York: Ronald Press, 1959), pp. 166-281; Sandeen, *The Roots of Fundamentalism*, pp. 81ff.; White, *History of the Warfare of Science with Theology*, 1:313-18; Clement Eaton, "Professor James Woodrow and the Freedom of Teaching in the South," *Journal of Southern History* 28 (February 1962): 3-17; *The Defence of Professor Briggs before the Presbytery of New York* (New York: Charles Scribner's Sons, 1893).

lennial conservatives, the fundamentalist label caught on as a designation for all opponents of modernism. To complicate matters further, conservatives and fundamentalists shared the common goal of defeating modernist heresy. Both fundamentalists and conservatives demanded that modernists be driven from orthodox denominations, although conservatives, unlike their more militant brethren, refused to categorize everyone who disagreed with them as a modernist. Fundamentalists sought to purge Darwinism from tax-supported schools through passage of anti-evolution laws, an idea that appealed to many conservatives, who responded by joining fundamentalists in an effort to cleanse the schools. The fight against modernism in churches and schools drew conservatives and fundamentalists together, prompting their opponents to interpret the anti-modernist movement as ideologically homogeneous.

Although not always apparent, three basic differences existed between fundamentalists and conservatives. Fundamentalists possessed a single-minded obsession with modernism, coupled with an intensity and fervor that disturbed many conservatives. Second, fundamentalists established the premillennial Second Coming of Christ as the cardinal test of orthodoxy, which ultimately led them to attack nonpremillennial conservatives as modernists in disguise. Finally, exhibiting a casual attitude toward denominational ties that shocked conservatives, fundamentalists advocated broad fellowship among like-minded Protestants, and, especially among Presbyterians and Baptists, revealed a readiness to break with the parent church to form separate religious bodies. Despite these differences, the joint effort to combat heresy and the lack of discernment by outsiders blurred distinctions between the two strains of antimodernism, enabling fundamentalists to overshadow traditional conservatism and fasten their name on the entire crusade against modernism.

Southern Baptists awakened to the dispute between conservatives and liberals long before the 1920s. With other Protestants they witnessed the American debut of Darwinism and higher criticism, but for several reasons they remained relatively uninvolved in the initial phase of the fight against modernism. In the first place, a Southern branch of the Baptist denomination had been organized only sixteen years before the Civil War, when a quarrel arose over sending slaveholders to foreign mission fields. With the Southern Baptist Convention in its infancy, its constituents occupied themselves with establishing a separate identity, only to be interrupted by the Civil War. In the postwar years, while Northern Protestants grappled with evolution and biblical criticism, the South's Baptists resumed the chore of establishing a denomination. At the same time, they threw themselves into the task of rebuilding a shattered society. The exigencies of Reconstruction—reentry into the Union, economic development, and racial adjustment—prevented Baptists from dwelling on purely religious topics and discouraged them from uniting with other conservatives in the fight against modernism. Even more important, in the late 1800s Southern Baptists presented an almost unrelieved front of orthodoxy. With virtually no evolutionists or higher critics among them, the South's Baptists felt unthreatened by modernism.[4]

One prominent case did arise in the late 1870s. In 1869 Dr. Crawford H. Toy became professor of Old Testament in the Southern Baptist Theological Seminary, then located in Greenville, South Carolina. Toy, a man of deep intellect and wide learning, soon incorporated Darwin's theory and the current methods of higher criticism into his studies. In 1877, after the Seminary's removal to Louisville, Kentucky, the discovery that Toy had begun instructing students in his adopted beliefs prompted President James P. Boyce to request that he stop such teaching. The professor agreed, but curious students, seeking out his well-known views, convinced Toy that he could not conscientiously teach the Old Testament without mentioning current intellectual developments. In May 1879, persuaded of the validity of his ideas, but unwilling to teach them against the wishes of his fellow Baptists, Toy resigned. In a spirit far removed from the bitterness of the 1920s, the board of trustees, "all in tears as they voted," accepted Toy's resignation.[5] "The mournful deed is done," John A. Broadus, professor of New Testament, wrote. "We have lost our jewel of learning, our beloved and noble brother, the pride of the Seminary."[6]

The absence of a witch hunt in the wake of this incident showed that Southern Baptists felt little fear of modernism in the late nineteenth century. Similar proof appeared in the denomination's willingness to allow William Poteat to expound his views undisturbed by the fury visited upon him in the 1920s. Poteat began his career at Wake Forest College in

---

[4]Robert A. Baker, *The Southern Baptist Convention and Its People, 1607-1972* (Nashville: Broadman Press, 1974), pp. 161-341.

[5]John A. Broadus, *Memoir of James Petigru Boyce* (New York: A. C. Armstrong and Son, 1893), pp. 260-63.

[6]John A. Broadus to Charlotte E. Broadus, 10 May 1879, in Archibald T. Robertson, *Life and Letters of John Albert Broadus* (Philadelphia: American Baptist Publication Society, 1901), p. 313.

1878 as a language tutor, shifting to the biology department two years later. The young professor soon found it impossible to reconcile his religious beliefs with current scientific findings. After a period of confusion and distress, he adjusted the discrepancies between science and scripture by concluding that biblical "science" represented the primitive attempts of an unscientific people to understand the mystery of life's origin.[7] Assured of his bearings, Poteat began teaching the theory of evolution to his biology classes and speaking and writing on the subject outside denominational circles. As early as 1893, in an article in the journal *Science*, he expressed his acceptance of evolution. In 1901 he further clarified his views in his first book, *Laboratory and Pulpit*. In May 1905, in a Colgate University lecture series devoted to the "new peace" between science and religion, Poteat rejected the biblical account of creation, contending that God had spent "aeons of waiting and travail" anticipating man's appearance in the unfolding of life. As late as 1915 these lectures could be published without provoking cries of outrage from Southern Baptists.[8]

Despite the absence of controversy, by the early twentieth century Southern Baptists had begun warily to eye the modernist threat to orthodoxy. Contributions by several Southern Baptists to *The Fundamentals*, a series of twelve pamphlets published between 1910 and 1915 by the wealthy Californians Milton and Lyman Stewart, demonstrated the denomination's awareness of the perils faced by conservatives. A. C. Dixon, a North Carolinian and pastor of Chicago's Moody Church, edited the first five volumes and joined three other Southern Baptists—E. Y. Mullins of Southern Seminary, and J.J. Reeve and Charles B. Williams, both professors in Southwestern Seminary—in contributing essays. In the third volume Mullins argued that the believer's religious experience proved the ultimate truth of Christianity.[9] In the same pamphlet Reeve attacked

---

[7]William L. Poteat, "My Approach to Religion," pp. 3-4, typescript of an address delivered to a Y.M.C.A. Conference in Blue Ridge, North Carolina, 15 June 1928, W. L. Poteat Papers.

[8]William L. Poteat, "The Effect on the College Curriculum of the Introduction of the Natural Sciences," *Science* 21 (31 March 1893): 170-72; *Laboratory and Pulpit: The Relation of Biology to the Preacher and His Message* (Philadelphia: Griffith and Rowland Press, 1901); *The New Peace: Lectures on Science and Religion* (Boston: Richard G. Badger, 1915), pp. 156-57.

[9]*The Fundamentals: A Testimony to the Truth* (12 vols.; Chicago: Testimony Publishing Co., n. d.), 3:76-85.

higher criticism for its affinity to Darwinism, advocated banishment of preachers tainted with modernism, and warned that a "subtle attempt to do away with the supernatural" threatened to destroy Christianity.[10] Dixon penned an appreciation of the Bible for volume five,[11] and Williams concluded Southern Baptist participation in *The Fundamentals* with an article in volume eight reiterating the "heinousness of sin."[12]

Two significant events accompanied the publication of these contributions to *The Fundamentals*; unimportant as isolated instances, they held vast symbolic meaning when viewed as precursors of the religious difficulties of the 1920s. In 1913 T. T. Martin published a work entitled *Redemption and the New Birth*. Although it focused on doctrinal matters, the book contained a brief attack on the University of Chicago for promoting modernism. Assailing three of the school's divinity professors for coauthoring a book questioning the importance of redemption from sin, Martin foreshadowed the later Baptist fear of modernism as an external threat to Southern orthodoxy.[13] A similar portent materialized the following year when the Texas *Baptist Standard*, edited by James Gambrell and Eugene C. Routh, charged Southern Seminary's W. O. Carver with denying the Virgin Birth.[14] The accusation was false, but it highlighted a larger truth: in the 1920s some Southern Baptists, goaded by fundamentalism's heated rhetoric, would transform modernism into an internal threat and turn upon their denomination for harboring heretics. A combination of these two interpretations—Martin's external menace, and Gambrell and Routh's internal peril—produced much of the difficulty experienced by Southern Baptists in the twenties.

The *Baptist Standard* impugned Carver's orthodoxy at a momentous time, for in August 1914 the armies of Europe's leading nations marched into war. The conflict between religious liberals and their conservative antagonists receded into the background as Americans turned their attention to the European struggle. The United States' entry into the war

---

[10]Ibid., 3:98-118.

[11]Ibid., 5:72-80.

[12]Ibid., 8:49-63.

[13]Thomas T. Martin, *Redemption and the New Birth* (New York: Fleming H. Revell Co., 1913), p. 85.

[14]William O. Carver, *Out of His Treasure: Unfinished Memoirs* (Nashville: Broadman Press, 1956), p. 72.

in 1917 demanded that domestic strife—political, economic, and religious—be quelled in order to focus on the defeat of the Central Powers. But the religious truce imposed by the war lasted only a short while, for on 11 November 1918, Germany signed an armistice. The war's conclusion released the energy the United States had poured into the crusade for democracy. Relieved of that emotional commitment, Americans resumed domestic quarrels that had been set aside by the need for wartime unity. For liberal and conservative Protestants alike this signaled renewal of the controversy that had been sidetracked by the war.

Although Southern Baptists resisted the immediate urge to join the crusade for orthodoxy, the First World War heightened their fear of modernism. Germany's defeat signified more than resolution of a global struggle in which democracy had bested absolutism. For by placing "her supreme trust in guns—in things material," the German nation had symbolized the spiritual poverty that accompanied modernism's reliance upon the rational and material powers of man, a writer suggested in the *Religious Herald*. The Allied armies by contrast had marched to war under the banner of Christ; this difference explained the victory over the Central Powers. Against the backdrop of German defeat and humiliation, God had spelled out a lesson for His people: Germany, one of modernism's breeding grounds, had been crushed by the United States, a repository of devout Christian faith.[15] Germany had been punished, as a group of Virginia Baptists observed, for "the sin of a perverted mental poise, the sin of hypocricy [sic], of sacrilege and idolatry, of skepticism and infidelity" and for her "organized propaganda of false teachers and false teachings; her higher criticisms and corrupt theology."[16]

The war had done more for Southern Baptists than to expose the poverty of "higher criticisms and corrupt theology." It had also stripped the scientific trappings from Darwinism, exposing its evil consequences. T. T. Martin spoke for many Baptists in identifying Germany as the most completely "Darwinized" country in the world. "Honorable Wm. E. Gladstone and others largely drove it out of England," Martin wrote. "Germany took it up and went wild over it, and it has doomed Germany."[17]

---

[15]*Herald*, 29 May 1919, p. 5; 10 July 1919, p. 5.

[16]Appomattox Baptist Association (Virginia), *Minutes*, 1920, pp. 12-13.

[17]Thomas T. Martin, *Evolution or Christ? Christ or Hell?* (n. p., ca. 1923), p. 33; *The Evolution Issue* (n. p., ca. 1923), p. 17.

Baptists ranging from E. Y. Mullins to A. C. Dixon constructed an argument that followed from Martin's premises. In Germany the "anti-Christ" Friedrich Nietzsche had refashioned the idea of survival of the fittest into an intellectual justification of the "blond beast," a "superman" unencumbered by traditional morality. Building upon the doctrine that the strong have the right to destroy the weak, Nietzsche had "hypnotized the German mind with his Pagan brute philosophy." Under the mad philosopher's spell Germany had developed a "national religion of militarism" that had sent her careening into the First World War. Modernism, in the form of the evolutionary concept of might makes right, had sparked a conflagration that had "deluged the world with blood," the argument concluded.[18]

The lessons of Germany's defeat, combined with prewar Baptist attitudes toward Darwinism and higher criticism, undergirded the denomination's attempts to grapple with fundamentalism and modernism in the 1920s. Southern Baptist attitudes toward the controversy existed on two levels. First, virtually all Southern Baptists recognized modernism as an alien force threatening to undermine orthodoxy. Within the denomination varying opinions existed on evolution and higher criticism, but scarcely anyone considered himself a modernist. Southern Baptist fundamentalists carried their reasoning to a second plane, transforming modernism from an outside danger into an internal menace. Evolution and higher criticism, they contended, had infiltrated Southern Baptist ranks. In the resulting confusion Baptists engaged the enemy on two fronts. The entire denomination combated modernism in its extreme forms, for all Southern Baptists rejected the higher criticism's proclivity for gutting the Scriptures and Darwinism's tendency to relegate God to an unimportant position. At the same time, a vocal minority combined this aversion to modernism with an attack on their fellow churchmen for failing to uphold the faith. The ensuing conflict disrupted the denomination more than anything else in the 1920s.

---

[18]Lee R. Scarborough, *Christ's Militant Kingdom* (New York: George H. Doran Co., 1924), pp. 70-71; Edgar Y. Mullins, *Christianity at the Cross Roads* (New York: George H. Doran Co., 1924), p. 12; Jessie W. Gibbs, *Evolution and Christianity* (Knoxville: pub. by the author, 1931), pp. 11-12; *News and Observer* (Raleigh, North Carolina), 31 December 1922, p. 5, clipping, Dixon Papers, Box 10; Amzi C. Dixon, *The Battle-lines between Christianity and Modernism* (London: The Bible League, n. d.), p. 28; Dixon to William Poteat, 11 January 1922, Dixon Papers, Box 10.

In dealing with the first level of Southern Baptist thinking on modernism—that it presented a threat from outside the denomination—one may begin with the reassertion of Southern sectionalism that emerged from this confrontation with modernism. Commenting on the Scopes trial of 1925, the Mississippi *Baptist Record* editorialized: "The second carpet-bag invasion has been repelled and East Tennessee has turned to reconstruction in the form of cooling the fires of religious and sectional prejudice which the Scopes evolution trial aroused."[19] Although cast in similar language, editor P. I. Lipsey's statement lacked the immediacy of the sectionalism of the late nineteenth century, for by 1925 the bonds of union had been reestablished. Reconciliation had proceeded steadily in the years after the Civil War, and reunion had been completed by the 1920s. Woodrow Wilson's election to the Presidency in 1912 had returned the South to the seat of national power, and in 1917 America had entered a war vigorously supported by Southerners. But this picture of national unity could be deceiving; the Southern sense of uniqueness and independence, formed by decades of antagonism and four years of bloodshed, had not been totally erased. The Civil War had aroused hostility and suspicion toward all things Northern and had "intensified" the South's "loyalty to what it had come to feel was uniquely its own."[20] In the third decade of the twentieth century the South remained reluctant to trade its distinctiveness for national conformity.

Religion served this sense of uniqueness especially well, for a glance at the American religious scene convinced the South that it remained the last bastion of Protestant orthodoxy. Joseph Dawson's observation that the South knew "nothing of the clamor of numerous isms which have turned the north and east and west into strange Babels" was correct.[21] Major defections from orthodox Protestantism had arisen and thrived outside the South; Transcendentalism, Mormonism, Spiritualism, and Christian Science had been founded by Northerners seeking new pathways to the divine. The rise of modernism reinforced Southern convictions because the region's Protestants observed that this latest deviation flourished best in the North, particularly in such places as the University of Chicago,

---

[19]*Baptist Record*, 6 August 1925, p. 4.

[20]Edwin McNeill Poteat, Jr., "Religion in the South," in William T. Couch, ed., *Culture in the South* (Chapel Hill: University of North Carolina Press, 1934), p. 253.

[21]Joseph M. Dawson, "Religion Down South," *Christian Century* 47 (25 June 1930): 811-12.

Columbia University, and Union Theological Seminary.[22] Southern Baptists believed, as a writer in the *Religious Herald* pointed out, that liberals had overrun the land north of the Mason-Dixon line. Scattered bits of God's truth had survived the conquest, but they lay buried beneath "piles of rubbish." But though modernism had triumphed in the North, the truth remained alive in the South, for Baptists had "a point of view that to us is saner, safer, and has proved to be more practical for kingdom-building," the *Herald's* correspondent added.[23]

Southern Baptists cited the Northern Baptist drift away from orthodoxy as proof of the prevalence of heresy in the North. The South's Baptists believed that God had not blessed the Northern denomination as richly as its Southern counterpart. The reason was clear: Southern Baptists had preserved their doctrinal purity, while Baptists in the North had embraced such heretical practices as alien immersion and open communion. These lapses might have been forgiven, but Southerners refused to excuse the modernistic leanings of the Northern church.[24] According to A. C. Dixon, modernist theology had gained in popularity among Northern Baptists and had even crept into the denomination's Crozer Theological Seminary in Chester, Pennsylvania.[25] Missouri Baptists did more than bewail this situation. Distressed with Northern modernism, they ended their dual alignment with Northern and Southern Baptists in 1919 by voting for sole affiliation with the Southern Baptist Convention.[26] This reassured Southern Baptists that they had correctly assessed conditions in the North.

Southerners reserved their fiercest denunciations for the University of Chicago, charging that the once-orthodox Baptist school had become a "satanic institution" harboring "infidelity, atheism, rationalism, and

---

[22]Rufus W. Weaver to John K. Williams, 22 April 1930, Rufus W. Weaver Papers, Dargan-Carver Library, Box 5; C. E. Hamric to A. T. Robertson, 26 September 1921, Robertson Papers, Folder 1921C.

[23]*Religious Herald*, 9 March 1922, pp. 8-9.

[24]Robert E. Smith, *Little Foxes in the Baptist Vineyard* (Waco: Press of Hill Co., 1923), p. 8; John C. Cowell to Frank Norris, 2 January 1930, Norris Papers, Box 5.

[25]Dixon to Reuben R. Saillens, 22 July 1924; Dixon to Curtis Lee Laws, 1924, Dixon Papers, Box 10.

[26]Missouri Baptist General Association, *Minutes*, 1919, pp. 90-91; Robert S. Douglass, *History of Missouri Baptists* (Kansas City, Missouri: Western Baptist Pub. Co., 1934), p. 382.

materialism." Modernists had turned the university into a "slaughter-house of faith" shunned by God-fearing Baptists who educated their children elsewhere.[27] W. B. Waff, a Baptist preacher in Mocksville, North Carolina, warned of the pitfalls awaiting those foolish enough to attend the school. Writing to A. T. Robertson, he cited the case of a "bright boy" from his church who had enrolled in the university and "got full of the rotten stuff that is taught there." His mind polluted with modernism, the young man had forsaken his religion for Unitarianism.[28] Similar stories of young men led astray convinced Southern Baptists that the University of Chicago and the Northern Baptist denomination had followed identical courses. Once bastions of orthodoxy, both had been undermined by modernism. From this environment one could expect Unitarians—or worse—to emerge.

Far from invoking pessimism, the opportunities presented by the nation's heresy actually encouraged Southern Baptists, who reasoned that the South, by providing a shelter for beleaguered orthodoxy, had reversed the terms of sectional debate. Since the early nineteenth century the South had been scorned as an anomaly constantly at odds with national purposes. In the 1920s Southern Baptists contended that the rest of the country had forsaken religious conservatism, leaving the South as the standard to which America must readjust itself. As the Home Mission Board stated: "The South constitutes the nursery, the training ground, the granary, the source of supplies, indeed, for our conquest in all lands."[29] Though worried over the state of American religion, Southern Baptists recognized a chance for their region to seize moral leadership of the nation. Opportunity and responsibility mitigated the anxiety produced by the modernist threat.

In criticizing modernism, Southern Baptists analyzed the broad impli-cations of the new departure, focusing particularly on its defects as a religious system. Baptists grounded their opposition to the new theology on what they conceived to be its rejection of the supernatural. The "fundamental" issue, according to E. Y. Mullins, lay "between Christianity which contains the elements of the supernatural and Christianity which

---

[27]J. E. Boyd to J. B. Cranfill, 20 July 1929, Norris Papers, Box 4; Thomas T. Martin, *Hell and the High Schools: Christ or Evolution, Which?* (Kansas City, Missouri: Western Baptist Pub. Co., 1923), p. 41.

[28]Waff to Robertson, 13 May 1923, Robertson Papers, Folder 1923C.

[29]SBC, *Annual*, 1924, p. 319.

contains nothing of the supernatural."[30] A. C. Dixon agreed, adding that belief in the supernatural divided orthodox Christians from modernists, for the latter had stripped supernaturalism from Christ and the Bible, leaving Christians with no basis for their faith.[31] This robbed Jesus of His divinity, reduced Him to a mere human being, and led to Unitarianism, Mullins asserted.[32] In the Stone Lectures, delivered at Princeton Theological Seminary in 1926, A. T. Robertson called the modernist attempt to undermine Christ the gravest issue facing Christians. "With Jesus knocked off his pedestal," Robertson warned, "there is nothing left worth contending for in such an emasculated Christianity."[33] Southern Baptists believed that modernist theologians, carrying their degradation of the deity a step beyond Unitarianism, had even dared to belittle God the Father. Though some modernists tried to "put God out of business," most of them, P. I. Lipsey said, pursued a more subtle course by cleverly chipping away at God's omnipotence.[34] The modernist deity—an impersonal force of "cosmic energy," bound by natural laws, and imprisoned in his own universe—contrasted sharply with the personal, all-powerful God worshiped by Southern Baptists.[35]

Modernism's second defect followed logically from its degradation of God and His Son: it elevated man to undeserved heights. To fill the void left by God's dethronement, modernism promoted "a self-reliant process of mental reasoning" that encouraged man to look within himself for solutions to life's mysteries. This produced a scoffing arrogance toward those who persisted in maintaining God's preeminence.[36] Baptists

---

[30]Mullins to E. B. Pollard, 12 March 1923, Edgar Y. Mullins Papers, Southern Baptist Theological Seminary, 1922-1923 Correspondence.

[31]Amzi C. Dixon, "What Is Fundamentalism?," sermon preached in the University Baptist Church, Baltimore, Maryland, 5 January 1924, copy in the Dixon Papers, Box 12.

[32]Edgar Mullins, "Modern Liberalism in Theology" (a lecture Mullins delivered on 22 March 1922, handwritten notes of which may be found on the endpaper of the University of Virginia's copy of Mullins's *The Christian Religion in Its Doctrinal Expression*).

[33]Archibald T. Robertson, *Paul and the Intellectuals: The Epistle to the Colossians* (Garden City: Doubleday, 1928), p. 60.

[34]*Baptist Record*, 21 April 1921, p. 4.

[35]William W. Weeks, *The Face of Christ* (Nashville: Sunday School Board, 1927), p. 189; Rufus W. Weaver, "The Baptist Opportunity in a Scientific Age," p. 4, typescript dated 5 February 1932, Weaver Papers, Box 11; George W. McDaniel, *The Supernatural Jesus* (Nashville: Sunday School Board, 1924), p. 125.

[36]Richard T. Vann, *The Things Not Seen* (Nashville: Sunday School Board, 1931), p. 53; *Herald*, 14 February 1924, p. 3; McDaniel, *The Supernatural Jesus*, p. 174.

deplored these modernist attitudes, insisting that God be left on His throne, and man remain His servant.

The third point in Southern Baptists' critique of modernism reinforced their concern over its glorification of man. They noted that modernism's adherents, through their lack of Christian character, proved the falsity of their lofty view of man. Modernists, George McDaniel said, attended church irregularly, contributed less to foreign missions, won fewer souls, and joined the ministry less frequently than their orthodox brethren.[37] The nation's modernist-saturated colleges and universities offered ideal laboratories for testing the new religion's ability to inspire men to rise to higher planes; the evidence, though fragmentary, suggested to A. C. Dixon that modernism had failed to produce superior character among the nation's youth.[38] But worse than its inability to develop men of superior traits, liberal Christianity had actually caused a "decline in standards of personal conduct," a Tennessee Baptist maintained.[39] In this vein, other Southern Baptists argued that recent religious trends threatened to destroy America's moral fiber by subverting the ethical code supported by conservative Protestants. Summarizing these fears, Victor Masters stated: "There is a real relationship between the immorality and lawlessness among the people . . . and the rationalistic and atheistic philosophy which has been seeking to poison America's heart."[40] Considering its failure to produce good Christians and its contributions to moral decline, modernism's high regard for man struck Southern Baptists as incongruous, if not dishonest.

Southern Baptists completed their assessment of religious liberalism by attacking its lack of a promise of eternal life. Modernism robbed humanity of its ultimate hope by rejecting the supernatural; only a God above natural law could care for man, direct his footsteps through life, and at last carry him to a better world beyond the grave. Realization of man's vision of eternal life depended upon the supernatural elements of Christianity: Christ's Virgin Birth, His atoning death, and His Resurrection and

---

[37]McDaniel, *The Supernatural Jesus*, pp. 181-82.

[38]Amzi C. Dixon, "A Mossback's Reply to Modernism," p. 2, ca. early 1920s typescript, Dixon Papers, Box 12.

[39]Gibbs, *Evolution and Christianity*, p. 174.

[40]Victor I. Masters, *Making America Christian* (Atlanta: Home Mission Board, 1921), p. 98.

Ascension.[41] This longing for eternity, as William Weeks pointed out, gave meaning to the Christian's earthly existence. "Grecianism," the modernist blend of science, philosophy, and reason, afforded some pleasure, Weeks admitted, but it failed its votaries at life's darkest hour. It "can lighten up the path that leads down to the grave but it has neither guide nor torch for those who are about to traverse its gloomy caverns."[42] Despite its promise of temporal joy attained through rationality, "Grecianism" failed to convince Southern Baptists that science or philosophy could cast aside the pall shrouding man's destiny. Only orthodoxy's promise of eternal life truly brightened human existence.

By analyzing the shortcomings of modernist religion, Southern Baptists attempted to clarify their own creed and to overcome modernism's tendency to "becloud one's thinking."[43] Because the urge to wrestle with modernism seized Baptists as diverse as farmers and professors, the denomination's response to the modernist challenge varied considerably. Those who heeded the counsel of such scholars as E. Y. Mullins viewed modernism as a dangerous foe, but one to be handled with reason and self-confidence. Until his death in 1927 Mullins directed his finely honed mind to a defense of orthodox Christianity. In a book published in 1924 he observed that orthodoxy had reached a "crossroads." Down one road continued the route God's people had traveled for centuries. The other fork followed a course marked out by modernists; only those desiring a Christian religion reduced "to the dimensions of an ethical movement or philosophic cult" should take this road. In criticizing current religious trends Mullins reiterated familiar themes: supernaturalism, God's omnipotence, Christ's divinity, and man's reliance on God.[44] But Mullins went beyond theological catchwords and met modernism on its own grounds, employing the tools of scholarship in his cogent examination of claims advanced by biologists, physicists, sociologists, psychologists, philosophers, and biblical critics. Mullins's book, *Christianity at the Cross Roads*, presented a calm and reasoned exposition of orthodoxy for those

---

[41]McDaniel, *The Supernatural Jesus*, pp. 57-58; Amzi C. Dixon, *Why I Am an Evangelical Christian and Not a Modernist* (Baltimore: University Baptist Church, ca. 1923), pp. 28-30.

[42]Weeks, *The Face of Christ*, p. 129.

[43]Charles T. Alexander to J. Frank Norris, 21 December 1929, Norris Papers, Box 1.

[44]Mullins, *Christianity at the Cross Roads*, pp. 22-23, 48, 233-34, 238-39.

troubled by the new departure in religion.

Following Mullins's example, many Baptists dealt intelligently with modernism, viewing it as antagonistic to orthodoxy, but refusing to panic. Other Baptists reacted differently; in their minds modernism assumed characteristics ascribed to Communism in a later era. They damned it as the root problem of their age, the source of all their difficulties, and the symbol for all their fears. The Reverend A. Reilly Copeland of Waco, Texas, typified the anxiety and discontent felt by these Baptists. To a fellow preacher Copeland wrote in 1927:

> Modernism is a worldwide system in scope, subtle in practice and damning in the end. As I understand modernism it is (1) Satanic in origin (2) ancient in historic age (3) materialistic in progress (4) fleshly in all desires (5) exalts human culture (6) deifies man (7) humanizes God (8) pen knife's [sic] revelation (9) mocks spiritual regeneration (10) denies blood bought redemption.[45]

In this passage Copeland repeated, though in less sophisticated fashion, themes found in the writings of Baptist scholars. He attacked modernism for debasing God and elevating man, criticized its lack of spirituality, and denounced its disregard of supernaturalism.

But in the next section of his letter Copeland launched into an irrational tirade that linked religious liberalism with every disturbing feature of modern thought and society:

> To be both exact and specific I will say that (1) Modernism in religion is New Theology (2) in education is *evolution* (3) in business is *communism* (4) in government is *anarchism* (5) in society is *lawlessness* (6) in amusement the *motion picture* (7) in entertainment the *modern dance* (8) in literature sex stories (9) in music the jazzy (10) in morals is *free lovism* (11) in the home disobedience to parents (12) in the community no respect for other's rights (13) in results worldwide confusion [,] wholesale corruption [,] increased bloodshed, and youthful crime wave.[46]

---

[45]Copeland to M. A. Gary, 21 September 1927, Norris Papers, Box 8.
[46]Ibid.; emphasis in the original.

The number of those who accepted this view cannot be determined, but its appeal must have been substantial, for it dramatically articulated the confusion felt by many Baptists in the 1920s. Those who accepted this all-encompassing interpretation fell prey to misguided men who, in their efforts to combat modernism, caused more grief among Southern Baptists than did orthodoxy's liberal detractors.

With their impassioned denunciations of modernism, Reilly Copeland and his fellow believers forced Southern Baptists to deal with liberal Christianity's right-wing antagonist, fundamentalism, thus setting the stage for a debate over modernism as an internal threat to the denomination. Although some Southern Baptists had flirted with the evolving fundamentalist movement before World War I, few had become deeply involved. By contrast, liberalism's success in the North had prompted many conservative Baptists there to embrace fundamentalism. William Bell Riley, pastor of the First Baptist Church in Minneapolis, and Curtis Lee Laws, editor of the *Watchman Examiner*, fought modernism within their own denomination and united with other Protestants to combat heresy on a larger scale. J. Frank Norris and A. C. Dixon, through their ties with Northern fundamentalists, carried the language and organization of national fundamentalism into the South.[47]

The establishment of a fundamentalist wing among Southern Baptists was a superfluous act. Southern Baptists had sampled modern religious trends sparingly before World War I, and in the 1920s they occupied the front lines of conservative Protestantism. L. L. Gwaltney estimated in 1940 that in the twenties fewer than one percent of the South's Baptists had questioned the Christian fundamentals of biblical inspiration and Christ's virgin birth, atonement, resurrection, and second coming.[48] A. Hamilton Reid, a Baptist preacher in Alabama during the twenties, stated in his 1967 history of Alabama Baptists that "almost all, if not all, Southern Baptist pastors" had remained true to the faith in the 1920s.[49] Contemporary statements reinforce the recollections of Gwaltney and Reid. Both George McDaniel, a prominent Baptist respected by fundamentalists, and

---

[47]Furniss, *The Fundamentalist Controversy*, pp. 103-18.

[48]Leslie L. Gwaltney, *Forty of the Twentieth or the First Forty Years of the Twentieth Century* (Birmingham: pub. by the author, 1940), p. 134.

[49]A. Hamilton Reid, *Baptists in Alabama: Their Organization and Witness* (N. p., 1967), p. 257.

T. T. Martin, ardent crusader against evolution, attested to the doctrinal soundness of Southern Baptists.[50] More important, Norris and Dixon exonerated the Baptist masses of heresy. To a leading European fundamentalist Dixon wrote: "I know that the Baptists of the South are overwhelmingly fundamentalist in their theology."[51] In 1930, after a decade of scouring his denomination for traces of modernism, Norris concluded that "there is no difference between my position... and the great body of Baptists."[52]

Norris and Dixon accompanied their praise of the Baptist masses with an indictment of the denomination's leaders. But these charges were false, for the beliefs of "modernist" Baptists scarcely resembled those of true proponents of the "new theology." Lee Scarborough, a regular victim of Norris's ire, advised his listeners in a frequently delivered sermon "to most soulfully accept, heartily believe, and loyally support, with our talents, our time, our money, and if need be our sacred lives, these glorious doctrines."[53] The "glorious doctrines" Scarborough stood ready to die for included the essential elements of conservative Protestantism. George Truett, another "modernist," swore fealty to Jesus Christ by reiterating every point in the traditional view of the Messiah.[54] Baylor University's President Samuel P. Brooks, focal point of Texas fundamentalist attacks during the twenties, frequently proclaimed his orthodoxy, on one occasion calling himself "an old time Baptist, a believer in the Book from cover to cover."[55]

Brooks, along with Scarborough and Truett, drew fire from fundamentalists in the Southwest; in the East, North Carolina's William Poteat furnished a target for right-wing sharpshooters. But even Poteat, an avowed evolutionist, when "judged by the standards prevailing in the big cities, seems very orthodox," a correspondent of H. L. Mencken's *Ameri-*

---

[50]McDaniel, *The Supernatural Jesus*, p. 186; Thomas T. Martin, *The Dawson-Norris Issue; J. M. Dawson and Modernism: "The Inside of the Cup Turned Out"* (Jackson, Tennessee: McCowat-Mercer Co., 1932), p. 47.

[51]Dixon to Reuben Saillens, May 1922, Dixon Papers, Box 10.

[52]Norris to the Editor, *News-Globe* (Amarillo, Texas), 16 October 1930, Norris Papers, Box 1.

[53]Lee R. Scarborough, *Endued to Win* (Nashville: Sunday School Board, 1922), p. 138.

[54]George W. Truett, *Follow Thou Me* (New York: Ray Long and Richard, 1932), p. 59.

[55]Brooks to C. J. McCarty, 14 October 1924, Samuel P. Brooks Papers, Texas History Collection, Baylor University, Waco, Texas, File Di-Faculty.

can Mercury observed.[56] As proof of his loyalty to the old beliefs, Poteat affirmed Christ's divinity and proudly called himself a "fundamentalist" because he insisted upon "essential necessary truth."[57] As the *American Mercury* noted, unorthodox Southern Baptists were not really very unorthodox.

To insist upon the conservatism of Southern Baptists does not rule out the existence of a few bona fide modernists, as fundamentalists discovered when they turned their attacks on denominational colleges. Henry Fox, dismissed as professor of biology from Mercer University in 1924, issued a statement that left no doubt of his deviation from conservative standards. He conceived of God as a spiritual force of "Love and Truth" and proclaimed himself an agnostic on the topic of God's "objective existence." Expressing a lack of "positive conviction" as to Christ's divinity, the professor called the incarnation and atonement "speculative theological doctrines." He dismissed the subject of biblical inspiration as irrelevant to all but scholars and suggested that insufficient proof of the virgin birth existed "to warrant a layman holding any decisive opinion on the question."[58] By virtue of his position and the controversy surrounding his dismissal, Professor Fox's views gained wide attention across the South. Others agreed with him, but their obscurity protected them from fundamentalists. A Florida Baptist, for example, asked Poteat why the denomination continued "to cling to so many really foolish teachings," while a former Wake Forest student renounced "all childish beliefs in the myths and legends of the ancient world."[59] These statements would have shocked rank-and-file Baptists, but Poteat's correspondents kept their views tucked away, to be revealed only to those who could be trusted to agree, or at least, as in Poteat's case, to understand.

Despite the presence of a few genuine modernists, the Southern Baptist denomination constituted a bastion of orthodoxy, defying the winds of theological change buffeting America in the 1920s. This conser-

---

[56]James D. Bernard, "The Baptists," *American Mercury*, 7 (February 1926): 137.

[57]Poteat to W. M. Ginn, 9 September 1927, W. L. Poteat Papers; Poteat, quoted in Richard T. Vann, *What Have Baptist Colleges to Do with Fundamentalism and Modernism?* (N. p., n. d.), p. 5.

[58]*Messenger*, 29 October 1924, pp. 10-11.

[59]E. A. Harrill to Poteat, 31 January 1928; Charles H. Utley to Poteat, 5 January 1929, W. L. Poteat Papers.

vatism shaped the denomination's attitudes toward the fundamentalist movement and led conservatives to differentiate their own orthodoxy from the militant views championed by fundamentalists. Distinguishing traditional religious conservatism from its fundamentalist first cousin presented an awesome task in the twenties and has furnished an endless source of contention among scholars ever since. Conservatives trod a treacherously narrow path, for in rejecting fundamentalism they had to avoid the appearance of endorsing modernism. Southern Baptist scholars, denominational leaders, and others contended that fundamentalism employed the wrong methods in its defense of orthodoxy. With friends such as fundamentalists, many conservatives insisted, orthodoxy needed no enemies.

Reasons for Southern Baptist unwillingness to embrace fundamentalism are readily apparent. In the first place, many Baptists disliked the movement's frantic acrimony. E. Y. Mullins criticized fundamentalists for injecting this element into religious debate. In an address opening the 1925-1926 session at Southern Seminary, he urged that: "The attitude of calm faith, of fair dealing, of firm confidence in the safety and security of God's truth is the winning attitude."[60] Rufus Weaver insisted that fundamentalists had forfeited their standing as good Baptists. Denouncing "controversial, bitter, narrowminded and domineering" men, Weaver advised Baptists to emulate the ideal believer who "is tolerant but uncompromising in loyalty to his convictions."[61] Weaver and Mullins voiced the sentiments of many Southern Baptists who, while refusing to compromise with modernism, condemned the heated defense of orthodoxy promoted by William Bell Riley or, closer to home, J. Frank Norris.

On 13 September 1926, a Baptist minister in Harlan County, Kentucky, graphically illustrated a second reason for Southern Baptist suspicion of the fundamentalist movement. On that date the Reverend J. R. Black conducted a public book burning in which disagreeable volumes fueled the bonfire.[62] For some Baptists the Reverend Black's actions furnished an explanation for fundamentalist militance: his behavior

---

[60]E. Y. Mullins, "Christianity in the Modern World," *Review and Expositor*, 22 (October 1925): 476.

[61]Weaver, "The Baptist Opportunity in a Scientific Age," p. 5-6.

[62]Maynard Shipley, *The War on Modern Science: A Short History of the Fundamentalist Attacks on Evolution and Modernism* (New York: Alfred A. Knopf, 1927), pp. 125-26.

showed his fear of facing facts that conflicted with his rigid beliefs.[63] Baptist scholars in particular looked uneasily upon this tendency to deny Christians the right to deal with new ideas in a careful, intelligent fashion. "Such Fundamentalism is the best ally of Modernism," Mullins warned, "because Modernism rejoices in nothing so much as in silencing the voice and stilling the pen of the Christian scholar and thinker."[64] Fundamentalist book burners threatened to do just that by compromising "Christianity before the intelligence of the world."[65]

Finally, many Southern Baptists resented the fundamentalist demand for adherence to a unique interpretation of Christian orthodoxy. Premillennialism presented the most obvious example of this dogmatism, but it also appeared in fundamentalist haggling over the atonement. Exactly how, fundamentalists asked, had Christ's death atoned for man's sins? Many Baptists dismissed the question as irrelevant; salvation, they said, came from the "stupendous fact" of Christ's suffering for lost humanity and not from theoretical discussion of the atonement.[66] William Poteat's comment to his brother summed up this attitude: "Things seem to be pressing me to adopt somebody's theory of the atonement, a thing which I do not feel disposed to do, for I don't think the New Testament has one. I prefer to leave the matter where Jesus left it—the birth by the Spirit is like the mystery of the wind."[67] A number of Baptists looked with similar disfavor upon fundamentalist hairsplitting over the "mysteries of the wind."

Despite these objections, some Southern Baptists remained unsatisfied with anything less than the uncompromising militance of fundamentalism. These people went far beyond their brethren in their intense preoccupation with modernism, and they made it clear that Christianity had been split into two implacably opposed camps. A. C. Dixon, fundamentalist crusader since the 1890s, contended that for centuries a conflict had been raging "between the clouds of unbelief and the light of faith."[68]

---

[63]William L. Poteat, "Culture and Restraint," in *Youth and Culture* (Wake Forest: Wake Forest College Press, 1938), p. 141.

[64]*Herald*, 23 July 1925, pp. 22-23.

[65]William L. Poteat, *Can a Man Be a Christian To-day?* (Chapel Hill: University of North Carolina Press, 1925), pp. 35-36.

[66]Vann, *The Things Not Seen*, p. 86.

[67]William L. Poteat to Edwin M. Poteat, 8 March 1920, W. L. Poteat Papers.

[68]Dixon, *The Battle-lines between Christianity and Modernism*, pp. 18-19.

Behind this warfare loomed Satan who had masterminded the age-old attempt to destroy Christianity. To further this end the Evil One had authored and promoted modernism, which fundamentalists had now engaged in a life-and-death struggle. J. Frank Norris maintained that the controversy had begun with Lucifer's fall from grace and would continue until God vindicated fundamentalism by destroying the devil. The issues must be "clearly defined" and men must be forced to choose sides, Norris argued.[69] S. J. Betts, a North Carolina ally of Norris, criticized those who refused to join the fundamentalist movement, insisting that there could be no fence straddlers in the battle between Satan's error and God's truth.[70] Finally, Clarence P. Stealey, editor of the Oklahoma *Baptist Messenger*, expressed the fundamentalist attitude toward those who tried to remain neutral: "You may depend upon it that in almost every instance where you hear an expounder place the emphasis on the fact that he is a Baptist and neither a fundamentalist nor a modernist he is either a modernist or has friends who are that he would protect."[71] No middle position existed, fundamentalists said. Satan had established modernism, and God had countered with fundamentalism; refusal to join God's forces constituted treason. Lines had to be drawn and terms defined: good versus evil, God versus Satan, fundamentalism versus modernism.

This fundamentalist quest for ideological clarity actually produced confusion within the Southern Baptist Convention because it disrupted the denomination's united conservative front. Contending that they represented the only authentic anti-modernism, J. Frank Norris and his followers sought to rally Southern Baptists to their cause. But regardless of what fundamentalists asserted, virtually all Southern Baptists rejected higher criticism and Darwinism. Granted, a few members of the denomination employed scholarly methods in their study of the Bible and others adhered to the scientific explanation of life's origins. But even most of these men, modernists in the eyes of fundamentalists, staunchly opposed modernism and considered themselves conservative Protestants. An examination of Baptist attitudes toward evolution and higher criticism demonstrates the denomination's essential conservatism; at the same time, it shows the interaction of fundamentalists and conservatives as they attempted to define Baptist orthodoxy.

---

[69]*Searchlight*, 5 June 1924, p. 1.

[70]S. J. Betts, *Criticism of Dr. Poteat's Book Recently Published* (N. p., ca. 1925), p. 12.

[71]*Messenger*, 12 December 1923, p. 8; 7 September 1927, p. 1.

CHAPTER 6

Southern Baptists and the Bible

The modernists' revision of orthodoxy included a critical look at the Bible. Employing methods raised to new levels of effectiveness by nineteenth-century German higher critics, modernists questioned the sanctity of the Holy Canon. Within its pages they found not the literal, infallible word of God, but an imperfect human document, valuable for the aid it rendered man in his quest for religious truth. Modernists transformed the Bible into a reference work to be consulted by those in need of spiritual guidance. This infuriated many Protestants who, unlike Roman Catholics, lacked the institutional authority of pope and universal church. The Reformation's heirs looked to the Bible alone for religious authority; to question it implied an attack on the foundations of Protestantism. Liberal Protestants adjusted their thinking to the new views, but conservatives refused to alter their conception of the Bible.

Although the liberal interpretation gained formidable strength in the North, tradition held sway in the South, especially among the region's Baptists. Southern Baptists elevated the Bible far above other facets of their religion; veneration of the Scriptures constituted the rule, not the exception. Two books published in the 1920s delineated the denomination's stand. In 1923 Harvey E. Dana, professor of New Testament in Southwestern Seminary, defended *The Authenticity of the Holy Scriptures*, and a year later Edwin C. Dargan, editorial secretary of the Sunday School Board, published *The Bible Our Heritage*. Both men exalted the

Bible, Dana discerning in it an "authoritative moral standard," a "source of rich and ennobling experience," and the world's "only hope of redemption."[1] Dargan, describing the Bible's glories, wrote: "The whole sum and substance of religion in its most intense personal realization and in its broadest universality is expressed and enjoined in this fadeless Word of God."[2]

Apart from such direct appreciations, Southern Baptists revealed their devotion to the Bible in the images and metaphors they used to describe it. The Bible assumed lifelike characteristics in Baptist thinking; it became a living organism that "bled" when wounded by modernist attacks. This prompted Baptists to personalize God's word, to conceive of it as a friend to be protected from its enemies. Switching to another image, Baptists visualized the Bible as a "gigantic storehouse" of "riches" and a "granary of the soul" filled with "food in inexpressible abundance." The turmoil of the 1920s induced Baptists to express metaphorically the Bible's stability. To counter "winds of false doctrine" threatening to capsize the ship of orthodoxy, George McDaniel urged Baptists to cling to the Scriptures, the "Christian's chart and compass on the sea of life." In a similar vein, McDaniel wrote of the Bible: "There it stands like Jackson at Manassas, 'a stone wall.' " Finally, to those spiritually ill from the strife of the 1920s the Bible offered balm, for it contained "the medicine for every sickness."[3]

Southern Baptist fundamentalists shared the denomination's reverence for the Scriptures, their views often forming an indistinguishable part of the larger Baptist effort to save the Bible from modernism. But broad agreement with their brethren failed to conceal the greater intensity and dogmatism exhibited by fundamentalists. All Southern Baptists honored the Bible as authoritative for Christian experience, but an added pugnacity characterized a Kentucky fundamentalist's boast to J. Frank

---

[1]Harvey E. Dana, *The Authenticity of the Holy Scriptures: A Brief Story of the Problems of Biblical Criticism* (Nashville: Sunday School Board, 1923), pp. 19-23.

[2]Edwin C. Dargan, *The Bible Our Heritage* (Nashville: Sunday School Board, 1924), p. xiv.

[3]John R. Sampey, *The Heart of the Old Testament: A Manual for Christian Students* (Garden City: Doubleday, Doran, 1928; original publication, 1909), p. 224; Arthur Flake, *Building a Standard Sunday School*, 4th ed. (Nashville: Sunday School Board, 1942; original publication, 1922), pp. 71, 73; Lee Scarborough, *Endued to Win* (Nashville: Sunday School Board, 1922), p. 64; George W. McDaniel, *The Supernatural Jesus* (Nashville: Sunday School Board, 1924), pp. 189, 203-204.

Norris that he no longer studied anything but his Bible. He further suggested that by way of purification, every Baptist preacher ought to be imprisoned for forty days, with nothing but his Bible and a diet of bread and water. Upon his release "give him a drink of tiger[']s blood, and then let him preach to his deacons," the writer advised.[4]

Norris could appreciate the Kentuckian's proposal, for in 1930 he counseled a young preacher that "if I had one word above another to say to every young minister it would be 'study your Bible, study your Bible, and then study your Bible.' "[5] The Scriptures furnished the final word on all matters, Norris contended; when they failed to thunder their authority the Christian should proceed with caution.[6] Norris's church implemented his views by discarding all "man-made literature" in order to concentrate on God's word. This housecleaning included the study aids produced by the Sunday School Board in Nashville, since Norris believed that "you can't learn the Bible with such junk."[7]

Whether fundamentalists or not, all Southern Baptists agreed that the higher criticism of the Bible presented a problem. At the bottom of their assessment of biblical criticism lay the belief that one must approach God's word with reverence and humility, constantly aware of the difference between it and the uninspired works of man. Many Baptists insisted that "reasoned and calm confidence" rather than "flaw-picking" should guide the Christian in his study of the Scriptures.[8] In accepted Southern fashion, A. C. Dixon boosted the Bible onto a pedestal alongside womanhood and excoriated those who dared to impugn the integrity of either.[9] Although Dixon and the fundamentalists placed greatest emphasis on keeping God's message unsullied, all Southern Baptists demanded that the Holy Book be handled with care.

The "atrocities" committed by liberals especially incensed Baptist fundamentalists. Labeling modernist methods of biblical study "destruc-

---

[4]D. B. Clapp to Norris, 9 July 1930, Norris Papers, Box 7.

[5]Norris to J. H. Brewster, 3 February 1930, Norris Papers, Box 2.

[6]Norris to F. K. Campbell, Jr., 2 May 1930, Box 5.

[7]*Searchlight*, 30 December 1920, p. 2; J. Frank Norris, *Inside History of the First Baptist Church, Fort Worth, and Temple Baptist Church, Detroit: Life Story of Dr. J. Frank Norris* (n. p., n. d.), p. 118.

[8]Dargan, *The Bible Our Heritage*, pp. 101-102.

[9]Amzi C. Dixon, "A Mossback's Reply to Modernism," p. 18, ca. early 1920s typescript, Dixon Papers, Box 12.

tive criticism," A. C. Dixon warned in 1920 of the menace to Southern religion.[10] In a pamphlet published that same year, he assailed higher critics, denouncing their "claims" as "moths which are eating away the texture of faith and character." In the first place, Dixon charged, higher criticism had undermined belief in the supernatural, had banished God from the world, and had deified natural law. Second, the modernist view of the Bible had seduced college teachers, had turned America's schools into hotbeds of heresy, and had made skepticism respectable. Finally, Dixon said, these teachings had weakened the consciences of untold numbers of "good men," leading them into "fraud and dishonesty."[11] Dixon cogently depicted fundamentalist apprehension, while proving to the satisfaction of many Baptists that higher criticism formed part of the modernist campaign to pollute the wellsprings of Christianity.

Dixon and other fundamentalists articulated the troubled thoughts of the Baptist masses who believed that the new departure in biblical study represented a deadly thrust at their religion. They cared nothing for the rights of scholarship; only the preservation of an unblemished Bible mattered. Many Baptists reasoned that since fundamentalists defended the Scriptures most vigorously the denomination should heed their example. As an Arkansas Baptist said in defense of J. Frank Norris: "He should not be condemned for attacking *sin* and it *is sin* for any men or set of men to attack the scriptures as is being done today."[12] In their evaluation of higher criticism, Southern Baptist fundamentalists spoke for an overwhelming majority of their fellow churchmen; on this issue extremism engulfed the denomination.

The denomination's leading intellectuals joined their fellow Baptists in condemning "destructive criticism." Robert Pitt denounced higher critics for their dogmatism, writing that the

> so-called "Higher Critics" have frequently—indeed usually— insisted upon the acceptance of their more or less probable guesses as final, and in no department of Biblical study and research, of which we have any knowledge, has there been

---

[10]Dixon to Reuben A. Torrey, 24 July 1920, Dixon Papers, Box 9.

[11]Dixon, *Myths and Moths of Criticism: An Examination of the Moths and Their Doings* (Los Angeles: Bible Institute of Los Angeles, ca. 1920), pp. 3, 8-10.

[12]Jeff Reynolds to Lee Scarborough, 8 April 1922, Lee R. Scarborough Papers, Southwestern Baptist Theological Seminary; emphasis in the original.

exhibited quite so much of arrogance and intolerance of opposing views.[13]

Pitt admitted that scholars had the right to examine the Bible—a right many Baptists denied—but he contended that too often this had degenerated into destruction of traditional beliefs. "Beyond all question," he charged, Christian faith had been weakened and biblical authority undermined by recent trends.[14]

Southern Baptist seminary professors also lent their prestige to the attack on higher criticism. A. T. Robertson, Southern Seminary's New Testament expert, exposed higher criticism's bias against Christ's divinity and argued that this "critical prejudice against the theological Christ has animated the long search for the historical Jesus."[15] Despite these abuses, Robertson acknowledged the validity of scientific analysis when conducted in the proper spirit. E. Y. Mullins agreed with Robertson that scientific methods should be employed in ascertaining the historical facts of the New Testament, but, he added, many proponents of this technique had been unscientific in their efforts to rid the New Testament of its supernatural elements.[16] Southwestern Seminary did not go unrepresented in this assault on the Bible's detractors, for in his book of 1923 Harvey Dana charged that unscientific biblical critics had shown their "deep-seated and violent prejudice against revealed religion."[17]

Although the denomination's leading thinkers were as orthodox as the fundamentalists on this issue, two important differences existed. In the first place, non-fundamentalists refused to panic at modernist challenges, remaining relatively free of the fears that haunted fundamentalists, and exuding confidence in the enduring strength of the Scriptures. William Poteat, for example, remarked that the Bible's teachings about Christ would survive because the Saviour was an "essential" that scientific inquiry could not destroy.[18] George Truett posited another essential that could not

---

[13]*Herald*, 4 September 1919, p. 10.

[14]*Herald*, 1 April 1920, p. 10.

[15]A. T. Robertson, "The Christ of the Logia," *Contemporary Review* 116 (July 1919): 208.

[16]Edgar Y. Mullins, *Christianity at the Cross Roads* (New York: George H. Doran Co., 1924), pp. 177-78, 180, 183.

[17]Dana, *The Authenticity of the Holy Scriptures*, p. 28.

[18]Poteat to Walter Lippmann, 13 May 1929, W. L. Poteat Papers.

be denied by the critics; in the Scriptures "we find revealed our own
experience," and this, he said, validated God's word.[19] Finally, W. T.
Conner maintained that modernist aggression remained harmless as long
as men continued to find God in the Scriptures. The stamp of scientific
approval mattered little; "a man no more needs to wait on the conclusions
of critics to be religious than he needs to wait for the dietician to settle all
scientific questions concerning food before eating his dinner," Conner
concluded.[20]

By realizing that the Bible could not be hidden from the scrutiny of
highly trained minds, Conner and others differed from fundamentalists on
a second point. These men reasoned that Christians should welcome
serious biblical study, for it would acquit orthodoxy of the accusation that it
rested on superstition and error. Southern Baptists who defended the right
to approach the Bible through the mind as well as the heart comprised a
lonely band. On their left flank they had to ward off modernist forays, while
on the right they had to cope with Baptists who disapproved of subjecting
the Scriptures to the critical eye of scholarship. A number of Baptists, filled
with reverence, but equally committed to the pursuit of truth, chose to
brave these difficulties.

E. Y. Mullins pursued this course in *Christianity at the Cross Roads*.
Although deploring the results of much biblical criticism, he maintained
that "the true method of approach to the New Testament is that of a sound
historical criticism, combined with spiritual appreciation of its contents."
The New Testament must pass the test of modern research, Mullins added,
or "it cannot permanently retain its influence."[21] Harvey Dana, while
denouncing the tendencies of higher criticism, warned that "the dogmatiz-
ing of an overzealous orthodoxy may win the sanction and applause of the
masses, but it fails utterly to satisfy the mind of the real thinker." Dana
believed that the worst defense of the Bible lay in shielding it from
intelligent inquiry; the Christian must allow science to examine the
Scriptures, guarding always, of course, against anti-Christian movements
masquerading in scientific garb. "We must meet a scientific approach with

---

[19]George W. Truett, *Follow Thou Me* (New York: Ray Long and Richard, 1932), p.
69.

[20]W. T. Conner, *A System of Christian Doctrine* (Nashville: Sunday School Board,
1924), p. 109.

[21]Mullins, *Christianity at the Cross Roads*, p. 185.

a scientific response," Dana concluded.[22] No one better illustrates this attitude than A. T. Robertson, a Baptist capable of meeting erudite critics on their own ground. Robertson, who believed that "obscurantism is no answer to radicalism," encouraged his students to deal intelligently with the theories of such thinkers as Ernest Renan and Thomas Huxley. In his own work Robertson upheld a commitment to "rigid scientific research into the facts," confident that the Bible had nothing to hide from its examiners.[23]

A number of men outside the academic world circulated these views to a larger audience. Richard Vann of North Carolina suggested that in employing reason and common sense in interpreting the Bible Baptists shared some of the attributes of rationalism. If not, Vann said, Southern Baptists might as well fill their seminary professorships with "Holy Rollers."[24] Both L. L. Gwaltney and Robert Pitt encouraged their readers to move beyond abject veneration of the Scriptures. Pitt deplored the condemnation of critical inquiry into the Bible and commended efforts to discover exactly what the writings taught "in the light of their history, their authorship and their full literary content."[25] Gwaltney felt that "serious biblical scholars and good men" who had delved into the Scriptures had strengthened rather than weakened orthodoxy.[26]

These reassurances were insufficient for the Baptist masses, who glared suspiciously at those displaying anything short of total awe and reverence toward the Bible. By taking this position, most of the South's Baptists failed to appreciate the efforts of conservative scholars who employed critical analysis in defense of the Bible. Recognizing the inadequacy of adoration, these men applied scholarly standards to the Bible, and after concluding their examination announced that God's word had passed the test. Edwin Dargan, for example, after surveying the earliest biblical

---

[22]Dana, *The Authenticity of the Holy Scriptures*, pp. 15-16.

[23]A. T. Robertson, *The Minister and His Greek New Testament* (New York: George H. Doran Co., 1923), pp. 84-85; *Syllabus for New Testament Study: A Guide for Lessons in the Classroom*, 5th ed. (London: Hodder and Stoughton, 1923; original publication, 1915), pp. 113-14, 123; "The Christ of the Logia," pp. 199, 201.

[24]Richard T. Vann, *What Have Baptist Colleges to Do with Fundamentalism and Modernism* (n. p., ca. 1925), p. 9.

[25]*Herald*, 4 September 1919, p. 10.

[26]Leslie L. Gwaltney, *Forty of the Twentieth or the First Forty Years of the Twentieth Century* (Birmingham: pub. by author, 1940), pp. 123-24.

manuscripts, reported that no other ancient book possessed so well attested a text as the Bible.[27] Harvey Dana used archaeological findings to vindicate biblical history.[28] John R. Sampey, the denomination's leading Old Testament specialist, countered higher critics by reaffirming his belief in the Mosaic authorship of the Pentateuch and Isaiah's claim to the book bearing his name.[29] Finally, A. T. Robertson confirmed Luke's authorship of the Acts of the Apostles and one of the Gospels, dismissed attempts to attribute Colossians to someone other than Paul, and upheld the validity of Matthew's and Luke's accounts of the life of Christ.[30] For Robertson, as for Sampey, Dana, and other learned Baptists, the Bible confirmed what the humblest believer felt in his heart: the Scriptures were reliable and unshakable.

Southern Baptist scholars' defense of the Bible may appear mistaken and outdated in the light of later findings, but in the 1920s their work represented a courageous attempt to demonstrate the compatibility of piety and intellect. For while these men pursued their studies, the deep-rooted animus of the Baptist masses toward learning fed the flames of fundamentalist denunciation and created anxiety over outside conspiracies to undermine revealed religion. Tendencies within higher criticism did threaten the Southern Baptist faith, but the denomination's scholars understood the new methods and used them to validate orthodox claims. But because most of the South's Baptists saw only evil in opening the Bible to research, they harbored suspicions toward orthodox scholars and stirred restlessly over an alien mode of thought they could not understand. Fundamentalism thrived in this atmosphere, and charges of Baptist modernism, though largely untrue, gained credibility.

While the discussion of higher criticism revealed the dominant conservatism of Southern Baptists, it also uncovered varying definitions of orthodoxy. This pattern repeated itself in Baptist attitudes toward the doctrines of biblical inspiration and literalism. The dispute over inspira-

---

[27]Dargan, *The Bible Our Heritage*, p. 46.

[28]Dana, *The Authenticity of the Holy Scriptures*, pp. 26-28, 50.

[29]Sampey, *The Heart of the Old Testament*, pp. 73-74, 169.

[30]A. T. Robertson, *Luke the Historian in the Light of Research* (New York: Charles Scribner's Sons, 1920), p. 15; *Paul and the Intellectuals: The Epistle to the Colossians* (Garden City: Doubleday, Doran, 1928), p. 24; *The Mother of Jesus: Her Problems and Her Glory* (Grand Rapids: Baker Book House, 1963; original publication, 1925), p. 71.

tion involved the problem of determining how God had influenced the authors of the Scriptures. Modernists settled the matter by comparing the inspiration of the Bible's writers to that felt by poets, painters, and musicians. For example, modernists observed that the Bible's poets had undergone the same imaginative transformation experienced by Shakespeare or Wordsworth. Or, to cite a second case, the same worshipfulness that had compelled the psalmist to sing praises to God had led Bach to compose the *Mass in B Minor*. Modernists wasted little time on the question of inspiration, preferring to emphasize the Bible's principles rather than engaging in controversy over how the books had been written. Conservatives resisted liberal Christianity's humanization of inspiration, interpreting it as part of an endeavor to destroy the Bible's authority. By denying the divine inspiration of the Scriptures, modernists placed the Bible on a level with human creations, conservatives charged. This could not go uncontested; to anti-modernist Protestants, whether fundamentalists or not, divine inspiration remained one of "the most fundamental of the fundamentals of the faith."[31]

Southern Baptists unanimously agreed that God had inspired certain men to write the books of the Bible and had watched over them as they prepared their works. Although Baptists concurred on the *fact* of God's divine inspiration, the *mechanics* proved to be troublesome. Reacting to modernist efforts to place the Bible alongside man's other creations, fundamentalists stressed God's role almost to the exclusion of the writers' part. They denied that the writers had influenced one another, that research had preceded composition, or that such mundane experiences as dreams had affected the authors. Fundamentalists eliminated temporal influences that might have swayed a writer in his choice of subject or use of words; the Bible, they argued, contained exactly what God had wanted, expressed in precisely the words He had spoken.[32] As J. Frank Norris's congregation stated in its confession of faith, the Bible "does not contain and convey the word of God, but IS the very Word of God."[33]

Elevation of the supernatural at the expense of man's role led Southern Baptist fundamentalists to adopt the theory of verbal inspiration. God had

---

[31]J. Frank Norris to Isaac E. Gates, 29 October 1930, Norris Papers, Box 16.

[32]J. H. O'Neall to Frank Norris, 2 February 1931, Norris Papers, Box 31.

[33]*Confession of Faith of the First Baptist Church,* Fort Worth, Texas (N. p., ca. 1923), p. 14.

spoken directly to his penmen in their native language. To J. Frank Norris's way of thinking this reduced the authors to "vessels or channels through which the Divine thought came."[34] Oklahoman Charles T. Alexander clearly spelled out the fundamentalist position in a letter to Norris.

> The question after all is this: HAS GOD ACTUALLY SPOKEN TO THE INTELLIGENCE OF THE HUMAN RACE SO THAT HUMANITY CAN GET GOD'S THOUGHTS? If so God must have used the only vehicle human beings have for the transmission of thought from one mind to another. That vehicle is language. But language, apart from words, cannot exist. How could God speak except with words [?] And how could He speak through an inspired, or chosen, man except through that man's vocabulary of words? There is so much foolishness in argumants [sic] against "verbal inspiration" as if there could be any other kind. The position that says the inspiration of the Bible lies back of and beyond the words etc. means this: Our Bible is not the word of God, but somehow just CONTAINS THE WORD OF GOD! That is Modernism, pure and simple.[35]

Accepting the logical conclusion of this chain of thought, fundamentalists proclaimed their adherence to the "dictation theory."[36] In effect, they argued that God had sat in heaven reading a prepared manuscript to stenographers who had transcribed every word and punctuation mark. With the theory of verbal inspiration through dictation, fundamentalists assured the impossibility of equating the Bible with other works of man.

Some Baptists responded to this theory with the same calm assessment that they gave to the debate over higher criticism. Granting the unique and divine character of the Scriptures, they refused to insist upon a single method of inspiration. Robert Pitt voiced this opinion in warning Baptists against using finely wrought theories to measure orthodoxy. God's method of inspiration, Pitt said, lay outside the realm of "human knowledge and existence" and resisted man's feeble efforts at definition.[37] Edwin

---

[34]*Fundamentalist*, 13 December 1929, p. 1.

[35]Alexander to Norris, 20 December 1929, Norris Papers, Box 1.

[36]S.J. Betts, *Criticism of Dr. Poteat's Book Recently Published* (N. p., ca. 1925), p. 6.

[37]*Herald*, 27 December 1923, p. 11.

Dargan acknowledged God's inspiration, but refused to describe its exact nature, writing that "there is room for much difference of opinion as to many details concerning the mode, the extent, and the results of the divine inspiration."[38] These men argued that orthodoxy's most important task lay in defending the reality of God's presence with the Bible's authors and not in expounding dogmatic theories of inspiration.

Fundamentalist insistence upon the theory of verbal inspiration created a dilemma for denominational leaders. Some readily accepted the fundamentalist view because it comported with their own beliefs. W. R. White, secretary of missions for Texas, publicly avowed that the Scriptures "were just as much the very word of God as if He had written every word in heaven and handed the Bible down to man ready-made."[39] Most Baptist spokesmen refused to embrace this formula, choosing instead to speak of inspiration in general, noncontroversial terms. E. Y. Mullins, for example, avowed that though "inspired men wrote the Bible," the mechanics of God's communication with these writers remained a mystery.[40] George Truett expressed the attitude of many Baptist preachers. Avoiding the question of how God had influenced the Bible's authors, the Dallas pastor thought it sufficient to proclaim his "unwavering belief in the holy scriptures as Divinely inspired of God."[41] The end, not the means, interested Truett and his colleagues; the technicalities of inspiration were best avoided.

Some non-fundamentalists felt compelled to deal more directly with fundamentalist "bibliolatry" by attacking it outright.[42] In this vein, William Poteat argued that the Bible provided no basis for the idea of dictation.[43] Two of the denomination's leading thinkers, W. T. Conner and A. T. Robertson, contested the theory by stressing the freedom God had accorded the Bible's authors. "Man was as free and as truly himself," Conner wrote, "as if God had nothing to do with the giving of the message

---

[38]Dargan, *The Bible Our Heritage*, pp. 21-22.

[39]Quoted in W. N. Webb to Lee Scarborough, 5 May 1930, Scarborough Papers.

[40]E. Y. Mullins to Frank Norris, 3 July 1924, Mullins Papers, 1924-1925 Correspondence.

[41]Truett to W. F. Matheny, 27 March 1930, Truett Papers.

[42]E. Y. Mullins, "Why I Am a Baptist," *Forum* 75 (May 1926): 727.

[43]William L. Poteat, *Can a Man Be a Chrisitan To-day?* (Chapel Hill: University of North Carolina Press, 1925), p. 71.

and putting it into written form."[44] Robertson even allowed an occasional human error to creep into Holy Writ.[45]

Some of the most telling criticism of verbal inspiration came from two Baptists who deeply resented the manipulation of God's word. Joseph Dawson denied that the Bible's writers had served as stenographers. If God had dictated his thoughts why, Dawson asked, did the Gospel accounts of the life of Christ differ in style and content? Moreover, God must have been careless in His dictation, for when New Testament writers quoted the Old Testament they seldom got the wording correct.[46] Richard Vann considered the argument over verbal inspiration incredible. How could fundamentalists advance such a thesis when the Scriptures they venerated had come from a seventeenth-century translation? Even a return to the ancient manuscripts solved nothing, Vann said, for "the people ought to know, also, that our present Greek and Hebrew texts, which formed the basis of our English Bible, were made up of some two thousand manuscripts, more or less incomplete, and no two exactly alike."[47] Reason dictated to Vann that it would be difficult to find God's original words in this jumble of sources, even assuming the validity of the fundamentalist contention.

The probing critiques offered by Poteat, Conner, Robertson, Dawson, and Vann came as no surprise, for these men formed part of the denomination's intellectual elite. The quality of their minds enabled them to penetrate fundamentalist theory and to expose its half-formed opinions and illogical suppositions. But even more impressive are the fleeting glimpses one catches of resistance to fundamentalist dogma on a different plane. The Reverend Joe H. Hankins of Childress, Texas, an "average" Baptist preacher with no seminary training, contested fundamentalist claims, writing to a supporter of J. Frank Norris that:

> I want you to know that you are no better "Fundamentalist"
> and neither is Norris than I, and thousands of others who do not
> nor never believed in the verbal inspiration of the scriptures. If

---

[44]Conner, *A System of Christian Doctrine*, p. 119.

[45]Robertson, *Luke the Historian*, p. 41.

[46]Joseph M. Dawson, *The Light that Grows: Sermons to College Students* (New York: George H. Doran Co., 1923), pp. 43-44.

[47]Vann, *What Have Baptist Colleges to Do with Fundamentalism and Modernism*, p. 12.

> God had to make a phonograph or stenographer out of a man to
> speak His message, then why did He ever use a man at all?
> Why did He not do like He did about the Ten Commandments,
> write them with His own finger?[48]

Hankins argued that God had inspired the writer's mind, leaving him free
to express God's truths in his own words.[49] As the Reverend Hankins
demonstrated, the denomination's elite held no monopoly on opposition
to the dictation theory.

A second problem of biblical study concerned literalism. To what
degree, men asked as they perused the Bible, did its words mean exactly
what they said? Modernists found no difficulty in offering an answer, for to
them only the Bible's ethical and spiritual principles mattered. Guided by
this canon, modernists jettisoned many parts of the Bible beloved by
Protestants. They reinterpreted the creation story, cast doubt on the
miracles, and undercut the prophetic writings. Liberals appealed to the
spirit rather than to the letter of the Bible, contending that the mere
existence of a statement did not guarantee its literal truth.

Orthodox Protestants found the problem more troublesome. If the
Bible had come from God through His chosen writers, how could fallible
human beings question the meaning of the text? When the Bible stated
that a "great fish" had swallowed Jonah or that Moses had parted the Red
Sea with his rod, conservatives usually accepted the statement as literal
truth. No other possibility existed for fundamentalists who, believing that
God had dictated His words to penmen, rejected the possibility that the
Lord had confused His people by speaking figuratively. God had promulgated simple truths in easily understood language, and man dared not twist
and interpret the words; he must accept them as they stood, fundamentalists concluded.

Accepting "the whole Bible just like it is written," Southern Baptist
fundamentalists employed literalism as another test of orthodoxy. If
Christians would adopt their method of Bible study all problems of
interpretation would cease, fundamentalists argued, for when read literally, as God intended, the Scriptures presented no difficulties. This belief
led fundamentalists to question the orthodoxy of those who confessed

---

[48]Hankins to R. R. Cumbie, 14 December 1929.

[49]Hankins to Cumbie, ca. December 1929, Norris Papers, Box 9.

uncertainty over the meaning of a given text.[50] As a Texan declared: "If you question the Bible in any one or more important facts you will question it on everything and it will soon be we will have no Bible that we can trust."[51]

Literalism's appeal reached into every corner of the denomination, commanding the assent of most Southern Baptists. Distinctions between fundamentalists and other Baptists blurred, as both groups rushed to affirm their acceptance of the Bible "from lid to lid."[52] Southern Baptists believed, as an outsider observed, that "what is in the Bible is absolutely and immutably true."[53] On this point fundamentalism carried the field, and, as with Baptist reaction to higher criticism, extremism swept the denomination. Lee Scarborough and George Truett, both of whom abhorred fundamentalism, attested to the widespread popularity of literalism among Southern Baptists. Scarborough declared his acceptance of every miracle recorded in the Bible and defended the story of Jonah as an actual occurrence.[54] Truett, as a contemporary recalled, frequently testified "as solemnly as if under oath that he believes it [the Bible] every word, just as it reads, miracles and all."[55] Truett and Scarborough reflected the sentiments of their followers; rank-and-file Baptists read the Bible literally, unwilling to surrender a single word in the "Old Book."

Ironically, Southern Baptist fundamentalists, the denomination's most extreme literalists, actually followed a figurative interpretation at times. Granted, when the Bible spoke of the sun standing still for Joshua or of Christ raising Lazarus from the dead, fundamentalists nodded their heads in assent. But in their bizarre reading of the prophetic books, especially those dealing with Christ's second coming, they forsook literalism. For premillennialism made the Bible, in J. Frank Norris's words,

---

[50]J. Frank Norris to Lawrence D. Byers, 3 February 1930, Norris Papers, Box 2; Fred W. Barnaclo to W. W. Chancellor, 22 October 1927, Norris Papers, Box 2; A. T. Camp to Norris, 27 October 1931, Norris Papers, Box 5.

[51]J. S. Allen to the editor, *Baptist Standard*, 27 January 1930, Norris Papers, Box 2.

[52]The Reverend J. T. Kincannon, quoted in Thomas L. Sydnor (ed.), *Living Epistles: The Old Guard* (Danville, Virginia: published by the author, 1924), 115.

[53]James D. Bernard, "The Baptists," *American Mercury* 7 (February 1926): 146.

[54]Lee R. Scarborough, *The Tears of Jesus: Sermons to Aid Soul-Winners* (Grand Rapids: Baker Book House, 1967; original publication, 1922), pp. 91-92.

[55]James B. Cranfill, *From Memory: Reminiscences, Recitals, and Gleanings from a Bustling and Busy Life* (Nashville: Broadman Press, 1937), pp. 128-29.

"entirely a different book."[56] Norris illustrated this in a sermon purporting to give the "correct rendering" of Ezekiel 38:1-7. In the Frank Norris version of the Bible the passage read:

> Son of Man, set thy face against Gogue, the emperor of Germany, Hungary, etc., and Autocrat of Russia, Muscovy and Tobolski, and prophesy against him, and say, Thus saith the Lord, Behold I am against thee, O Gogue, Autocrat of Russia, Muscovy and Tobolski, and I will turn thee about, from the north parts, and all thine army, horses and horsemen, and all of them accoutred with all sorts of armor even a great company with bucklers and shields, all of them handling sword, among whom shall be Persians, Ethiopians, and Libyans; all of them with shields and helmuts. French and Italians, Circassians, Cossacks and the Tartar hordes of Usbeck and many people not particularly named besides.[57]

Introducing Frenchmen, Italians, and "the Tartar hordes of Usbeck" into a document written centuries before the birth of Christ cast serious doubt on fundamentalists' literalism. But they failed to perceive the contradiction; along with most of their fellow churchmen, they vigorously defended the doctrine of biblical literalism.

Fewer Baptists spoke out against literalism than against verbal inspiration, but a number of men seconded China missionary Gordon Poteat's call for a "saner view" of the Bible.[58] L. L. Gwaltney took up the cause of this small band. Gwaltney had entered Richmond College in 1899 a firm believer in the Bible's literal accuracy, but had soon changed his mind, realizing that the Scriptures included "poetry, simile, metaphor, parables, allegories and visions which contain great truths, but which were not intended to be taken as literal facts."[59] Seminary professors A. T. Robertson and W. T. Conner, through their rejection of biblical literalism, enabled a few young Baptists to undergo the transformation experienced by Gwaltney. Robertson labeled the theory a "half-truth,"[60] and Conner

---

[56]Norris to Roy L. Puckett, 11 December 1931, Norris Papers, Box. 32.

[57]*Fundamentalist*, 30 August 1929, p. 5.

[58]Poteat to Z. T. Cody, 23 July 1926, Robertson Papers, Folder 1926B.

[59]Gwaltney, *Forty of the Twentieth*, p. 120.

[60]Robertson, *The Minister and His Greek New Testament*, p. 84.

cautioned his students to "beware the dictionary" in their study of Holy
Writ.[61] Robertson's colleague and president, E. Y. Mullins, also protested
against the literalists. Writing in 1923, he said:

> Figures of speech, metaphors and all sorts of literary media
> for communicating truth are to be found in it [the Bible], and a
> great part of the controversial matter grows out of a literal
> interpretation of passage which anyone with a good literary
> sense would have no difficulty with whatever.[62]

In Robert Pitt Virginia Baptists boasted one of the denomination's
most outspoken foes of literalism. Pitt delighted in combing the Scriptures
for figurative passages with which to taunt literalists. Quoting Revelation
7:1—"And after these things I saw four angels standing on the four corners
of the earth"—Pitt concluded that the earth must be flat. He seized upon
Revelation 6:13, with its prophecy of stars falling upon the earth, as proof
that, regardless of the findings of astronomers, the earth was larger than
the stars.[63] In addition to his own parodies of literalism, Pitt published
articles by like-minded men. Edward B. Pollard, a Virginian teaching in
Pennsylvania's Crozer Seminary and a frequent contributor to the *Religious Herald*, authored a controversial article in September, 1919, entitled
"On Taking the Bible Literally." Pollard indicted literalists for teaching
science from the Scriptures, distorting the prophecies, employing the
Bible's statements as "legislative regulations," and misunderstanding
biblical imagery. Literalists, Pollard concluded, threatened to change the
Bible from a book "that breathes and glows" into a "stale, arid, flat,
unprofitable" work.[64] The *Religious Herald*, through Pollard's articles and
Pitt's editorials, served as a focal point for antiliteralism during the 1920s.

Those who advocated Gordon Poteat's "saner view" applied themselves to the practical task of explaining the Bible. In particular, they
rejected the literal reading of the word "day" in Genesis, and on numerous
other points they dissented from the popular interpretation. Professor C.
S. Fothergill of Baylor accepted the account of the Great Flood, but argued

---

[61]Conner, quoted in Stewart A. Newman, *W. T. Conner: Theologian of the Southwest*
(Nashville: Broadman Press, 1964), p. 108.

[62]Mullins to T. O. Mabry, 7 June 1923, Mullins Papers, 1923-1924 Correspondence.

[63]*Herald*, 28 May 1925, p. 11.

[64]*Herald*, 25 September 1919, pp. 4-5.

that Noah's ark, if built according to specifications, could not have held the number of animals listed in the Bible.[65] John R. Sampey, a thoroughly orthodox Baptist, took a critical view of Job's story, placing it somewhere between history and fiction.[66] Sampey remained undisturbed that the book did not contain a verbatim rendering of the dialogue between Job and his friends, for "the message of the book is substantially the same, whether we conceive of it as a parable, or literal history, or history worked over with poetic embellishment."[67] Sampey, Fothergill, and their colleagues felt no compulsion to worship the Bible's every word; granting its overall validity, they could question the literal truth of inessentials.

---

[65]Fothergill, Letter of Resignation, 5 November 1924, Brooks Papers, File Di-Faculty.

[66]Sampey, *The Heart of the Old Testament*, p. 43.

[67]John R. Sampey, *Syllabus for Old Testament Study*, 4th ed. (New York: George H. Doran Co., 1922; original publication, 1903), p. 116.

CHAPTER 7

The Evolution Controversy

Modernists offered a second challenge to conservative Protestants with the theory of biological evolution. In a sense, the evolution debate formed part of the controversy over the Bible, for in applying their methods to the Scriptures, higher critics dealt harshly with the Genesis account of creation, interpreting it as an example of the Bible's use of myth. But more important, scientists fleshed out the theory proposed by Charles Darwin in the nineteenth century, lifting the question of man's origins out of the realm of biblical exegesis and making it a problem in its own right.

Southern Baptists opposed the doctrine of evolution as adamantly as any Protestants. Benjamin A. Copass, professor of Old Testament in Southwestern Seminary, correctly observed in 1922: "If I am not mistaken Baptists are set against the theory of evolution."[1] Support for Copass's statement came from every corner of Southern Baptist territory in the 1920s. State conventions in North Carolina, Kentucky, Mississippi, Texas, and Louisiana vigorously assailed Darwinism, with Louisiana Baptists calling it a "soul-destroying, Bible-denying and God-dishonoring theory."[2] Although some members of the denomina-

---

[1]Benjamin A. Copass to Lula Pace, 9 November 1922, Brooks Papers, File Di-Faculty.

[2]North Carolina, *Annual*, 1925, pp. 29-30; Kentucky, *Proceedings*, 1923, pp. 76-77;

tion couched their opposition in more sophisticated terms, the vast majority of Southern Baptists agreed with these sentiments.

The thinking of the denomination's leaders coincided with the mass opinion expressed in state convention meetings. E. Y. Mullins and George Truett, both presidents of the Southern Baptist Convention in the 1920s, accepted their denomination's stand on evolution, with Truett taking offense on one occasion at the mere suggestion that he did not accept the creation story as recounted in Genesis.[3] Lee Scarborough expressed his thoughts even more explicitly, pointing out in a 1924 book that he accepted even the story of Eve's creation from Adam's rib.[4]

The opinions of Scarborough and Mullins, both of whom were seminary professors, demonstrated that not only illiterate or poorly educated Baptists opposed Darwinism. Yet education did seem to increase susceptibility to the blandishments of evolutionary thought; after all, Southern Baptist colleges harbored most of the denomination's evolutionists. But even in the colleges, education and evolution did not go hand in hand; despite the presence of a few evolutionists, Southern Baptist colleges remained orthodox. The faculty of Tennessee's Union University typified this sentiment in proclaiming that "we believe in Jehovah as the creator of the heavens and the earth, and all things therein and utterly repudiate any theory contrary to such origin of things whether it be called evolution or by any other name." Although Baylor University employed several evolutionists, it hardly qualified as a hotbed of heresy. The editor of the student newspaper stated in 1922 that the entire student body adhered to creationism, and several years later thirty-two Baylor graduates denied that the school's professors advocated Darwinism.[5] Baylor and Union showed that the educated elite generally conformed to the views held by less learned Baptists.

Mississippi, *Proceedings*, 1925, p. 32; Texas, *Annual*, 1922, p. 13; Louisiana, *Annual*, 1922, p. 29.

[3]Mullins to T. W. Callaway, 20 July 1925, Mullins Papers, 1925-1927 Correspondence A-L; Truett to Clarence Stealey, 3 March 1926, Truett Papers.

[4]Lee R. Scarborough, *Christ's Militant Kingdom: A Study in the Trail Triumphant* (New York: George H. Doran Co., 1924), p. 53.

[5]*Herald*, 9 February 1922, pp. 4-5; George D. Tyson to James B. Cranfill, 12 April 1922, Pat M. Neff Papers, Neff Division, Texas History Collection, Baylor University, Governor Correspondence, 1922; ca. mid-1920s statement drawn up by Baylor graduates attending Southwestern Seminary, Scarborough Papers.

This unanimity created problems for fundamentalists, who found it difficult to distinguish their own antievolutionism from that of non-fundamentalists. For example, in setting forth its view of the creation of life, J. Frank Norris's congregation adopted a position that most Southern Baptists accepted. Norris's church asserted that: (1) the author of Genesis had written in literal language; (2) God had formed man in the divine image; (3) long periods of development had played no part in man's creation; and (4) God had created all life instantaneously and had established the immutability of species.[6] As this shows, fundamentalists found themselves part of a larger Baptist company in their rejection of Darwinism. Unable to distinguish themselves ideologically, they relied upon imaginative rhetorical denunciations to establish their position. Style, not substance, mattered to evangelist "Cyclone Mack" McLendon, who said in a frequently delivered sermon:

> Let the college professors of the institutions of this country teach that your father was a muskrat and your mother an o'possum and your great aunt a kangaroo and the toads and scorpions and lizards and snakes and the snapping turtles your illustrious predecessors. My father was God.[7]

Although the tone of McLendon's tirade appeared more often among fundamentalists, most Southern Baptists found it useful in expressing their hatred of Darwinism. As with the reaction to higher criticism, extremism characterized the Southern Baptist attitude toward Darwinism.

The reasons for this rejection of Darwinism fall under three headings. First, Baptists attacked the theory for undermining orthodox Christianity. The second point, closely related to the first, focused on the relationship between evolution and Baptist moral standards. Finally, Baptists objected to Darwinism on scientific grounds. Taken together, these comprise the Baptist critique of the theory of evolution; religiously, morally, and scientifically the South's Baptists found the doctrine false and abhorrent.

For Southern Baptists the dispute over Darwinism involved far more than the validity of a scientific theory; at stake was "the eternal destiny of

---

[6]*Confession of Faith of the First Baptist Church*, Fort Worth, Texas (n. p., n. d.), p. 23.

[7]Baxter F. McLendon, *The Story of My Life and Other Sermons* (Bennettsville, South Carolina, 1923), p. 66.

souls," for evolution opposed everything Christians cherished.[8] With evolution threatening the foundations of their faith, Southern Baptists directed their attention to the theory's religious meaning. In the first place, they identified Darwinism with ideas antagonistic to Christianity. J. Frank Norris suggested that the evolutionary theory formed the latest outcropping of "infidelity," cleverly disguised in the trappings of science.[9] The Oklahoma *Baptist Messenger* agreed and, in addition, linked evolution with "paganism."[10] For most Southern Baptists "paganism" was nothing more than a convenient term with which to castigate evolutionists, but T. T. Martin invested the word with deeper meaning by relating it to the evolutionary views expounded by Greek philosophers centuries before the birth of Christ. Martin, along with Tennessean Jessie Gibbs, discovered further affinities between the evolutionary strain in ancient philosophy and the pantheism that had also appealed to the ancient world. Pantheism, with its worship of a god indwelling in nature, and Darwinism, with its emphasis on the natural world, complemented one another and led to the same results: a diminished God bound to the processes of the natural world.[11] Although their logic sometimes went awry, Baptists dimly perceived that the theory of evolution had originally arisen in an environment alien to Christianity.

If evolutionists damned themselves by the company they kept, they convicted themselves even more clearly in their attitude toward the Bible, Baptists argued. Evolutionary scientists contradicted God's word when they spoke of the development of life over millions of years, for the first chapter of Genesis clearly stated that God had created the earth and all its life forms in six twenty-four hour days. It mattered little to Baptists that no scientific explanation existed for this feat; if the Scriptures recorded it Christians must accept it.[12] This attitude could not be trifled with, as a

---

[8]J. E. Boyd to F. M. McConnell, 6 March 1929, Norris Papers, Box 4; Mississippi, *Proceedings*, 1925, 32.

[9]Norris to W. H. Bridges, 16 January 1931, Norris Papers, Box 2.

[10]*Messenger*, 27 June 1923, p. 8.

[11]Thomas T. Martin, *The Evolution Issue* (n. p., ca. 1923), pp. 16-17; Martin, *Hell and the High Schools: Christ or Evolution, Which?* (Kansas City, Missouri: Western Baptist Publishing, 1923), pp. 65, 143; Jessie W. Gibbs, *Evolution and Christianity* (Knoxville: pub. by the author, 1931; original publication, 1930), p. 57.

[12]*Herald*, 3 June 1926, p. 23. This attitude showed up clearly in the movement to get the Southern Baptist Convention to declare its unequivocal support of the Genesis

Baptist teacher in West Texas learned when he lost his job for suggesting that the creation "days" might be long periods of time.[13]

For the majority of Southern Baptists the Genesis account presented no difficulty; the Bible meant exactly what it said. But a number of ardent antievolutionists had some inkling of the problems raised by a literal reading of the word "day." George McDaniel, for example, left the time span involved in creation indeterminate in order to give geologists room to speculate.[14] T. T. Martin suggested that the first three "days" of creation had encompassed millions of years, since God had not created the sun until the fourth day, thereby providing a demarcation between periods of time. The sun's appearance had divided the last four days of creation week into twenty-four hour segments, Martin stated.[15]

Although a few Baptist antievolutionists questioned the literalness of the creation days, few doubted that the theory of evolution threatened the Scriptures. T. T. Martin charged that evolutionists had accused the Bible of "lying" when it referred to the immutability of species. Darwinists had also scorned the Bible's statement that God had fashioned Adam in His own image, Martin added.[16] Baptists viewed the theory of evolution as an ally of higher criticism in the modernist war on God's sacred book; by denying the validity of Genesis, evolutionists undermined scriptural authority.[17] Genesis and Darwinism could not be reconciled; to proclaim the truthfulness of one consigned the other to the intellectual scrapheap. As the Southern Baptist Convention stated in 1922: "One can understand both the Bible and evolution and believe one of them, but he cannot

---

account of creation. At the 1926 meeting the delegates adopted George McDaniel's statement that: "This Convention accepts Genesis as teaching that man was the special creation of God, and rejects every theory, evolution or other, which teaches that man originated in, or came by way of, a lower animal ancestry" (SBC, *Annual*, 1926, p. 18). For a good discussion of the events leading up to this statement see Robert A. Baker, *The Southern Baptist Convention and Its People, 1607-1972* (Nashville: Broadman Press, 1974), pp. 398-99.

[13]W. W. Freeman to A. T. Robertson, 15 December 1922, Robertson Papers, Folder 1922B.

[14]George W. McDaniel, *The Supernatural Jesus* (Nashville: Sunday School Board, 1924), p. 191.

[15]Thomas T. Martin, *The Second Coming of Christ* (n. p., ca. 1922), pp. 7-8.

[16]Martin, *Hell and the High Schools*, p. 44.

[17]*Record*, 5 March 1925, p. 2.

understand both and believe both."[18]

A vicious attack on Jesus Christ accompanied Darwinist criticism of the Scriptures, Southern Baptists charged. Acceptance of the theory of evolution and worship of Christ were incompatible because Darwinism destroyed faith in Him as Messiah and Saviour. "How could Christ be evolved in the human species and be in a special sense the Son of God?" Baptists asked.[19] Evolutionists and orthodox Christians held sharply contrasting conceptions of Jesus Christ, orthodoxy worshiping Him as God made flesh, born into the world to redeem men from sin, while Darwinists robbed Christ of His divinity.[20] Martin graphically portrayed these contrasting views by accusing evolutionists of replacing the Son of God with "the bastard, illegitimate son of a Jewish fallen woman."[21]

By undermining the Bible and degrading Christ, evolutionists destroyed the significance of God's churches, A. C. Dixon pointed out. Despite their imperfections, the local churches embodied the principles expounded in the Bible and illustrated by Christ's life. With the Bible interpreted as nothing more than a collection of ancient writings and Christ reduced to the level of humanity, the rationale for the church disappeared. It ceased to be a body of believers striving for eternal life, becoming instead, a human creation bereft of spiritual import.[22] Inexorably the logic of evolutionary thought proceeded to its destination: first the Bible, then Jesus Christ, and finally the church—all snatched away by Darwinists bent on robbing Christians of their religion.

The results of Darwinist depredations had already appeared: "almost every day" Baptist parents reported children lost to the faith, their minds polluted by Darwinism.[23] Five thousand American scientists, responding to a questionnaire circulated by Professor James Henry Leuba of Bryn Mawr College, offered additional proof of the destructiveness of evolutionary thought, T. T. Martin said.[24] Admitting that they had once

---

[18]SBC, *Annual*, 1922, p. 35.

[19]Edwin Poteat to William Poteat, 4 March 1923, W. L. Poteat Papers.

[20]Account in the Raleigh, North Carolina, *News and Observer*, of a sermon preached by A. C. Dixon on 31 December 1922, clipping, Dixon Papers, Box 10.

[21]Martin, *The Evolution Issue*, 16.

[22]*News and Observer*, 31 December 1922, p. 5.

[23]John W. Porter, *Evolution—A Menace* (Nashville: Sunday School Board, 1922), pp. 84-85.

[24]Martin, *Hell and the High Schools*, pp. 140-41.

been orthodox Christians, over half of the respondents confessed that they no longer believed in a personal God or eternal life. A. C. Dixon discerned the same pattern in the life of the great infidel himself, Charles Darwin. The father of modern evolutionary theory had been raised a devout Christian, Dixon observed, but barren speculation had blotted out his spirituality.[25] Armed with these examples, Baptists felt justified in their hatred of evolutionists, whom they considered to be emissaries of Satan, "Christianity suck[l]ed soul-murderers," and "wicked" people.[26]

Darwinian hostility toward Christianity precluded the possibility of uniting the two to form a hybrid known as "Christian evolutionism," most Southern Baptists said. The term implied a contradiction; by definition one had to choose between Christianity and evolution. Evolution's emphasis on natural law denied such Christian essentials as divine inspiration and miracles. Trying to harmonize Darwinian naturalism with Christian supernaturalism inevitably alienated one from orthodoxy.[27] In the minds of most Baptists, "Christian" and "evolutionist" were mutually exclusive terms.

Although Baptist antievolutionists denied the possibility of combining Christianity and Darwinism, they sometimes admitted that belief in a vaguely defined supreme being could be grafted onto the theory of evolution. The result, something called "theistic evolution," closely resembled the atheistic form, for both taught that life had evolved through a time-consuming process. Baptists decried the theistic evolutionist's attempts to fit God into this framework by attributing the initial spark of life to the Creator; a deity limited to the creation of a blob of protoplasm fared poorly among a people who worshiped a God who had fashioned man with his own hands.[28] Baptists appreciated the honesty of atheists who, admitting their rejection of God, formulated their theories without outside help. Theistic evolutionists, by contrast, perverted the Christian God by incorporating a pale replica into an ill-conceived theory.

---

[25]*News and Observer*, 31 December 1922, p. 5.

[26]Amzi C. Dixon, *The Battle-lines between Christianity and Modernism* (London: Bible League, ca. 1924), p. 21; Martin, *Hell and the High Schools*, p. 51; Landrum P. Leavell, *Pupil Life with Hints to Teachers* (Nashville: Sunday School Board, 1919), p. 81.

[27]"The Menace of Evolution," *Southwestern Evangel* 10 (April 1926): 18; Porter, *Evolution*, pp. 28-29.

[28]Martin, *Hell and the High Schools*, p. 63.

A. C. Dixon considered these men worse than atheists, for by injecting
God into the evolutionary process they made him responsible for the
suffering inherent in the struggle for survival.[29] T. T. Martin excoriated
theistic evolution for being as "Bible-denying, Christ-dethroning, and
soul-destroying" as the godless variety and concluded that one "damn[ed]
a student as certainly as" the other.[30] North Carolinian S. J. Betts established a cause and effect relationship between the two theories, writing
that "theistic evolution is the kindergarten for athetistic [sic] evolution,
and ultimately leads to agnosticism and infidelity."[31] Identifying theistic
evolution as the training ground for atheism enabled Baptists to assert
that all true evolutionists denied God's existence.[32] Through this reasoning antievolutionists deprived their opponents of the right to use God,
glossed over the gradations of evolutionary thought, and condemned all
evolutionists as wicked assailants of orthodoxy.

Satisfied that they had correctly taken the religious bearing of Darwinism, Southern Baptists turned to a discussion of its moral implications. This was closely related to their rejection of Darwinism as
anti-Christian because Southern Baptists derived their moral precepts
from Christianity. The moral critique began with the warning that
Darwinism's triumph would destroy current standards of behavior. With
God's sovereignty diminished man would fashion a new moral code in
the perverse depths of his mind. A world attuned to evolutionary theory
would be far more evil than the present debased state of mankind,
Baptists continued. Materialism would erase all traces of spirituality,
giving free rein to instinct and physical gratification. Passions would go
unchecked, for in the evolutionist's world the words "evil" and "sinful"
had no meaning. With the concept of sin banished there would be no
guilt, and without a sense of wrongdoing man would run wild. The moral
obligation to conquer one's sinful self would be discarded by Darwinists
intent on freeing man from Christian influence, Baptists concluded.[33]

---

[29]Dixon, *Battle-lines*, p. 29.

[30]Martin, *Hell and the High Schools*, pp. 31, 63.

[31]S. J. Betts, *Criticism of Dr. Poteat's Book Recently Published* (n. p., ca. 1925), p. 10.

[32]William Poteat to John L. Hill, 2 March 1929, W. L. Poteat Papers.

[33]James M. Carroll, *A History of Texas Baptists: Comprising a Detailed Account of
Their Activities, Their Progress and Their Achievements* (Dallas: Baptist Standard,

Baptists seldom tired of reciting the disasters that would befall a world deprived of Christian morality. Evolutionists' tampering with Genesis would tear the institutions of marriage and the family from the fabric of Western society, since both had been initiated with Adam and Eve and recorded in the Bible for man's edification. Released from the constrictions of marriage, men would indulge in every sexual excess imaginable. Other vices and crimes would flourish as well, for the collapse of the moral code would inaugurate a reign of lying, stealing, and killing.[34] Jessie Gibbs discerned a portent in the celebrated Chicago murder case of Nathan Leopold and Richard Loeb. These two college students, their minds depraved by the evolutionary philosophy, had murdered young Robert Franks as a "scientific experiment," Gibbs said. The crime had been more than a bizarre aberration; "this same cynicism, animalism, inability to think, godlessness, and lawlessness characterize the general spirit of our times. They are the evil fruit of an evil philosophy," Gibbs concluded.[35]

Reasoning from the idea of survival of the fittest, Baptists accused evolutionists of exalting brute force, of pitting man against man in an endless war for existence that would reduce humanity to its basest level and extinguish love, mercy, and compassion. Natural selection's weeding out of the unfit spelled misery and degradation, not the advancement promised by evolutionists.[36] To expose the moral consequences of evolutionary struggle, Southern Baptists applied the theory in ways not always intended by its proponents. T. T. Martin suggested that industrialists could justify oppression of laborers by invoking the right of the strong to crush the weak. If followed strictly, John W. Porter of Kentucky argued, the theory would encourage the killing of the "aged and infirm" to accelerate evolutionary processes. Why provide hospitals, orphanages, insane asylums, and homes for the elderly when the unfit impeded progress?[37] Finally, Southern Baptists contended that "evolution logi-

---

1923), p. 1000; "The Menace of Evolution," p. 18; *News and Observer*, 31 December 1922, p. 5; Gibbs, *Evolution and Christianity*, p. 190.

[34]*Record*, 21 June 1923, p. 5; Martin, *Hell and the High Schools*, pp. 139-40; *News and Observer*, 31 December 1922, p. 5.

[35]Gibbs, *Evolution and Christianity*, p. 94.

[36]Dixon, *Battle-lines*, p. 27; Gibbs, *Evolution and Christianity*, p. 53.

[37]Porter, *Evolution*, p. 61; Martin, *Hell and the High Schools*, pp. 132-33.

cally and inevitably leads to war." The idea of the survival of the fittest, which had prompted Germany to precipitate World War I, continued to encourage strife among nations. Antievolutionists found this ironic; for evolutionists, expounding the dictum of progress through struggle, increased the likelihood of global warfare, thereby paving the way for mankind's destruction.[38] There could be no compromise with a theory that diverged so sharply from Christian ethical standards.

The weakest part of the antievolutionist critique lay in the attempt to discredit the theory of evolution on scientific grounds. Put bluntly, Baptist antagonists of evolution lacked the knowledge to discuss scientific theory intelligently. Few genuine scientists belonged to the denomination, and those who did refused to support hardline antievolutionism. This failed to deter the foes of evolution, who plunged into the world of science, there to flail about and look ridiculous.

Many Baptists insisted that Darwinism was unscientific. T. T. Martin and George McDaniel, preachers largely innocent of scientific knowledge, expressed this viewpoint, Martin calling evolution "an unproven theory, that is not science at all," and McDaniel referring to the "illogical conjectures" and "audacious dogmatisms" of evolutionists.[39]

Southern Baptists argued that evolutionists discredited their findings by employing faulty methods. Emile O. Kaserman, professor of biology in Oklahoma Baptist University, used this argument against Charles Darwin, contending that the Englishman's proclivity for speculation at the expense of experimentation cast doubt upon his findings.[40] A. C. Dixon, claiming to be a disciple of Sir Francis Bacon, alleged that scientists had rejected Bacon's injunction to "sit at the feet of Nature and accept what she teaches" in favor of a pre-Baconian method of forcing the facts of the natural world into a preconceived mold.[41]

Baptists also leveled their fire at science's use of hypotheses. At best, antievolutionists granted their opponents the right to use them, only to

---

[38]Porter, *Evolution*, p. 88; A. C. Dixon to William Poteat, 11 January 1922, Dixon Papers, Box 10; Gibbs, *Evolution and Christianity*, pp. 109-110.

[39]Martin, *Hell and the High Schools*, p. 72; McDaniel, *The Supernatural Jesus*, pp. 192-93.

[40]*Messenger*, 22 June 1921, p. 2.

[41]Amzi C. Dixon, *Why I Am an Evangelical Christian and Not a Modernist* (Baltimore: University Baptist Church, ca. 1923), p. 18.

charge that Darwinists had clung blindly to these suppositions long after conflicting facts had been discovered. More often, Southern Baptists completely misunderstood the purpose of hypotheses. Equating them with wild conjectures, they denounced evolution as a "hypothesis—a guess—without a fact in the Bible or in nature to support it."[42] By denying the theory of evolution the support of science, many Baptists compensated for their own scientific ignorance and enabled the humblest among them to claim intellectual parity with the most learned scientist.

Emboldened by this flat dismissal of Darwinism from the halls of science, Southern Baptist antievolutionists ventured into the theory's specifics, focusing particularly on Darwinism's denial of the immutability of species. Evolutionists, pointing to the development of one species from another, argued that present plants and animals had evolved from life forms lower on the evolutionary scale. Antievolutionists refused to accept this, basing their argument on the statement in Genesis that each species produces "after his kind." God had created distinct categories of life and had preserved them intact over six thousand years. Evolutionists had failed to prove the development of species, the antievolutionist argument continued; they had discovered no transitional stages in the fossil record and had been unable to find the missing link between man and his simian ancestors. The average Baptist farmer understood the resistance of species to change; he knew that turkey eggs produced turkeys, not chickens, and that wheat, not oats, grew where wheat had been sown. "If transmutation has been the method, if one species originated from a different species, why does not transmutation go on before our eyes?" one antievolutionist asked.[43] Finally, T. T. Martin dismissed the idea of the progression of species as another example of Darwinism's scientific carelessness, arguing that proponents of the theory had falsely concluded that the possession of common features indicated that one species had evolved from another.[44]

Baptists buttressed their case against Darwinism by maintaining that scores of scientists, awakening to their errors, had abandoned the theory.

---

[42]*Record*, 14 December 1922, p. 4; Appomattox, *Minutes*, 1921, pp. 22-23.

[43]Betts, *Criticism of Dr. Poteat's Book*, p. 5; Martin, *The Evolution Issue*, pp. 27-28; William D. Nowlin, *Fundamentals of the Faith* (Nashville: Sunday School Board, 1926; original publication, 1922), pp. 164-65; McDaniel, *The Supernatural Jesus*, p. 197.

[44]Martin, *Hell and the High Schools*, p. 89.

Recitations of the names of eminent scientists who had forsaken their faith in evolution ignored William Poteat's exposure of one such list that contained two unknown scientists, five men who had not made the statements attributed to them, seven who had won fame in non-biological fields, and six who had been dead for more than forty years.[45]

In asserting the imminent demise of evolutionary science, Baptists flaunted their ignorance of current biological theory. Darwin's idea of natural selection had undergone intense scrutiny in the early twentieth century, but Baptists failed to comprehend that though scientists had questioned this facet of Darwinism, they remained committed to the idea of evolutionary progression.[46] Untutored in the fine points of science, Southern Baptists seized this rift in scientific ranks as evidence of the falsity of the theory of evolution. Southern Baptists thus stood indicted of carelessness and ignorance born of overeagerness; they wanted to believe that evolutionists had erred, and this wish, with a little prompting, became reality for them.

Although the denomination's rigid antievolutionism made dissent difficult, it did not completely blot out differences of opinion. One group of dissenters rejected the theory of evolution but deplored many of the ideas and methods of hardline antievolutionists. In the first place, these moderate creationists took issue with the general condemnation of science that frequently accompanied antievolutionism. Most Baptist antievolutionists pledged their faith in science, arguing that the "true" variety supported their position and that their fight lay only with the perverted views of evolutionists. But implicit in this contention lay an animus toward all science, for by the 1920s virtually the entire scientific community had adopted evolution as a working hypothesis. Perhaps a few men successfully maintained this distinction between truth and perversion, but for the average Southern Baptist, hatred of evolution produced antagonism toward science, or at least toward scientists. Although antievolutionists contended that Darwinism had been discredited and that leading scientists had rejected it, they continued to harbor suspicions toward men who tampered with the mysteries of God's

---

[45]Martin, *Hell and the High Schools*, p. 106; William L. Poteat, "Evolution," *Biblical Recorder*, 19 April 1922, p. 3, clipping, W. L. Poteat Papers.

[46]W. C. Curtis, "Evolution Controversy," in Jerry R. Tompkins ed., *D-Days at Dayton: Reflections on the Scopes Trial* (Baton Rouge: Louisiana State University Press, 1965), pp. 80-81.

creation.[47]

Styling themselves friends of both religion and science moderate creationists urged that in dealing with Darwinism one must preserve a friendly attitude toward science. To promote this attitude moderate creationists stressed science's rights of investigation. The *Southwestern Evangel*, a journal published by Southwestern Seminary, warned that those who barred science from sacred areas raised questions about the truthfulness of Christianity. The powers of the mind must not be dismissed, the journal editorialized; the right to seek truth through scientific means must be defended. E. Y. Mullins, the most prominent moderate creationist, advised his brethren not "to usurp the task of science." Baptists who shared Mullins's attitude believed that orthodox Christians should approach hostile scientists with the intention of witnessing for Christ. Bitter assaults on the rights of science served only to exacerbate tensions between it and religion.[48]

Moderate creationists tried to draw science and religion closer by muting the polarities set up by hardline antievolutionists. This entailed no compromise of principles; rather, it showed that a more realistic stance could be taken in order to calm the denomination's anxieties over Darwinism. An important step lay in convincing Southern Baptists that the Bible did not contain ultimate truth outside the field of religion. Baptists should not ascribe final authority to the Scriptures in such areas as geology, chemistry, and astronomy, Mullins advised. In a similar spirit, Richard Vann urged his fellow churchmen to remember that the revelation in Genesis had been given to a people unequipped to cope with twentieth-century science. Moses had couched his thoughts in the primitive language of his day, and his writings must not be wrenched from that context, Vann maintained. Robert Pitt added a final warning to those who based the Bible's validity on its pronouncements in peripheral areas. Recalling that John Wesley had wrongly insisted that the Bible authenticated the existence of witches, Pitt advised Baptists to control their penchant for overextending the Bible's authority.[49] Moderate creation-

---

[47]William L. Poteat, *Can a Man Be a Christian To-Day?* (Chapel Hill: University of North Carolina Press, 1925), p. 33.

[48]"God and Science," *Southwestern Evangel* 9 (October 1924): 27-28; E. Y. Mullins, "Christianity in the Modern World," *Review and Expositor* 22 (October 1925): 488; Rufus W. Weaver, "Science and Religion," p. 3, typescript notes of a sermon preached in Atlanta, Georgia, on 5 April 1925, Weaver Papers, Box 11.

[49]*Herald*, 22 May 1919, p. 4; 4 September 1924, p. 3; Richard T. Vann, *What Have*

ists feared this tendency, realizing that in staking the Bible's reputation on its scientific validity antievolutionists had dragged the Holy Scriptures into an area where they did not belong. In reaction to this, moderate creationists adopted as their motto: religion from the Bible and science from the laboratory. By remaining true to this dictum, they hoped to preserve the Bible's credibility.

This refusal to treat the Scriptures as a textbook of science produced a flexible attitude toward the Genesis account of creation. Moderate creationists declined to press for a literal reading of the word "day," maintaining that they could allow God more than six days to fashion the world without losing their faith. The Creator had worked outside man's conception of time, they argued; day, week, month, year held no meaning for Him.[50] This appeared self-evident to Robert Pitt, who stated that "no intelligent person of full age in our time believes that the world was made in six days."[51] Those who agreed with Pitt derived support from a number of revered figures in Southern Baptist history. Pitt singled out the nineteenth-century patriarchs James B. Boyce and F. H. Kerfoot, and Lee Scarborough mentioned B. H. Carroll, founder of Southwestern Seminary, as another opponent of six-day literalism.[52] The support of such men of unquestioned orthodoxy strengthened moderate creationists in their convictions and, added to their Bible study, convinced them that they had correctly refused to abide by a literal reading of Genesis.

Moderate creationists discovered a remarkable correspondence between their interpretation of creation and the hypothesis advanced by evolutionists. They responded to the evolutionist's emphasis on aeons of development with their own contention that God had transcended man's conception of time.[53] Even more important, the Genesis order of creation duplicated the evolutionary charting of the appearance of life; God had created plants and animals first and had capped His work by fashioning man. Sensing this similarity, Mullins wrote:

Baptist Colleges to Do with Fundamentalism and Modernism?, (n. p., ca. 1925), p. 13.

[50]John R. Sampey, *The Heart of the Old Testament: A Manual for Christian Students* (Garden City: Doubleday, Doran, 1928; original publication, 1909), pp. 16-17.

[51]*Herald*, 6 May 1926, p. 11.

[52]*Herald*, 20 May 1926, p. 11; Lee Scarborough to Joseph Dawson, 5 December 1927, Joseph M. Dawson Papers, Texas History Collection, Baylor University.

[53]Sampey, *The Heart of the Old Testament*, pp. 16-17.

Nature ascends from lower to higher stages. Progress is the key to the meaning of all the processes of nature. She begins with the crystal. She mounts upward to the plant. From the plant she rises to the animal. From the animal she ascends to man, and there the process abruptly ends.[54]

Mullins implied that the author of Genesis had understood the hierarchical arrangement of the natural world, and that evolutionists had mistakenly assumed that each level had evolved from the one below it. Instead of ranting at Darwinist perfidy in distorting nature's testimony, moderate creationists contented themselves with observing that in a backhanded way the theory of evolution confirmed the broad outlines of the Genesis account.

This calm attitude permitted moderate creationists to discern the gradations of evolutionary thought and to realize that not all exponents of the doctrine wished to destroy Christianity. John W. Jent, professor of sociology at Oklahoma Baptist University, conceded that such "fair and broad-minded" evolutionists as Columbia University botanist W. C. Curtis posed no threat to orthodoxy. In defending the evolutionist's right to worship God, Z. T. Cody, editor of the South Carolina *Baptist Courier*, wrote that "evolution does not even by implication deny religion." With his friend William Poteat in mind, Richard Vann extended Cody's reasoning by arguing that an evolutionist could be an orthodox Baptist.[55] Moderate creationists maintained an open mind toward evolutionists, insisting that one could fuse Christianity and evolution into a sound philosophy. At the same time, they refused to embrace the doctrine themselves and demanded that atheistic evolution be refuted. As E. Y. Mullins stated: "I have not the slightest fear of evolution if it is correctly stated. Of course in its naturalistic form it is fatal."[56] Such views earned moderate creationists a unique position within the Southern Baptist denomination, assuring them the suspicion of hardline anti-Darwinists and the gratitude of Baptist evolutionists.

---

[54]E. Y. Mullins, *Spiritualism—A Delusion* (Nashville: Sunday School Board, 1920), pp. 47-48.

[55]John W. Jent, *After Fifty-Eight Years: An Autobiography* (Shawnee, Oklahoma: pub. by the author, 1935), p. 54; *Herald*, 9 March 1922, p. 6; Vann, *What Have Baptist Colleges to Do with Fundamentalism and Modernism?*, p. 10.

[56]Mullins to R. H. Pitt, 30 July 1925, Mullins Papers, 1925-1927 Correspondence M-Z.

Baptist evolutionists, "sifted all about" among the forces of antievolutionism, formed the denomination's second group of dissenters.[57] This small body of men adhered to a mild evolutionism which accepted God as the Creator who had employed a process of development to produce the earth and its inhabitants. In many ways they differed little from moderate creationists. Both rejected a literal reading of Genesis, and both considered the earth older than six thousand years. But moderate creationists refused to go beyond this point. Although they dismissed the theory that God had produced the world instantaneously, they continued to believe that each act of creation had been carried out by God and had involved no process of evolutionary development. Moderate creationists stood on the threshold of evolutionary thought, but neither desired nor attempted to enter the evolutionist's world. Baptist evolutionists, though often vague, stepped beyond moderate creationism. They stressed the gradual development of life, overseen, of course, by God, and more important, they usually called themselves evolutionists. But diversity existed within the group; some evolutionists remained close to moderate creationism, while others, notably William Poteat, adopted evolutionary thought in its entirety. Whatever their scientific opinions, Baptist evolutionists remained religiously conservative, defending orthodox Christianity while dissenting from the denomination's strident antievolutionism.'

Many of these evolutionists taught in the denomination's colleges, most notably at Baylor University in Waco, Texas. Baylor's involvement in the debate over evolution produced a cloud of rhetoric that obscured the scientific views of alleged evolutionists. Evolutionism definitely existed in Baylor, although it hardly constituted the "godless" Darwinism the university's critics complained about. With antievolutionists raging against heresy, and Baylor's defenders insisting that none of the faculty taught evolution, the problem became one of definition. Baylor students, denying they had been subjected to evolutionary teachings, restricted their definition to the idea that man had descended from lower organisms.[58] In this sense, Baylor probably contained no evolutionists; most of Baylor's "heretics" recoiled at linking man to the higher apes, but in other respects they accepted the theory of evolution. They preferred to remain

---

[57]William Poteat to Virginius Dabney, 15 June 1931, W. L. Poteat Papers.

[58]Undated statement of Baylor graduates attending Southwestern Seminary, Scarborough Papers.

vague, contenting themselves with references to the process of development and avoiding the specifics of evolutionary theory.

The difficulties of ferreting out the exact views of Baylor's evolutionists become apparent in considering three members of the faculty: Lula
Pace and L. O. Bradbury, both of the biology department, and sociologist
Grove S. Dow. Professors Pace and Bradbury freely admitted their
acceptance of evolution, stating to an investigating committee: "Creation
is a process, and evolution may be defined as God's method in this
process." At the same time, Dr. Pace reaffirmed her belief "that God
created all things, and that each produces after its kind." For a scientist
Dr. Pace was unusually confused over the meaning of the term evolution,
or else she simply wished to keep a foot in both camps. Professor Dow's
Introduction to the Principles of Sociology, published by the Baylor press
in 1920, contained enough evolutionary influence to warrant Dow's
classification as an evolutionist.[59] Despite these deviations, Dow, Pace,
and Bradbury offered no threat to orthodox Christianity; their scientific
views strengthened rather than weakened the faith of students who came
under their charge.[60] The tentative, at times reluctant, probing of scientific theory by Baylor's evolutionists represented nothing more than the
efforts of a handful of scholars to understand the origins and development of life.

A similar quest prompted Southern Seminary's W. O. Carver and
A. T. Robertson to risk the ire of militant antievolutionists. Taking
advantage of the freedom granted by President Mullins, they sought to
emancipate Baptists from their rigid conception of orthodoxy. Carver
adopted a vague belief in evolution which asserted that God had initially
created life and had sustained its development in accordance with natural
law.[61] Although Robertson generally displayed more caution than his
outspoken colleague, he suggested that Christians troubled by the relationship between science and religion should read the works of an

---

[59]Texas, *Annual*, 1922, pp. 56-57; Pace to Benjamin Copass, 11 November 1922,
Brooks Papers, File Di-Faculty; "The Teaching of Evolution in the Baptist Institutions of
Texas," *Science* 55 (12 May 1922): 515.

[60]Charles D. Johnson to an unnamed correspondent, ca. 1924, Neff Papers, Governor
Correspondence, 1924.

[61]William O. Carver, *Out of His Treasure: Unfinished Memoirs* (Nashville:
Broadman Press, 1956), pp. 74-75.

English evolutionist named McKenna.[62] More important, Robertson confessed to his friend and biographer Everett Gill:

> I am willing to believe in it [evolution], I rather do, but not in atheistic evolution ... I say, write "God" at the top, and what if he did use evolution? I can stand it if the monkeys can ... If he did do it that way, He still did it.[63]

Evolutionary thought won converts outside educational institutions as well. A number of Baptist ministers, exposed always to the vagaries of popular opinion, courageously voiced their approval of Christian evolution. Gordon Poteat paid homage to the Genesis identification of God as the source of life, but dismissed the "speculative" details of the biblical account of creation.[64] Ashby Jones avowed his belief more explicitly, writing in the *Religious Herald* in 1925 that "many of us who are ministers of Christ, together with scores of physical scientists, accept as true the general theory of evolution." Jones's religious faith remained undisturbed, for evolution rendered additional proof of God's "continued presence in His universe."[65] The Atlanta pastor reiterated his position in an article in the *Atlanta Constitution*, declaring that the overwhelming preponderance of scientists accepted the theory of evolution, and advising untutored Christians not to interfere with geologists and biologists familiar with the intricacies of their disciplines.[66]

If Ashby Jones took a strong stand, Joseph Dawson of Waco, Texas, hedged a bit. In a conversation between Dawson and James B. Cranfill, a prominent foe of Darwinism, Dawson, according to Cranfill, "contemptuously" referred to the instantaneous creation of life as the "mud man theory." When reminded of this by Cranfill, Dawson denied being an evolutionist, insisting that the length of the creation days formed the only point of contention between them. Despite this denial, Dawson

---

[62]A. T. Robertson, *Luke the Historian in the Light of Research* (New York: Charles Scribner's Sons, 1920), p. 154.

[63]Everett Gill, *A. T. Robertson: A Biography* (New York: Macmillan Co., 1943), p. 181.

[64]Poteat to Z. T. Cody, 13 September 1926, Robertson Papers, Folder 1926B.

[65]*Herald*, 12 November 1925, p. 2.

[66]Edwin Mims, *The Advancing South: Stories of Progress and Reaction* (New York: Doubleday, 1926), p. 14.

gave reason to suspect him of evolutionary leanings; after all, Cranfill, an honorable and intelligent man, can hardly be accused of lying. Moreover, Dawson revealed his admiration of a number of Christian evolutionists and admitted that the theory, if proven true, would not destroy the Bible. Dawson's inner convictions remained veiled, for he realized the dangers of taking an unpopular stand in controversy-racked Texas. But regardless of the degree to which he accepted evolution, Dawson sympathized with efforts to align orthodoxy with modern science.[67]

Evolutionary thought emanating from lectern and pulpit struck responsive chords among some Baptists. North Carolina possessed two of the denomination's most notable evolutionists. Both Josiah W. Bailey, editor of the *Biblical Recorder* from 1895 to 1907 and United States Senator from 1930 to 1945, and Clarence Poe, editor of the *Progressive Farmer*, had accepted the doctrine by the 1920s.[68] Less prominent Baptists took a similar course. Frank Hindren, a North Carolina attorney, found it impossible to believe that God had made man "a finished article at the start."[69] Early in 1923 Walter E. Tynes of Houston, Texas, declared that although he had not yet become a "positive evolutionist," the theory no longer frightened him.[70] Within a short time Tynes had made the transition, referring to man's creation as "an orderly process, which may properly be called either evolution or development as one may define the word."[71] The Mississippi *Baptist Record* supplied a final example of the spread of evolutionary thought. Signing himself "An Innocent Bystander," the author of a letter to the editor in 1921 defended the theory of evolution and denied that it conflicted with orthodox Protestantism.[72] This Mississippian chose to remain anonymous, for despite the acceptance of evolution by a number of Southern Baptists, the prudent individual refrained from trumpeting his beliefs too loudly.

---

[67]Cranfill to Dawson, 2 December 1927; Dawson to Cranfill, 3 December 1927; Dawson to P. J. Little, 26 July 1927, Dawson Papers.

[68]Clarence Poe, *My First Eighty Years* (Chapel Hill: University of North Carolina Press, 1963), pp. 114-15.

[69]Frank B. Hindren to A. T. Robertson, 18 September 1925, Robertson Papers, Folder 1925B.

[70]Walter E. Tynes to Robertson, 14 February 1923, Robertson Papers, Folder 1923A.

[71]Tynes to Samuel P. Brooks, 13 October 1924, Brooks Papers, File Di-Faculty.

[72]*Record*, 6 October 1921, p. 6.

Judged by this standard, William Poteat spent his life tempting fate; from the 1890s until his death in 1938 he proclaimed his acceptance of the theory of evolution in the classroom, from the public lectern, and in widely read books and articles. Amidst the turmoil of the 1920s he gained a reputation as the most fearless Southern Baptist advocate of evolution. Writing in the North Carolina *Biblical Recorder* in 1922, Poteat argued that both scholarship and the natural world confirmed Charles Darwin's thesis,[73] and on another occasion, he declared that Darwin's insights had become "as firmly established in scientific opinion as the law of gravitation or the Copernican astronomy."[74] Poteat spent little time quibbling over the length of the creation days or determining how God had participated in the evolutionary process; he chose instead to accept evolutionary theory in its entirety, including natural selection, the variability of species, and man's ascent up the scale of life. Contrast Poteat's words with the carefully hedged statements of most Baptist evolutionists:

> For life is Nature's goal and crown. Her struggle upward out of war and night into order and beauty, her wistful brooding for ages on the insensate elements, all her storm and pain find their compensation when Life first rises to view. It is lodged in a tiny cell. It is frail and simple and poorly equipped. But she takes it to her bosom, warms and guards it, feeds it with opportunity, establishes and diversifies it with struggle, until alga and moss and fern and rose, infusor and worm and insect and bird and man respond to her mother yearning from every nook of her wide domain.[75]

Poteat's bold advocacy placed him in a category by himself, earning him renown as the most thoroughgoing Southern Baptist evolutionist in the 1920s.

Poteat heightened this reputation by venting his wrath on antievolutionists, calling them "misguided men" who had shattered the "peace"

---

[73]William L. Poteat, "May a Christian Be an Evolutionist?," *Biblical Recorder*, 26 April 1922, p. 3, clipping in the W. L. Poteat Papers.

[74]"Liberty and Restraint," p. 4, typescript of an address delivered at Vassar College, 4 March 1927, Poteat Papers.

[75]Poteat, *Can a Man Be a Christian To-day?*, pp. 19-20.

forged by science and religion in the late nineteenth century. Antievolutionists had established "a false alternative" between the Bible and science, had extended the Scriptures beyond their authority, and had made it difficult for scientists to remain orthodox Christians. Despite his abhorrence of antievolutionism, Poteat understood its motivation, for he, too, cherished the religious truths that opponents of Darwinism sought to preserve. To put their minds at ease, Poteat reminded antievolutionists that the Bible and science agreed on the essential facts of the origins of life. Whatever science's attitude toward the natural world it could not "discredit faith," Poteat said, for religion lay outside the realm of science. Poteat impressed this distinction upon his students at Wake Forest, assuring them that their faith in God would not be destroyed when they discovered the workings of the natural world. Poteat's success at combining religious devotion with Darwinism witnessed to the compatibility of science and religion.[76] As scientist and man of God he wrote:

> And so I think of science as walking to and fro in God's garden, busying itself with its forms of beauty, its fruits and flowers, its beast and bird and creeping thing, the crystals shut in its stones, the gold grains of its sands, and coming now at length in the cool of the long day upon God himself walking in His garden.[77]

Those who feared for orthodoxy's safety at the hands of Baptist evolutionists needed only to turn to Poteat's reference to nature as "God's garden" to realize that Southern Baptist evolutionism presented no real danger.

Baptist evolutionists and moderate creationists understood this, for they realized that the real peril for their religion came from atheistic evolutionary thought. Warning that this would destroy Christianity, moderate creationists and evolutionists refused to compromise with those who discarded God, for His removal reduced the universe to a machine, stripped man of his spirituality, and imprisoned him in the

---

[76]William L. Poteat, "The Horizon of the Scholar," p. 2, typescript abstract of the Phi Beta Kappa Oration at the University of the South, 9 June 1930, W. L. Poteat Papers; *Can a Man Be a Christian To-day?*, pp. 34-35; "Evolution," p. 3; Poteat to George Pennell, 25 January 1929, Poteat Papers; George W. Paschall, *History of Wake Forest College*, vol. 3: *1905-1945* (Wake Forest: Wake Forest College Press, 1943), p. 122.

[77]Poteat, "Liberty and Restraint," p. 25.

chains of natural law. This "New Mechanism" or "Monistic Naturalism" contradicted everything Baptists cherished, McNeill Poteat and Rufus Weaver observed. These men realized that the crucial issue of the twentieth century transcended the debate between evolutionists and special creationists; it involved a clash between two conceptions of science, the one following in God's footsteps, the other deposing God, reducing man to his animal nature, and deifying the material world. Baptists who dissented from hardline antievolutionism envisioned their task as saving "humanity from hopeless imprisonment in a cruel and merciless world" created by "godless science;" to them it seemed foolish and harmful to rant against every form of evolutionary thought regardless of its attitude toward God, man, and the world.[78]

But most Southern Baptists viewed the problem differently, arguing that the theory of evolution, however qualified with references to God, represented one of the most malign influences in the modern world. These Baptists put their fear and revulsion into practice by joining the crusade to outlaw the teaching of Darwinism in the nation's tax-supported schools.[79] But their involvement in this movement did not stem from a desire to destroy the public schools; quite to the contrary, Southern Baptists supported public education, arguing that it had been nurtured by Christians to preserve American liberties. Their concern arose from the feeling that something had gone wrong with American education, that an alien influence had insinuated itself into the schools. In this vein, John M. Price, director of Southwestern Seminary's School of Religious Education, pointed out that "religious and moral" elements had been eased out of the educational curriculum.[80] Since such generalities

---

[78]Edwin McNeill Poteat, Jr., "Humanism," pp. 5-6, typescript of an address delivered in Raleigh, North Carolina, 8 November 1930, E. M. Poteat, Jr. Papers, Box 11; Rufus W. Weaver, untitled lecture delivered at American University in 1931, Weaver Papers, Box 6; Weaver, "The Baptist Opportunity in a Scientific Age," pp. 10-11, typescript dated 5 February 1932, Box 11.

[79]Surveys of the antievolution crusade appear in Kenneth K. Bailey, *Southern White Protestantism in the Twentieth Century* (New York: Harper and Row, 1964), pp. 72-91; Norman F. Furniss, *The Fundamentalist Controversy, 1918-1931* (New Haven, CT: Yale University Press, 1954), pp. 76-100; and Maynard Shipley, *The War on Modern Science: A Short History of the Fundamentalist Attacks on Evolution and Modernism* (New York: Alfred A. Knopf, 1927).

[80]South Carolina, *Minutes*, 1920, p. 33; Southern Baptist Education Association, *Proceedings*, 1929, 44.

failed to satisfy the search for a concrete villain, Baptists looked else-where, finding a focal point for their discontent in "godless science" clothed in the robes of evolutionary theory. In thus identifying Darwin-ism as the source of the crisis, Baptist antievolutionists claimed that they had found the roots of America's irreligion: the schools, as Victor Mas-ters complained, had been indoctrinating the youth with Darwinism and weaning them from old-time religion.[81]

T. T. Martin devoted more time and energy to the antievolution crusade than any other Southern Baptist, condemning Darwinist teachers in revival meetings, public lectures, books, and articles. Martin argued that teaching evolution to children constituted the most heinous crime imaginable, for it condemned youngsters to eternal damnation. Bootleggers, rapists, and murderers committed horrible deeds, but they left their victims' souls untouched. Evolutionists, on the other hand, by undermining faith in God, destroyed the spirit rather than the body and robbed men of the hope of eternal life. For the moral and religious well-being of the nation Darwinism should be barred from the schools, Martin urged.[82]

Martin next called upon the legal and constitutional sense of the American people. In his 1923 book *Hell and the High Schools* he cited separation of church and state as another reason for ridding the educa-tional system of evolutionary teachings. Baptists had willingly abided by the prohibition of religious instruction in the public schools, Martin wrote, but they objected to having their children filled with the irreli-gious drivel dished up by Darwinist teachers.[83] Despite its appeal, Mar-tin's argument ignored two important considerations. First, America's public schools had long been closely tied to Protestantism. The "wall" between church and state had kept the schools relatively free of sectarian-ism, but it had not excluded religious influences altogether. Particularly in the South, where teachers, administrators, pupils, and parents shared a common Protestant faith, schools had not been purely secular institu-

---

[81]Victor I. Masters, *The Call of the South* (Atlanta: Home Mission Board, 1920; original publication, 1918), pp. 158-59.

[82]Thomas T. Martin, *Viewing Life's Sunset from Pikes Peak: Life Story of T. T. Martin*, ed. by A. D. Muse (Louisville: pub. by the editor, n. d.), p. 78; Martin, *Hell and the High Schools*, pp. 149-50.

[83]Martin, *Hell and the High Schools*, pp. 17-18.

tions. Second, by placing the teaching of evolution in a religious context, Martin distorted the role of scientific inquiry. But antievolutionist Baptists ignored these objections, using Martin's constitutionalism to flay teachers of evolution.

Martin invoked American tradition once again in his appeal to the rights of the taxpayer in a democratic society. By omitting religious instruction and encouraging godless science, the state used Christian taxpayers' money to support ideas they found distasteful, Martin complained. The American way as expounded by Thomas Jefferson pointed in the other direction: a man should not be forced to render financial aid to a principle he opposed. Martin concluded from this that school teachers supported by public funds had no right to teach material conflicting with the taxpayers' cherished beliefs. As Martin observed: "There can be no middle ground; either THE ONE WHO GIVES THE PAY CHECK SHALL DECIDE WHAT SHALL BE TAUGHT, OR THE ONE WHO RECEIVES THE PAY CHECK SHALL DECIDE WHAT IS TO BE TAUGHT."[84]

Although irreligious, illegal, and un-American, Darwinism had permeated the public educational system, Martin reported. From primary schools through state universities unscrupulous teachers daily bombarded their charges with the evil theory.[85] Incensed by this brazen affront to orthodoxy, Martin promised that "THESE PAGAN FOLLOWERS SHALL NOT PRESS THEIR CROWN OF PAGANISM ON THE BROW OF AMERICAN YOUTH; THEY SHALL NOT CRUCIFY THE SOULS OF OUR CHILDREN ON THE CROSS OF THEIR VENEERED INFIDELITY."[86] Martin's rhetoric contained more than an idle threat, for he proposed practical ways of dealing with the problem. He advised Baptists to unite with other godly folk in applying pressure on local school boards. If these boards refused to cleanse the schools of heretical teachers and textbooks, they should be hounded from office. Finally, Martin said, antievolutionists should elect legislators who vowed to destroy the Darwinist influence.[87]

---

[84]Martin, *The Evolution Issue*, pp. 42, 44-45.

[85]Martin, *Evolution or Christ?*, pp. 33-34.

[86]Martin, *Hell and the High Schools*, pp. 10-11.

[87]*The Evolution Issue*, pp. 39, 46.

A number of moderate creationists disapproved of Martin's measures. John E. White, president of South Carolina's Anderson College, deplored the antievolutionists' readiness to use the papacy's action against Galileo as a model for state legislatures in dealing with recalcitrant teachers.[88] In his 1924 book, *Christianity at the Cross Roads*, E. Y. Mullins condemned the movement to ban evolutionary teachings, commenting that "nothing could be more ill-advised than for Americans to attempt to employ legislative coercion in the realm of scientific opinion."[89] Exhibiting the courage demanded of Baptist dissenters, Mullins reiterated his position in a New Orleans speech that received nationwide publicity.[90]

While applauding their moderate colleagues, the denomination's evolutionists contributed their own thoughts on the campaign against Darwinism. William Poteat denounced the conversion of legislatures into forums for the exhibition of scientific ignorance, warning that unless intelligent men moved quickly the chains of obscurantism would be fastened upon the minds of American students. Poteat detected a sad irony in the failure of Baptists, long the proponents of religious liberty, to realize that in legalizing the antievolutionist reading of Genesis they would violate the First Amendment's prohibition against "an establishment of religion."[91] In 1921, an "Innocent Bystander" from Mississippi offered antievolutionists insight into the futility of their efforts. Barring the theory from state schools would solve nothing, he argued; he had been protected from Darwinism in Mississippi College, an orthodox Baptist institution, yet had been converted to the theory through casual reading after leaving school. If he, the product of sheltered orthodoxy, had adopted evolutionary views what good would it do to outlaw the theory, he asked?[92] Ignoring this question, Baptist antievolutionists plunged ahead with their plans to purify America's educational system.

---

[88]*Herald*, 9 February 1922, pp. 4-5.

[89]E. Y. Mullins, *Christianity at the Cross Roads* (New York: George H. Doran Co., 1924), p. 66.

[90]Isla M. Mullins, *Edgar Young Mullins: An Intimate Biography* (Nashville: Sunday School Board, 1929), p. 162.

[91]William L. Poteat, "In Praise of Ignorance," pp. 5, 7 (handwritten note on back of page), typescript of an address delivered in Charleston, South Carolina, 22 December 1925, W. L. Poteat Papers; "Liberty and Restraint," pp. 2-4, 13.

[92]*Record*, 6 October 1921, p. 6.

The mixed results of this plunge appear in a state-by-state survey of Baptist involvement in the antievolutionist movement.

In the coastal states extending from Maryland to Florida the campaign generated considerable heat but produced few results. Maryland, the northern outpost of this tier of states, experienced little difficulty with the antievolutionist movement. The state's Baptists were subject to moderate influences that scarcely touched believers farther south. To the north lay Pennsylvania, whose Baptists were unencumbered by the arch-conservatism that burdened so many Southern states, while to the immediate south Virginia provided another example of moderation. As pastor of Baltimore's University Baptist Church from 1921 to 1925, A. C. Dixon tried to offset these influences. But he spent too short a time in Maryland to alter Baptist opinion, and during his brief pastorate the affairs of national and international fundamentalism consumed much of his energy. More important, Dixon shied away from the movement to enact antievolution laws, thus depriving the crusade of his complete cooperation. Finally, Marylanders of all denominations remained calm during the 1920s, and the state's educators and politicians paid scant attention to the occasional entreaties of antievolutionists.[93]

Like her neighbor, Virginia remained relatively free of agitation. A Methodist clergyman changed his mind about introducing an antievolution bill into the legislature after discovering the futility of such a gesture. Journalist Virginius Dabney pointed out why, writing that in the Old Dominion "anyone who attempts to hamper scientific research by an appeal to Scripture receives only loud guffaws and is speedily laughed out of court."[94] Singling out Robert Pitt, editor of the *Religious Herald*, and the Richmond *News-Leader*'s Douglas S. Freeman for special praise, Dabney granted Baptists "the major share of the credit" for keeping the state free of antievolution laws;[95] and William J. Robertson, author of *The Changing South*, commended Virginia's Baptists for "rebelling against the old intolerance."[96] Baptists more conservative than Pitt and

---

[93]Shipley, *War on Modern Science*, pp. 150-52. The position of Maryland Baptists emerges from a reading of the state convention records and from the books, articles, and personal correspondence of A. C. Dixon.

[94]Virginius Dabney, "Virginia," *American Mercury* 9 (November 1926): 354-55.

[95]Dabney, *Liberalism in the South* (Chapel Hill: University of North Carolina Press, 1932), p. 306.

[96]William J. Robertson, *The Changing South* (New York: Boni and Liveright, 1927), p. 100.

Freeman, notably George McDaniel, pastor of Richmond's First Baptist Church, also kept the peace, refusing to advocate legal measures against Darwinism.

A search for the basis of this revolt "against the old intolerance" leads to three conclusions. First, the example of such men as Pitt, Freeman, and McDaniel made it difficult for extremists to gain a hearing in Virginia. Second, Virginians prided themselves on a tradition of gentlemanly discourse that frowned on such unseemly conduct as political demagoguery, Ku Kluxism, and antievolutionism. Third, and most important, Baptists remained aware of the denomination's historic struggle to free religion from state interference. Although this sensitivity to church-state relations cropped up most noticeably in a discussion of compulsory Bible reading in the public schools, the logic employed by the Dover Baptist Association in rejecting the proposal applied to the evolution controversy as well. The state's most important Baptist association resolved in 1925:

> That the Dover Association [comprised of Richmond and surrounding rural areas] on behalf of the twenty-six thousand members of its churches reaffirms the historic opposition of Virginia Baptists to any meddling by the State in matters concerning religion, and respectfully protests to the General Assembly against the passage of any such law on the grounds that it would be an improper interference by the State in the realm of religion, and a violation of the principles of religious liberty, and the complete separation of the spheres of church and State as embodied in the constitution of the Commonwealth.[97]

By refusing to be caught up in the antievolution passion, Virginia Baptists remained true to the principles enunciated by the Dover Association.

The Carolinas presented a study in contrasts, North Carolina experiencing a bitter controversy over evolution, with South Carolina escaping her neighbor's turmoil. North Carolina struggled with the issue throughout the 1920s, the crisis reaching a climax in 1925 when the lower house of the legislature defeated an antievolution bill. Amidst this

---

[97]Dover Baptist Association (Virginia), *Minutes*, 1925, p. 31.

upheaval, T. T. Martin, president of the Anti-Evolution League of North America, descended on the state to organize an interdenominational drive to outlaw the teaching of evolution. William Poteat placed his influence squarely in Martin's path, and such important Baptists as Richard Vann and Livingston Johnson, editor of the *Biblical Recorder*, stood beside him. Their opposition paid off; Martin failed to rally sufficient support to force passage of an antievolution law, and the Baptist State Convention refused to advocate such a bill. Moderates triumphed in North Carolina, but only after a prolonged struggle.[98]

South Carolina's Baptist convention similarly declined to press for an antievolution law. Z. T. Cody, editor of the *Baptist Courier*, showed no sympathy for antievolutionism, and Anderson College's John White also opposed the movement. More important, William J. McGlothlin, president of Furman University and one of the state's most respected Baptists, offered no encouragement to the crusade. Finally, other than abortive attempts to force laws through the legislature in 1921 and 1928, South Carolina's antievolutionists remained relatively quiet. This spared the state's Baptists from the controversy experienced by North Carolinians, enabling them to pursue a moderate course more easily.[99]

In both Georgia and Florida anti-Darwinists campaigned against the teaching of evolution. Between 1923 and 1925 the Georgia house of representatives grappled with the issue, twice killing prospective laws. The Florida legislature, responding to the entreaties of William Jennings Bryan, approved a resolution in 1923 condemning the teaching of Darwinism. In 1925 and 1927 the senate saved the state from further antievolution legislation by rejecting bills passed by the house.[100]

Although unsympathetic with Darwinism, Georgia's Baptists made no official effort to obtain legislative prohibition of the theory. Individual Baptists approved of the crusade's goals, but the state organization refused to endorse them. Leading Georgia Baptists such as Louie D. Newton, editor of the *Christian Index*, Ashby Jones, and Rufus Weaver

---

[98]Willard B. Gatewood, "The Evolution Controversy in North Carolina, 1920-1927," *Mississippi Quarterly* 17 (Fall 1964): 205; Suzanne K. Linder, "William Louis Poteat and the Evolution Controversy," *North Carolina Historical Review* 40 (Spring 1963): 135-57; Poteat to Virginius Dabney, 15 June 1931, W. L. Poteat Papers.

[99]*Herald*, 9 February 1922, pp. 4-5; Poteat to Dabney, 15 June 1931; Furniss, *The Fundamentalist Controversy*, p. 79.

[100]Furniss, *The Fundamentalist Controversy*, pp. 80, 84.

strove successfully to keep the state's Baptists from answering the call of extremism.[101]

Lacking such leadership, Florida Baptists announced their position early in the decade when in 1921, following the advice of Bryan, they implored the legislature "to prevent all teaching in our public schools and State University which would destroy the faith of [our] own boys and girls in the Bible."[102] This resolution was the only formal endorsement of antievolution legislation made by Southern Baptists in the Atlantic coastal states. The moderation that prevailed in Maryland, Virginia, the Carolinas, and Georgia best expressed the sentiments of the area's Baptists.

Baptists in Alabama, Mississippi, Kentucky, and Tennessee voiced their intention to use the state to crush Darwinism, with only Alabama's Baptists failing to support the drive wholeheartedly. Although antievolutionists managed to get bills before the legislature in 1923 and 1927, Alabama escaped the upheaval experienced by other states of the middle South. This allowed the state's Baptists to take a more detached stance, free from the constant controversy that kept Baptists aroused in Tennessee, Kentucky, and Mississippi. But beyond this, Alabama Baptist leaders showed a moderation similar to that of their counterparts in the Atlantic coastal states. L. L. Gwaltney deserved much of the credit, for during the 1920s he placed the state's Baptist journal on the side of moderation. Some Alabama Baptists urged the enactment of an antievolution law, but on the whole, the state's Baptists rejected this as an improper way to deal with Darwinism.[103]

Mississippi's Baptists followed a different course. Led by T. T. Martin and encouraged by P. I. Lipsey of the *Baptist Record*, they embraced the antievolution movement. As early as 1922 the Baptist pastors of Simpson County requested the appointment of a committee to examine public school textbooks for heretical ideas. Two years later, armed with proof that the books taught the theory of evolution, the committee warned educational superintendents to rid the schools of offensive books and

---

[101]Poteat to Dabney, 15 June 1931; Weaver, "The Baptist Opportunity," pp. 5-6.

[102]Florida, *Annual*, 1921-1922, pp. 89-90.

[103]Furniss, *The Fundamentalist Controversy*, p. 80. For Baptist antievolutionists' lack of success on the state level see the annual reports of the Alabama Baptist State Convention.

teachers and pleaded with the legislature to protect Mississippians from "anti-Christian teaching."[104] In 1926 Martin carried the fight to the state legislature, daring the lawmakers to reject the proposed antievolution bill and then "go back to the fathers and mothers of Mississippi and tell them . . . you turned their children over to a teaching that God's word is a tissue of lies."[105] Responding to such pressure, the legislature prohibited the teaching of evolution in tax-supported schools. Mississippi Baptists rejoiced, Lipsey remarking that "friends of the bill and all who are opposed to the teaching of evolution have reason to be grateful to those who have fought for it from start to finish."[106]

Few Mississippi Baptists dared to question their denomination's involvement in the antievolution crusade. In Kentucky, by contrast, divergent strains of Baptist thought existed openly. Although the state contained such uncompromising conservatives as John Porter, Victor Masters, and Boyce Taylor (editor of *News and Truths*), it also boasted the men of Southern Seminary—Mullins, Robertson, Carver, Sampey— and other spokesmen for moderation. But the opposition of these men did not prevent Kentucky Baptists from participating in the movement to enact an antievolution law. On 6 December 1921, Porter, leader of Kentucky's Baptist antievolutionists, persuaded the state mission board to establish a committee to spearhead the legislative drive. The movement gained momentum a month later when William Jennings Bryan addressed antievolutionists in Lexington. Following Bryan's oration, the Reverend W. L. Brock, pastor of the city's Immanuel Baptist Church, introduced a resolution calling on the legislature to outlaw the teaching of evolution, higher criticism of the Bible, and other forms of "atheism and infidelity." A sympathetic lawmaker placed the proposal before the lower house.[107]

In an attempt to forestall action injurious to scientific research, Mullins had a countermeasure introduced in the senate which omitted reference to evolution, but asked the state not to employ teachers "who shall directly or indirectly attack or assail or seek to undermine or weaken

---

[104]Mississippi, *Proceedings*, 1922, p. 28; 1924, p. 27.

[105]Shipley, *War on Modern Science*, p. 65.

[106]*Record*, 4 March 1926, p. 4.

[107]Alonzo W. Fortune, "The Kentucky Campaign Against the Teaching of Evolution," *Journal of Religion* 2 (May 1922): 227-29.

or destroy the religious beliefs and convictions" of students. This bill represented an honest attempt to preserve the rights of science, while calming the Baptist masses. A few contemporaries, notably William Poteat, understood Mullins's motivation, but most people interpreted his action to suit their prejudices. Baptist antievolutionists viewed Mullins's compromise as further proof of his vacillation; non-Baptist liberals construed it as abetting the antievolutionist cause. In any event, Baptists and their allies were too weak to force their will on the state legislature: between 1922 and 1928 six bills entered the hopper, but none survived.[108]

The people of Tennessee wrote a different ending to their story: in 1925 the legislature prohibited the teaching of evolution in state schools. As early as 1923 Tennessee Baptists had warned teachers and administrators to beware of the intrusion of anti-Christian ideas into the schools, and when the legislature passed the antievolution bill Baptists acclaimed it.[109] Between the passage of the act in March of 1925 and official Baptist approval in November, an event occurred that spilled over Tennessee's borders and stirred the nation's interest. From 10 to 21 July Americans riveted their attention on the small southeastern Tennessee town of Dayton, where John T. Scopes, Clarence Darrow, and William Jennings Bryan enacted the drama known as the "Scopes Monkey Trial."

Southern Baptists' admiration for Bryan predetermined their attitude toward the trial; Bryan, the champion of rural America, the common man, and "old-time religion," held a special claim to Baptist loyalty. Regardless of their opinion of the antievolution crusade, Southern Baptists respected Bryan for his devotion to civic and moral righteousness.[110] Armed with this predisposition and horrified by the inroads evolutionary theory had made into the land of orthodoxy, most Southern Baptists saw the Scopes trial from only one perspective. The tawdriness, charlatanry, and indecisiveness associated with the trial escaped the South's Baptists; to them, goodness had vanquished evil. J. Frank Norris wrote: "It is Moses challenging Pharaoh; it is Elijah arraigning Ahab; it is Paul

---

[108]Ibid., p. 233; William Poteat to Edwin Poteat, 9 February 1922, W. L. Poteat Papers; *Searchlight*, 21 August 1925, p. 1; Albert C. Dieffenbach, *Religious Liberty: The Great American Illusion* (New York: William Morrow, 1927), pp. 103-104; Furniss, *The Fundamentalist Controversy*, pp. 82-83.

[109]Tennessee Baptist Convention, *Annual*, 1923, p. 40; 1925, p. 53.

[110]Martin, *Hell and the High Schools*, pp. 18-19; Alabama, *Annual*, 1925, p. 34; *Herald*, 16 March 1922, p. 14.

defying Nero; it is Martin Luther hurling his thesis [sic] at Pope Leo X. It is the greatest battle of the centuries."[111]

Southern Baptists who saw the folly of employing the state to crush science viewed the proceedings less ecstatically. A. T. Robertson dismissed it as a disgraceful display of extremism,[112] and Mullins wrote that "it would be laughable, if it were not so serious in some of its aspects."[113] The Scopes trial vindicated the beliefs of neither side, L. L. Gwaltney concluded; it left both Darwinists and their antagonists looking ridiculous.[114] Robert Pitt summarized these feelings when he wrote:

> There can be no doubt that public opinion all over the land is disgusted with the Scopes Trial. The whole proceeding has been turned into a roaring farce. No serious impression has been made by it upon intelligent public sentiment. The chief actors in it have apparently been anxious to exploit the interest which it has aroused in procuring the limelight for themselves. The whole business is pitiful, humiliating, distressing. Let our people rest assured that neither the truth of revealed religion nor any just claims of science have been in the least degree affected by this overadvertised case.[115]

Although Baptists farther west boasted nothing as exciting as the Scopes trial, they were enthusiastic over prospects of proscribing the teaching of evolution. Louisiana Baptists began their campaign in 1922, appointing a committee to ferret out public school textbooks containing the theory. Interest increased in 1925 when T. T. Martin, fresh from the Scopes trial, invaded Louisiana to win another legislature for God. Baptists continued to press for the elimination of unacceptable textbooks, advising educators in the fall of 1925 to find books free of the theory of evolution. In June of 1926 Louisianians saw their hopes for an antievolution law partially realized when the house approved a bill banning

---

[111]*Searchlight*, 24 July 1925, p. 1.

[112]Archie Robertson, *That Old-Time Religion* (Boston: Houghton-Mifflin Co., 1950), p. 21.

[113]Mullins to John R. Sampey, 9 July 1925, Mullins Papers, 1925-1927 Correspondence M-Z.

[114]Leslie L. Gwaltney, *Forty of the Twentieth or the First Forty Years of the Twentieth Century* (Birmingham: pub. by the author, 1940), pp. 139-40.

[115]*Herald*, 23 July 1925, p. 23.

evolutionary teachings; to the dismay of Baptists, the senate shelved the measure the next day. Blocked on the legislative front, Baptists turned to the state education board, beseeching its members to throw out Darwinist textbooks and silence offending teachers. No doubt influenced by such pleas, Louisiana's superintendent of education issued a directive in 1927 forbidding public school teachers to present the theory of evolution to their students. This satisfied the state's Baptists, who ceased to agitate for an antievolution law.[116]

Arkansas Baptists' zealous advocacy of proscriptive laws placed them in the forefront of Southern Baptist antievolutionism. In December of 1926 they went "on record as favoring the passage of a law to prohibit the teaching of the theory of evolution in the tax-supported schools of the state." On 9 February 1927, the Arkansas house of representatives voted favorably on an antievolution bill, only to have the senate table it. Incensed by such temerity, the Reverend Ben M. Bogard initiated a petition campaign to force a referendum in the fall of 1928. Although Bogard belonged to the American Baptist Association, a group that had seceded from the Southern Baptist Convention in 1905, the Arkansas Baptist State Convention endorsed his petition campaign in November of 1927 and advised its constituents to vote only for antievolutionist candidates. Bogard collected the necessary signatures, and in the fall of 1928 the people of Arkansas approved antievolution legislation by a vote of 108,000 to 63,000.[117]

Missouri Baptists showed greater circumspection in their call for repressive legislation. Without mentioning evolution, they noted in 1924 that public school teachers had been questioning the Bible's inspiration and attacking evangelical religion. Demanding an end to this, Baptists

---

[116]Louisiana, *Annual*, 1922, p. 29; 1925, pp. 36-37; 1926, pp. 20-22; Martin, *Viewing Life's Sunset*, p. 31; Furniss, *The Fundamentalist Controversy*, pp. 93-94.

[117]Arkansas, *Proceedings*, 1926, p. 94; 1927, p. 89; Furniss, *The Fundamentalist Controversy*, p. 94. Virginia Gray, in "Anti-Evolution Sentiment and Behavior: The Case of Arkansas," *Journal of American History* 57 (September 1970): 352-66, contends that "in counties with a high percentage of Baptist church members, the electorate did not tend to vote for the ban on evolution." This does not necessarily conflict with my findings, for even if Baptists did not vote in large numbers for the antievolution bill, they still could have opposed evolutionary teachings. As Mrs. Gray admits: "Low voter turnout in areas of supposedly high antievolution sentiment means that in this case group sentiments were not automatically turned into action." Mrs. Gray's statistics do not prove that Arkansas Baptists did not oppose the teaching of evolution; rather, they raise the question of why antievolution Baptists did not go to the polls in larger numbers.

suggested that they unite with other denominations in pushing for a law prohibiting "any act or word of irreverence or disrespect of the Bible before the children in the public schools."[118] In addition, they advised Baptist preachers to contact legislators in behalf of the measure. But Missouri Baptists failed to get their views written into law; in 1927 the legislature rejected an antievolution bill and made no attempt to enact a more general law protecting the sanctity of evangelical Christianity.[119]

The states of Oklahoma and Texas contained some of the most vocal Baptist antievolutionists in the South. Oklahoma's crusaders looked to Texas, especially to J. Frank Norris, for aid and inspiration in their struggle against Darwinism. Norris's Oklahoma allies—Charles Alexander, Mordecai Ham, and Clarence Stealey—promoted antievolutionism in their state. In November 1921, before other states had acted, Oklahoma's Baptists advised educators to guard against "anti-Christian" teachers and textbooks, backing up their advice with the warning that "we will bend every effort to discover, expose, and expel any such book or instructor."[120] When the legislature banned Darwinian textbooks in 1923 Stealey congratulated the lawmakers for their "manhood," and a few months later the *Baptist Messenger's* editor commended the University of Oklahoma for firing an unorthodox professor. When the legislature repealed its textbook ban in 1926 antievolutionists countered by introducing another bill. The *Messenger* quickly endorsed the measure, for Stealey had been working with several legislators on a similar bill. The lower house tabled the bill, and most of Oklahoma's Baptists, weary of the constant agitation that had characterized Stealey's editorship, allowed the issue to die.[121]

Baptist opponents of Darwinism, led by J. Frank Norris, worked diligently to drag Texas into the antievolution orbit. The delegates to the state Baptist convention in 1921 appointed a committee to scrutinize textbooks. But most Baptists, influenced by the moderation of such men as Lee Scarborough, George Truett, and Samuel Brooks, rejected the idea of legislating against evolution. Unhampered by such doubts, Norris

[118]Missouri, *Minutes*, 1924, p. 117.

[119]Furniss, *The Fundamentalist Controversy*, pp. 95-96.

[120]Oklahoma, *Minutes*, 1921, p. 103.

[121]*Messenger*, 28 February 1923, p. 9; 27 June 1923, p. 8; 19 January 1927, p. 1; Furniss, *The Fundamentalist Controversy*, p. 83.

carried the fight to the Texas house of representatives in 1923, hoping to persuade the lawmakers to prohibit the teaching of evolution in tax-supported schools. Although the senate refused to bring the bill to a vote, Governor Miriam E. Ferguson, acting as head of the state textbook commission, compensated for this lapse in 1925 by banning Darwinist textbooks. Moderates managed to prevent the state's Baptists from lending official support to the antievolution movement, but not before many Texans had seconded Norris's demands for legislative action.[122]

In examining Southern Baptist attitudes one is tempted to agree with W. J. Cash's contention that the antievolution crusade constituted an "authentic folk movement" supported by an "overwhelming majority of the Southern people."[123] Cash's statement is true when applied to general opposition to the theory of evolution, for most Southerners, Baptists included, rejected the idea. But did opposition to Darwinism necessarily lead to advocacy of antievolution laws? Among Southern Baptists this did not always prove to be true; their support of antievolution legislation varied from state to state, depending on the moderation of Baptist leadership and the degree to which antievolutionism became embroiled in politics. Although most Southern Baptists disagreed with the theory of evolution, not all believed, as Cash implied, that throwing the issue into the political arena solved anything. Indeed, Baptists played a significant role in maintaining freedom of teaching in many Southern states.

After analyzing the Baptist response to the theory of evolution the nagging question remains: Did the problem warrant the attention lavished on it in the 1920s? Without doubt, evolutionary thought, especially when part of a world view that dispensed with God, conflicted with Southern Baptist beliefs. In the context of the 1920s Darwinism assumed frightening proportions. It became more than just a disagreeable scientific theory; combined with the other dangers of the decade—social Christianity, higher criticism, Catholicism, urbanism, and inter-denominationalism—it appeared to be part of Satan's effort to destroy the gospel message. Moderate creationists and evolutionists tried to put the matter into perspective, reminding Baptists that more important tasks confronted their denomination than denouncing Darwinism and

---

[122]Texas, *Annual*, 1922, pp. 85-87; *Searchlight*, 23 February 1923, p. 1; Furniss, *The Fundamentalist Controversy*, pp. 86-88.

[123]W. J. Cash, *The Mind of the South* (New York: Alfred A. Knopf Co., 1941), p. 346.

pressuring state legislatures. E. Y. Mullins summed up this position clearly when he wrote, in 1927, that:

> One of the greatest dangers facing us now is that Christian people will be diverted from their task of saving souls into lobbying around legislatures and making out a program for the statute book rather than a program for the salvation of the world.[124]

But such words often went for naught. Antievolutionism obsessed many Baptists, distracting them from world evangelization and promoting dissension and distrust within the denomination. Few issues unsettled Southern Baptists more than the struggle with the theory of evolution.

---

[124]Mullins to W. A. Sunday, 1 February 1927, Mullins Papers, 1925-1927 Correspondence M-Z.

CHAPTER 8

J. Frank Norris and Southern Baptist Fundamentalism

Most Southern Baptists saw Darwinism and higher criticism as external threats, components of an alien philosophy that Baptists rejected. Had the denomination's anxiety over modernism remained on this level Southern Baptists would have come through the fundamentalist modernist controversy relatively unscarred. Instead, the denomination's fundamentalists, led by J. Frank Norris, turned the controversy inward, accusing ministers, professors and church leaders of fostering modernism within the bosom of orthodoxy. Although Baptists survived this strife, their campaign of world evangelization suffered severely; in the midst of internal debate the South's Baptists frequently lost sight of the goal they had set for themselves at the end of World War I.

Southern Baptist fundamentalists leveled their earliest charges at evolutionists in the denomination's colleges. In 1920, with postwar solidarity still dominant, T. T. Martin launched an attack on William Poteat, indicting the biologist for corrupting the youth of North Carolina. Seeking the widest circulation for his accusation, Martin offered a series of articles to a number of Baptist journals, but found recipients only in Kentucky, Arkansas, and Louisiana. Norris soon followed Martin's example, initiating his prolonged dispute with Baylor University in an article criticizing Professor Grove S. Dow for promoting Darwinism in his book *Introduction to the Principles of Sociology*.[1] Norris's vendetta against Baylor and the attack on Poteat continued throughout much of the 1920s.

Expanding beyond these attacks, fundamentalists rebuked denominational leaders for their modernist proclivities. Especially in Texas, fundamentalists delighted in hurling charges at prominent Baptists. Norris accused Frank S. Groner, secretary of the executive board, of abetting the modernist cause by mishandling funds entrusted to him by rank-and-file Baptists. The "unholy trio"—Joseph Dawson, George Truett, and Lee Scarborough—provided a favorite target for Texas fundamentalists. They accused Dawson of denying the inspiration of the Scriptures; indicted Truett for welcoming unorthodox Northern Baptists into his pulpit; and assailed Scarborough for presiding over a nest of infidels at Southwestern Seminary.[2] Outside Texas, fundamentalists discovered another source of modernist subversion in Southern Seminary. They reproached several of the school's professors for their shortcomings: John R. Sampey for teaching "rank modernism" in a Bible commentary series; A. T. Robertson for speaking approvingly of evolution; and W. O. Carver for promoting unorthodox ideas on foreign missions.[3]

Fundamentalists complained that unorthodox leaders had undermined three important agencies of Baptist work, the Foreign Mission Board, the Sunday School Board, and the Baptist World Alliance. Norris and Victor Masters charged that the Foreign Mission Board, with the full knowledge of Secretary T. B. Ray, had compromised Baptist orthodoxy in China and had cooperated with Northern Baptists in protecting modernist missionaries.[4] Baptists in Kentucky, Oklahoma, and Texas, alarmed at "heretical teachings" in the literature published by the Sunday School Board, concluded that the board had succumbed to the wave of modernism engulfing the denomination.[5] A similar fate had befallen the Baptist

---

[1]*Herald*, 1 April 1920, p. 3; *Searchlight*, 21 October 1921, p. 1.

[2]*Searchlight*, 20 November 1925; *Fundamentalist*, 13 December 1929; Norris to William Riley, 7 March 1931, Norris Papers, Box 36; Orville S. Anderson to Lee Scarborough, 27 November 1931, Scarborough Papers.

[3]Norris to F. F. Gibson, 24 May 1929, Norris Papers, Box 16; Norris to Louis S. Chafer, 17 April 1928, Box 5; William Carver to Norris, 27 February 1933, Box 7.

[4]Norris to Mordecai Ham, 6 March 1928, Norris Papers, Box 18; Norris to Masters, 18 February 1931, Box 27.

[5]Kentucky, *Proceedings*, 1929, p. 21; W. H. Tennison to J. B. Weatherspoon, 20 June

World Alliance, a fraternal organization comprised mainly of Baptists from the United States, Canada, and Northern Europe. Fundamentalists injected their disenchantment with this organization into the proceedings of the Southern Baptist Convention; in 1928 they attempted to pass a resolution protesting the presence of leading liberals at the Alliance's 1928 meeting, and succeeded a year later in convincing the Convention to state that Southern Baptist participation in the Alliance implied no endorsement of "unscriptural views."[6]

Surveying this "evidence" of subversion, fundamentalists concluded that modernism posed an immediate danger to Southern Baptist orthodoxy; and that the work of the denomination's boards, colleges, and seminaries obviously had been undermined by a treacherous group of professors, ministers, and denominational leaders who had allied themselves with the foes of orthodoxy. Fundamentalists absolved the Baptist masses of responsibility for this turn of events; rank-and-file believers had kept the faith and had resisted modernist overtures. By employing a conspiracy theory which placed the blame on the denomination's elite, Baptist fundamentalists singled out easily recognizable villains upon whom to vent their frustration over the bewildering developments in modern religious thought. All was not well in the Baptist Zion of the South, and fundamentalists knew whom to blame.

Taken at face value, fundamentalist charges indicated that modernism abounded in Baptist schools, pulpits, and agencies. But fundamentalists misread the situation, for modernism had scarcely touched Southern Baptists. The denomination harbored no higher critics, and its few evolutionists taught a tame variety of evolutionary thought that posed no danger. Southern Baptist "modernists" proclaimed their allegiance to orthodoxy, and a comparison between them and liberals outside the denomination supported their claims. Those stigmatized as modernists differed in one major respect from other Baptists: they refused to panic over the modern world's antagonism toward orthodoxy, insisting that the faith be defended with the tools of reason rather than the weapons of invective. These Baptists carefully weighed the merits of higher criticism, borrowing from it whatever enabled them to understand the Bible

---

1931, Norris Papers, Box 40; R. H. Cunningham to Karl H. Moore, ca. 1931, Norris Papers, Box 27.

[6]SBC, *Annual*, 1928, p. 90; 1929, p. 22.

better. More important, they distinguished between Christian evolution-ism and evolutionary thought that enthroned naturalism and material-ism. In dealing intelligently with biblical criticism and the theory of evolution, allegedly modernistic Baptists maintained their faith in evan-gelical religion. By meeting liberals on their own grounds they showed that evangelicals could defend their views without recourse to fanaticism. Baptist "modernists" actually strengthened orthodoxy instead of weaken-ing it as fundamentalists charged.

How, then, account for the fundamentalist obsession with Southern Baptist modernism? In the first place, the sophisticated approach to religion taken by scholars troubled poorly educated Baptists. Untutored minds found it difficult to distinguish between Christian evolutionism and Darwinism, or between higher criticism and scholarly, but conserva-tive, analysis of the Bible. Although this inability to perceive intellectual distinctions produced unrest and suspicion among uneducated Baptists it did not necessarily lead them to attack their fellow churchmen. After all, the "modernists" commanded wide respect within the denomination. E. Y. Mullins, George Truett, and William McGlothlin presided over the Southern Baptist Convention at different times during the twenties; Robert Pitt, Livingston Johnson, Z. T. Cody, Louie Newton, L. L. Gwalt-ney, and F. M. McConnell edited Baptist journals; A. T. Robertson, W. O. Carver, W. T. Conner, and other scholars dominated Baptist seminaries; William Poteat, Rufus Weaver, and Samuel Brooks headed the denomi-nation's leading colleges; and McNeill Poteat, Ashby Jones, and Joseph Dawson were pastors of important Baptist churches. Most Baptists, in spite of their intense and often unthinking conservatism, supported these men and refused to believe that their leaders had surrendered to modernism.

Yet fundamentalism appealed to many Southern Baptists who, fear-ful of Darwinism and higher criticism, appreciated the unequivocal way in which fundamentalists fought orthodoxy's antagonists. Fundamental-ists banished the complexities of the modern world, simplifying issues and offering easy solutions to the problems that plagued orthodox Chris-tians. But this attraction failed to win the active support of most Southern Baptists; those who joined the fundamentalist movement remained a minority. The explanation for this lies with the five distinguishing characteristics of Southern Baptist fundamentalism. First, the movement cannot be understood without an analysis of J. Frank Norris, the guiding genius of Southern Baptist fundamentalism. Second, premillennialism furnished the most important theological doctrine of the movement. An interdenominational impulse, derived from the premillennial conception of the church, formed a third aspect of fundamentalism. Fourth, "ruralism" played a role in shaping the movement. Finally, fundamentalists advocated local autonomy, spontaneity, and democracy. These facets of Southern Baptist fundamentalism explain both its strengths and weaknesses.

J. Frank Norris furnishes a logical starting point for examining Southern Baptist fundamentalism. Norris first exhibited his dissatisfaction with the denominational program in his critical view of the Seventy-Five Million Campaign. In later years he contended that he had opposed the idea from its inception, and that because of his stand "denominational despots" had turned on him. But Norris's own statements disprove this, for he initially supported the fund drive. Although he complained that $100,000 represented too great a burden for his congregation, he approved the program and, in January 1920, praised Lee Scarborough for leading Southern Baptists to "the most notable victory in their history." Norris probably became disenchanted when he realized the difficulties involved in raising $100,000, especially since his church had undertaken a separate drive to erect a new building. Moreover, when Norris saw his church's contributions being funneled into Baptist colleges tainted with heresy he pulled out of the campaign, thereby earning the enmity of Baptist leaders.[7]

Norris widened this breach by joining the burgeoning nationwide fundamentalist movement. During the first two weeks of March 1920, Norris's church hosted a "Conference on Christian Fundamentals," featuring A. C. Dixon and William B. Riley, head of the World's Christian Fundamentals Association. In the fall of the same year Norris further antagonized Baptist leaders by severing ties with the Sunday School Board, declaring that because his congregation disagreed with statements in the board's literature the First Baptist Church of Fort Worth would study the Bible without "man-made" commentaries.[8] Norris happened

---

[7]J. Frank Norris, *Inside History of First Baptist Church, Fort Worth, and Temple Baptist Church, Detroit: Life Story of Dr. J. Frank Norris* (n. p., n. d.), p. 160; *Searchlight*, 16 October 1919, p. 2; 8 January 1920, p. 1; Norris to the Editor, Cleburne, Texas, *Morning Review*, 24 October 1927, Norris Papers, Box 7.

[8]*Searchlight*, 10 February 1920, p. 1; 16 December 1920, p. 2.

upon an issue in the spring of 1921 that led to further alienation from Southern Baptists. He discovered that modernism had found a foothold in nearby Dallas through the influence of John R. Rice, a professor in Southern Methodist University. Norris exposed Rice in a sermon published in the fledgling journal the *Searchlight*. Letters of praise convinced Norris that he had touched a vital issue and persuaded him to channel his full energies into the war on modernism. He next turned on Baylor University for harboring evolutionists; the congratulatory letters he received, coupled with the *Searchlight's* expanding list of subscribers, assured him of the wisdom of his decision.[9] Norris had charted his course, never to be deterred; he would spend the rest of the decade fighting modernism both inside and outside his denomination.

Norris brought a high sense of destiny to his task, believing that he had a "mission to perform" and a "command to obey." His followers encouraged him to consider himself chosen by God to cleanse the temple of orthodoxy, and Norris complied with their wishes by comparing himself to the prophets God had called to chastise the Jews. John the Baptist, the fearless prophet of the Judean wilderness, especially commanded Norris's admiration, and when accused of fanaticism Norris cited his similarity to those "righteous extremists" Jeremiah and Isaiah.[10] In reply to the charge that he was the "arch-Bolshevik of the Southern Baptist Convention," a reproach aimed at his methods and not his ideology, Norris placed himself in a long line of "Bolsheviks" who had stirred men from their lethargy: Moses, Abraham, Elijah, and Paul had shaken the ancient world with their "bolsheviking," Norris said. He saw affinities between his own struggle with Baptist authorities and the war waged on corrupt religious power by those notable "Bolsheviks" Savonarola, John Hus, and Martin Luther. Completing his recitation on the history of Bolshevism, Norris called up the memory of the "Arch-Bolshevik of the British Empire," George Washington. In a further effort to establish his greatness, Norris extolled the fundamentalist movement as one of the major religious revivals of history, lineal descendant of the Protestant Reformation, Puritanism, and the Great Awakening of the eighteenth century.[11]

---

[9]Ibid., 18 May 1921, p. 3; 16 December 1921, p. 2.

[10]M. H. Duncan to Norris, 27 August 1929, Norris Papers, Box 11; Norris to Isaac Gates, 12 November 1927; 30 March 1928, Box 16.

[11]*Searchlight*, 2 June 1922, p. 1; quoted in E. Ray Tatum, *Conquest or Failure? Biography of J. Frank Norris* (Dallas: Baptist Historical Foundation, 1966), p. 210.

Convinced of his divine calling, Norris contended that those who attempted to block the completion of his mission risked the wrath of God. Proof of this lay in the disasters that had befallen those who had crossed the Lord's messenger: bankruptcy, defrocking, suicide, insanity, and premature death had come to preachers, politicians, newspapermen, lawyers, and businessmen who had opposed him, Norris said.[12] Norris's self-esteem and sense of calling enabled him to wield vast influence among fundamentalists, but they also produced an overweening air of self-righteousness that irritated other Baptists.

Norris combined this self-rectitude with a love of controversy that transcended the normal Baptist affinity for doctrinal disputation. As the *Christian Century* remarked in 1924: "Dr. Norris is probably the most belligerent fundamentalist now abroad in the land."[13] Norris's fellow Baptists recognized this trait: Lee Scarborough declared it impossible to settle disputes with Norris,[14] and W. R. White, Texas's secretary of missions in the 1920s, recalled in 1965 that Norris had been "rather restless without some kind of fight."[15] Norris verified this judgment in both word and deed. He boasted to Scarborough, Truett, and Dawson that "the last thing in the world you want now is agitation and that is the first thing I want."[16] On another occasion Norris expressed disappointment over prospects of an early end to his dispute with the Baptist General Convention of Texas.[17]

At the root of this love of controversy lay a deep-seated need to be noticed, to be considered important in the world's eyes. Troubled by the memory of a rural childhood of poverty and obscurity, Norris strove to establish his identity. Whether people loved or hated him mattered little; even recognition by his enemies fed Norris's craving for attention. As he once commented: "If you can't say something good about me, say some-

---

[12]Norris, *Inside History*, pp. 11-18.

[13]"Texas Baptists Repudiate Dr. Norris," *Christian Century* 41 (25 December 1924): 1672.

[14]Scarborough to J. J. Taylor, 29 April 1922, Scarborough Papers.

[15]White to Donald G. Bouldin, 8 September 1965, copy in the appendix of Bouldin's "The J. M. Dawson—J. F. Norris Controversy: A Reflection of the Fundamentalist Controversy among Texas Baptists" (unpublished M. A. thesis, Baylor University, 1969).

[16]Norris to Truett, Scarborough, and Dawson, n. d., Norris Papers, Box. 2.

[17]Norris to Forrest Smith and C. V. Edwards, 24 September 1929, Scarborough Papers.

thing bad; but say something."[18] Norris's opponents discerned this flaw in his character and used it to discredit him, as when fellow Texan J. M. Mizzell suggested that the Fort Worth pastor's ambition to be "a HERO in BAPTISTS['] ranks" discredited him as a leader.[19] E. Ray Tatum, Norris's biographer and associate in the late 1940s, corroborated this testimony, showing that the fundamentalist leader welcomed controversy because it brought the recognition he so deeply desired.[20] In all fairness to Norris, it must be admitted that he used religious quarrels to broaden his ministry and carry God's message to larger crowds. But he found it impossible to separate his role as God's messenger from his need to nurture his own ambitions. The two causes were bound inseparably in Norris's mind, and controversy promoted both. Joseph Dawson understood this, remarking in 1965 that "Norris's trouble was not so much theological as psychological."[21]

Norris's deliberate promotion of controversy could be defended as a legitimate way of getting the fundamentalist message before the public; less excusable, in fact totally without justification, was his attempt to discredit his opponents by twisting their words. Norris carried this to such lengths that, as Samuel Brooks suggested, the *Searchlight* should have been renamed the "Smirchlight."[22] Grove Dow discovered this early in the 1920s. Dow's *Introduction to the Principles of Sociology* had undeniably been influenced by evolutionary thought, but Norris garbled the professor's words so badly that he emerged sounding like a militant Darwinist.[23] Dow's successor in the sociology department at Baylor, a thoroughgoing creationist named W. P. Meroney, fared no better at Norris's hands. In 1927 Norris launched an attack on Meroney, charging that the professor had written: "It is generally taken for granted that men inherited some guiding instincts from their beast ancestry."[24] Meroney

---

[18]Quoted in Tatum, *Conquest or Failure?*, p. 209.

[19]J. M. Mizzell to Lee Scarborough, 10 and 16 November 1926, Scarborough Papers.

[20]Tatum, *Conquest or Failure?* p. 204.

[21]Dawson to Donald Bouldin, 6 September 1965, copy in the appendix of Bouldin's "The J. M. Dawson—J. F. Norris Controversy."

[22]Brooks to Glenn Sneed, 27 July 1926, Brooks Papers, File Di-Faculty.

[23]Dow to President and Trustees of Baylor University, 7 December 1921, Brooks Papers, File Di-Faculty.

[24]R. E. Bell to Meroney, 21 August 1927, W. P. Meroney Papers, Texas History Collection, Baylor University, Box 1.

pointed out that the quotation came from a passage in William Graham Sumner's *Folkways* which Meroney had excerpted for use in a book of readings for his sociology classes. As Meroney charged, Norris's accusation resulted from either "gross ignorance . . . or a willful and malicious intent to misinterpret."[25] Given Norris's intelligence, the latter seems most likely. Another Texan, Joseph Dawson, served as Norris's victim on numerous occasions. Norris frequently distorted Dawson's book reviews in the *Dallas News*, and after reading an article by Dawson in the *Homiletic Review*, Norris falsely accused him of endorsing the views of the famous agnostic Robert G. Ingersoll.[26] A letter to Norris from Charles Alexander, one of his most trusted allies, offers further proof that he deliberately misrepresented the views of others. Calling Norris's attention to an article written by Powhatan James, George Truett's son-in-law, Alexander remarked: "This article may nesessitate some more surgical work. But I leave it to you for an 'Interpretation.' "[27] Perhaps Norris felt that such "surgical work" could be justified in the war on modernism. But this does not exonerate him; his attitude resembled the witch-hunt mentality too closely to deserve anything but condemnation.

The controversial figure of J. Frank Norris, whether villain, crusader for God, or more likely, a combination of the two, dominated Southern Baptist fundamentalism and became a volatile issue during the 1920s. Baptists throughout the South knew of Norris, and their acceptance or rejection of fundamentalism often hinged on their attitude toward him. His followers acclaimed him as a man of God called to lead Southern Baptists out of the morass of modernism, while his enemies considered him a terrible plague come to torment Baptists with destruction and disunity. In any case, Southern Baptists could not ignore J. Frank Norris; he formed the storm center of the most disturbing problem faced by the denomination in the 1920s.

If Norris provided the personal element in Southern Baptist fundamentalism, the premillennial interpretation of Christ's Second Coming served as its doctrinal focal point. Premillennialists warned that evil

---

[25]Meroney to Bell, 23 August 1927, Box 1.

[26]Joseph M. Dawson, *A Thousand Months to Remember* (Waco: 1964), pp. 131-32; Norris to Mat Harder, 3 February 1930, Norris Papers, Box 19.

[27]Alexander to Norris, 6 June 1928, Norris Papers, Box 1.

would increase in the world, to be conquered only by Christ's cataclysmic return to destroy the wicked. The Second Coming, the "Blessed Hope" that comforted God's people in their travail, would usher in the millennium, a thousand years of peace and righteousness that owed nothing to man's feeble efforts to reform the world. This doctrine had been popular throughout the nineteenth century, attaining its greatest fame in the Millerite movement in the 1840s. The twentieth century stimulated premillennial predictions of the world's doom; World War I, the chaotic 1920s, and the economic depression of the 1930s furnished the crisis and unrest that premillennialism flourished upon.[28]

J. Frank Norris, imbibing premillennialism from such men as James R. Graves, a nineteenth-century Baptist leader, William B. Riley, and Jasper C. Massee, a Baptist preacher in Boston, Massachusetts, began preaching it around the time of World War I. Explaining the war's impact on his theology, Norris wrote:

> We saw all the achievements of man come to naught; all the skill of man for the past six thousand years turning the world into an awful maelstrom, a seething furnace of destruction[;] foundations gave way, governments were overthrown, and we witnessed the utter helplessness of man.[29]

Men turned in despair to the Second Coming as the only solution to the world's misery, Norris said. Throughout 1919 and 1920 Norris filled his sermons and the pages of the *Searchlight* with the premillennial message, listing signs of the end of time, discussing the progression of events at Christ's return, and warning of "World Conditions Ripening for the Last Dictator, the Beast of Prophecy." During the 1920s articles by such leading premillennialists as Riley and T. T. Shields, pastor of Toronto, Canada's Jarvis Street Baptist Church, appeared in the *Searchlight* (renamed the *Fundamentalist* in 1927) along with Norris's articles and sermons. The onset of the Great Depression, with its breadlines, unemployment, and air of crisis, confirmed what Norris and other premillennialists had been preaching: society was moving toward the final cataclysm. Rising to the occasion, Norris bombarded his readers with

---

[28]W. R. White to Donald G. Bouldin, 8 September 1965.

[29]*Fundamentalist*, 29 August 1930, p. 4.

warnings of imminent destruction.[30]

In the early 1920s Baptist fundamentalists refrained from making premillennialism a test of orthodoxy. While admitting that premillennialists dominated the World's Christian Fundamentals Association, William Riley invited A. T. Robertson, well-known foe of premillennialism, to participate in the Association's 1921 meeting.[31] Later that year Norris expressed concern over Southwestern Seminary's opposition to premillennialism, but praised the school and assured President Scarborough that he meant no harm in criticizing the Seminary's position on the Second Coming. A. C. Dixon stated as late as 1924 that fundamentalism demanded no specific belief on the time of Christ's return.[32] This moderation receded as the fundamentalist position hardened in the struggle against modernism. Norris pointed the way, announcing in 1926 that he would no longer "mince words," but would henceforth use premillennialism to test the orthodoxy of his fellow Baptists.[33] He insisted that fundamentalists had to be premillennialists because only they could be trusted in the war on modernism. During the rest of the decade Norris maintained that his doctrine of the Second Coming provided an infallible test. This emphasis gained concrete form in 1931 with the organization of the Southwestern Premillennial Conference, which met in Fort Worth's First Baptist Church from 15 to 29 November, with almost two thousand delegates, most of them from the Southwest and Midwest. This venture's success prompted Norris to establish the Southwestern Premillennial Bible School.[34] By the end of 1931 Norris had made premillennialism the trademark of Southern Baptist fundamentalism.

Fundamentalists refused to permit neutrality on this issue, insisting that Baptists take a forthright stand. T. T. Martin criticized those who steered a middle course by simply acknowledging that they waited ex-

---

[30]Searchlight, 6 November 1919, p. 3; 19 September 1920, p. 2; 17 August 1923, p. 3; Fundamentalist, 29 April 1927, p. 1; 26 September 1930, p. 1.

[31]Riley to Robertson, 8 March 1921, Robertson Papers, Folder 1921B; Norris to Scarborough, 17 November 1921, Scarborough Papers.

[32]Amzi C. Dixon, "What Is Fundamentalism?," p. 3, sermon preached in the University Baptist Church, Baltimore, Maryland, 5 January 1924, Dixon Papers, Box 12.

[33]Searchlight, 8 January 1926, p. 1.

[34]Fundamentalist, 20 November 1931, p. 1; 27 November 1931, p. 1.

pectantly for Christ's return. Such persons were covert premillennialists, Martin said, fearful of standing up for their beliefs.[35] Texas fundamentalist M. H. Duncan drew the opposite conclusion, charging that those unwilling to declare themselves were postmillennialists in disguise.[36] Although A. C. Dixon maintained that a fundamentalist did not have to accept premillennialism, he left little doubt as to where believers should stand. Jesus had been a premillennialist, Dixon said, for he had warned his followers that he would reappear when they least expected it and had said nothing about a millennium preceding His return.[37]

Fundamentalists combined this insistence on a clearcut division with an attack on postmillennialism. This doctrine formed one of the evils of modern religion, they charged, for it glorified denominationalism over congregational freedom, stressed education instead of evangelism, and advocated working for the betterment of a doomed world. Worst of all, the postmillennial camp contained evolutionists, higher critics, and the entire Roman Catholic Church. Fundamentalists drew the obvious conclusion: only premillennialists could be trusted, for all other Christians bore the marks of modernism and Catholicism.[38]

Fundamentalists set themselves at odds with many Baptists by demanding that Christians accept their interpretation of the Second Coming. In the first place, Southern Baptists possessed an orthodox source of postmillennialism in the writings of the late B. H. Carroll, founder of Southwestern Seminary. Although Baptists admired Carroll, few openly espoused his position in the 1920s: at Southwestern Seminary, for example, only W. T. Conner preserved the founder's millennial views.[39] In addition, a few other Southern Baptists, William Poteat in particular, came to postmillennialism through the Social Gospel's advocacy of earthly reform as the precursor of the millennium.[40]

---

[35]Thomas T. Martin, *The Second Coming of Christ* (n. p., ca. 1922), pp. 6-7.

[36]M. H. Duncan, "Law and Grace: His Second Coming," pp. 1-2, undated typescript, Norris Papers, Box 11.

[37]Amzi C. Dixon, "Why I Am a Premillennialist," *Moody Bible Institute Monthly* (August 1925): 536, clipping, Dixon Papers, Box 12.

[38]*Fundamentalist*, 21 August 1931, p. 7; Martin, *The Second Coming of Christ*, pp. 6-7.

[39]W. T. Conner, *A System of Christian Doctrine* (Nashville: Sunday School Board, 1924), p. 533.

[40]William L. Poteat, *The Way of Victory* (Chapel Hill: University of North Carolina Press, 1929).

While most Baptist leaders rejected postmillennialism, they also dismissed the opposing theory as unnecessary for orthodox Christianity. They downgraded the millennial issue, taking an "amillennial" position that combined belief in Christ's return with a refusal to place it either before or after the millennium.[41] Realizing the potential disruptiveness of premillennialism, denominational spokesmen advanced a noncontroversial view with which most Baptists could agree. The confession of faith approved in 1925 by the Southern Baptist Convention proclaimed the certainty of Christ's return, but refused to furnish a timetable.

> The New Testament teaches in many places the visible and personal return of Jesus to this earth. . . . The time of his coming is not revealed. . . . It is the duty of all believers to live in readiness for his coming and by diligence in good works to make manifest to all men the reality and power of their hope in Christ.[42]

This statement accurately portrayed the views of leading Baptists. E. Y. Mullins, for example, stated that "no one can make out from the New Testament beforehand exactly what the millennium is to be."[43] Oklahoma Baptist University's John Jent, in another typical statement, spoke for many Baptists when he asserted: "I do not regard the Millen[n]ium or Second Coming as a FUNDAMENTAL DOCTRINE."[44]

In spite of the popularity of their views, amillennial Baptists could not dismiss premillennialism as merely the bizarre theory of a handful of fanatics. Fundamentalists claimed widespread support for their position, a Louisianian announcing that "the masses of Baptist people in the South are premillennialists."[45] Toward the end of the 1920s, as premillennialists stepped up their campaign, Baptist preachers found vast audiences eager to hear of the earth's coming destruction. Norris, the most popular of these doomsayers, exclaimed that Texas had been seized by a premil-

---

[41]Emmett H. Cantwell, "Millennial Teachings among Major Southern Baptist Theologians from 1845 to 1945" (Th. M. thesis, Southwestern Baptist Theological Seminary, 1960), p. 90.

[42]SBC, *Annual*, 1925, p. 73.

[43]Mullins to J. Frank Norris, 3 July 1924, Mullins Papers, 1924-1925 Correspondence.

[44]Jent to Lee Scarborough, 28 April 1922, Scarborough Papers.

[45]W. H. Horton to Lee Scarborough, 27 March 1922, Scarborough Papers.

lennial fervor that "is sweeping the state like a prairie fire."[46] Norris can be faulted for his usual extravagance, but his statement contains an essential truth: premillennialism appealed to many Southern Baptists. The premillennial message held out alluring simplicities to people confused by such portentous events as World War I and the Depression. Fundamentalists capitalized on the unrest and uncertainty of the 1920s; their claims proved to be more than idle boasting.

Ultimately the significance of premillennialism lay not in the number of Baptists who accepted it, but in how those who did related it to their broader religious views. Fundamentalists allowed it to overshadow everything else, premillennialism becoming the test of orthodoxy and the single ray of light in a world of darkness. The doctrine thus alienated them from their fellow Baptists. Non-fundamentalist Baptists who adopted premillennialism managed to take it in stride, integrating it into their religious system without becoming obsessed with it. P. I. Lipsey and James Gambrell personified this strain of Baptist thought. Both men handled premillennialism with discretion, careful not to become preoccupied with it or to allow it to drive a wedge between them and other Baptists. Gambrell cautioned against extremism, illustrating his warning with the story of a Mississippian who became so caught up in an attempt to divine signs of the end of time that he identified the seven-headed, ten-horned beast of Revelation as Mississippi College, a Baptist school with seven departments and ten teachers.[47] In contrast to fundamentalists, Lipsey and Gambrell continued to fellowship with Baptists who refused to commit themselves on the millennial issue. All Southern Baptist fundamentalists were premillennialists, but, as Lipsey and Gambrell showed, not all premillennialists accepted the militant, uncompromising views of fundamentalism.

Fundamentalists further distinguished themselves from other Baptist premillennialists by teaching a variety known as dispensationalism. Dispensationalism arose in England in the 1840s, expounded by John Nelson Darby and the Plymouth Brethren. This doctrine reached the United States at mid-century and gradually displaced the premillennialism of the Millerites. By the twentieth century it had become the dominant strain of American premillennialism, attaining its most thorough

---

[46]Norris to U.S. Pawkett, 1 August 1931, Norris Papers, Box 34.

[47]*Messenger*, 4 August 1920, p. 4; *Record*, 13 April 1922, p. 4.

expression in the reference Bible published by C. I. Scofield in 1909. Scofield divided world history into seven ages or *dispensations*, each beginning with God's establishment of a covenant with man and ending with God's judgment upon mankind for failure to abide by the agreement. Dispensationalists believed that man now dwelt in the sixth dispensation, soon to be ended by the Second Coming and establishment of the millennium, the seventh and final period in the earth's history.[48]

Fundamentalists readily embraced this innovation. J. Frank Norris, for example, urged Baptists to read the Scofield Bible, because "there can be no adequate understanding or rightly dividing of the Word of God except from the standpoint of dispensational truth." Other fundamentalist leaders similarly advertised their acceptance of dispensationalism by using and promoting Scofield's volume. Clarence Stealey touted the book in the *Baptist Messenger* and stocked it in the journal's bookstore. T. T. Martin, owner of two well-thumbed Scofield Bibles, displayed their influence in his book *The Second Coming of Christ*. In addition to Scofield, fundamentalists also derived dispensational teachings from the writings of James R. Graves, the most prominent Southern Baptist premillennialist of the nineteenth century.[49]

Dispensationalism's most important feature for Baptist fundamentalism was its conception of the Church. The "Church" in dispensational language referred not to Baptists, Methodists, Presbyterians, or Episcopalians, but to the faithful few whom God gathered out of these denominations to await the Second Coming. This teaching weakened denominational loyalties, for dispensationalists believed that God's chosen ones should fellowship together, regardless of their ties with institutional churches. Dispensationalists did not necessarily interpret this to mean that the saved should form an interdenominational organization; rather, they believed that a bond existed among the righteous that led to an ebbing of denominational consciousness.[50]

---

[48]Ernest R. Sandeen, *The Roots of Fundamentalism: British and American Millenarianism, 1800-1930* (Chicago: University of Chicago Press, 1970), pp. 59-102; C. Norman Kraus, *Dispensationalism in America: Its Rise and Development* (Richmond: John Knox, 1958), pp. 19, 43, 72, 104, 115-17.

[49]*Searchlight*, 12 February 1926, p. 1; *Messenger*, 11 October 1922, p. 14; Thomas T. Martin, *Viewing Life's Sunset from Pikes Peak: Life Story of T. T. Martin*; ed. A. D. Muse (Louisville: pub. by the editor, n. d.), p. 223; Martin, *The Second Coming of Christ*, p. 15; Duncan, "Law and Grace," p. 5.

[50]Kraus, *Dispensationalism in America*, pp. 106-109.

Baptist dispensationalist A. C. Dixon frequently ignored denominational barriers, contending that "the mission of the Spirit and the gospel is to gather out a people" for the day of Christ's return. Dixon played an active role in the early interdenominational effort to combat modernism, participating in Bible conferences, being pastor of the Moody Church in Chicago from 1906 to 1911, and editing the first five volumes of *The Fundamentals*. After World War I he cooperated with the World's Christian Fundamentals Association, lectured at the Bible Institute of Los Angeles, and raised funds for the Paris Tabernacle, an interdenominational institution established by French fundamentalist Reuben Saillens. As pastor of Baltimore's University Baptist Church from 1922 until his death in 1925, Dixon labored to impress Baptists with the need to "join with other evangelical churches" in offering "testimony to the fundamentals of Christianity." He further promoted this effort by welcoming into his pulpit such prominent non-Baptists as William Jennings Bryan and Princeton Professor Robert Dick Wilson. Although he began and ended his career as a pastor of Southern Baptist churches, A. C. Dixon, true to dispensationalist dictates, refused to restrict his ministry to Baptists.[51]

J. Frank Norris also looked beyond his denomination, but unlike Dixon, he agonized over the conflict between his identification as a Southern Baptist and his desire to forge a broader alliance of God's people. Throughout the 1920s he fluctuated between these two poles. Following accepted fundamentalist practice, he established a Bible institute in Fort Worth in 1920, featuring such non-Baptist guest lecturers as Presbyterian Mark A. Matthews, Anglican J. Stuart Holden, and James M. Gray of the Moody Institute. In the early 1920s Norris entered the highest ranks of interdenominational fundamentalism, playing an important role in the World's Christian Fundamentals Association and establishing ties with fundamentalists of other churches. He became increasingly disenchanted with the Southern Baptist Convention and began to envision a new Baptist body, cleansed of modernism and headed by himself.[52] His cooperation with interdenominational fundamentalism

---

[51]Dixon, "Why I Am a Premillennialist," 536; Dixon to Reuben Saillens, 1 April 1922, Dixon Papers, Box 10; Dixon to Members of the University Baptist Church, 1922, Box 30; Helen Dixon, *A. C. Dixon: A Romance of Preaching* (New York: G. P. Putnam's, 1931), p. 286; leaflet announcing a series of lectures delivered by Wilson, Box 30.

[52]*Searchlight*, 27 May 1920, p. 1; Tatum, *Conquest or Failure?*, p. 198.

and his attacks on Southern Baptists led to his ouster from the Baptist General Convention of Texas. Following his expulsion, he alternated between asserting his strong ties with the denomination and calling for a complete break with Southern Baptists.[53] On the one hand, he continued to attend the annual meetings of Texas Baptists and remarked in 1929: "I expect to stay with the Baptists, have never had any other intention, and if anything I am stronger in that conviction today than ever."[54] At the same time, he contended that "denomination" was an unscriptural term, insisted that he harbored no desire to rejoin the Texas convention, and predicted: "I think there is a complete separation coming everywhere, and it is only a question of time until the fundamentalists of all denominations will be together." Norris's vision of a broader fellowship won out; in 1931 he announced that premillennialists could no longer participate in the Southern Baptist program, and three years later he established a new religious organization, the Premillennial Baptist Missionary Fellowship.[55] But as the name indicates, Norris retained his ambivalence even in the act of breaking with Southern Baptists. His dispensationalist side convinced him of the need for a community of fellow believers, but he could not reject his Baptist heritage completely in the interests of a broad union of fundamentalists.

The majority of Southern Baptists rejected such challenges to denominationalism, for they believed that "a denominationalized Christianity . . . is yet the strongest expression of Christianity."[56] Entering the twenties with a heightened sense of mission, they maintained that their denominational organization would best serve to spread God's truth to a sin-filled world. Nothing must be done to divide or weaken the Southern Baptist Convention, they argued. The first challenge came from Christianity's left wing, from liberals advocating church union in the interests of fellowship among Protestants. During 1919 and 1920 Baptists battled

---

[53]Texas, *Annual*, 1923, pp. 18-24; Norris to E. M. Francis, 11 July 1927, Norris Papers, Box 13.

[54]Norris to Luther J. Holcomb, 27 September 1929, Norris Papers, Box 17.

[55]*Fundamentalist*, 22 April 1927, p. 8; Norris to George Truett, Lee Scarborough, and Joseph Dawson, n. d., Norris Papers, Box 2; Norris to W. W. Bustard, 12 December 1927, Box 2; *Encyclopedia of Southern Baptists*, 2 vols. (Nashville: Broadman Press, 1958). 2:983.

[56]Lee R. Scarborough, *Christ's Militant Kingdom: A Study in the Trail Triumphant* (New York: George H. Doran Co., 1924), pp. 137-38.

these proponents of interdenominationalism, especially those affiliated with the Inter-Church World Movement. This defensiveness continued throughout the decade, leading Baptists to reject cooperation with the Federal Council of Churches and other ecumenical organizations. Within the denomination, Baptists looked suspiciously upon men such as McNeill Poteat, who considered taking a post with the interdenominational Christian Literature Society and advocated employing non-Baptist teachers in China's Shanghai Baptist College. Few Baptists agreed with Poteat; the official policy remained one of non-cooperation with movements to encourage Christian unity.[57]

Most Southern Baptists viewed the right-wing challenge as hostilely as they did the liberal threat. J. B. Rounds, Oklahoma's secretary of missions, called fundamentalism the "fly in the ointment" of Baptist denominationalism.[58] Criticism of Southern Baptist fundamentalism's leading spokesmen, Dixon and Norris, also attested to concern over the undermining of Baptist loyalty. James Love publicly assailed Dixon, asserting that "the denomination wants its orthodoxy championed in the name of the denomination and within the denomination."[59] Even Dixon's efforts to unite Southern Baptist fundamentalists met rebuff; two Marylanders rejected his overtures, arguing that the proposed union would create discord within the denomination.[60] Norris received even harsher rebukes. Eugene Alldredge charged him with deliberately weakening the denomination to make it easy prey for interdenominationalism.[61] Lee Scarborough labeled Norris a heretic who accepted Campellites and Methodists into his church without rebaptism, promoted Protestant union, and allowed a Methodist preacher to occupy the pulpit of Fort Worth's First Baptist Church.[62] Attacks on interdenomina-

---

[57]George Truett to C. W. Knight, 27 February 1929, Truett Papers; T. B. Ray to Edwin McNeill Poteat, Jr., 30 March 1926, E. M. Poteat, Jr., Papers, Box 1; Poteat to Ray, 29 June 1928, Box 1.

[58]*Messenger*, 5 April 1928, p. 8.

[59]*Herald*, 3 January 1924, p. 4.

[60]R. H. White to Dixon, 10 January 1924; W. H. Baylor to Dixon, 9 January 1924, Dixon Papers, Box 11.

[61]Alldredge to L. L. Gwaltney, 21 November 1922, Alldredge Papers, Box 13; *Messenger*, 1 March 1922, p. 14.

[62]Scarborough to J. D. Sandifer, 25 November 1921; Scarborough to T. T. Martin, 21 January 1922, Scarborough Papers.

tionalism came from other than critics of Dixon and Norris; fundamentalists also testified to the compelling force of church loyalty. Clarence Stealy—fundamentalist and dispensationalist—reproved the World's Christian Fundamentals Association for its interdenominationalism and insisted that a union of anti-modernist forces would have to await the conversion of all fundamentalists to the Baptist faith.[63]

As Stealey's position suggests, most Baptist fundamentalists stopped short of Norris's solution: a new religious fellowship based on premillennialism. When Norris set up his organization in 1934 he took with him few of the men who had joined his crusade against modernism. The ties with the Southern Baptist Convention were too strong for most fundamentalists to break. Norris's attitude toward the Baptist denomination both strengthened and weakened his movement. His emphasis on the community of interests among fundamentalists did indeed give his followers a sense of participation in a broad-based crusade for Christ. But Norris's break with the Southern Baptist Convention alienated many of his followers and sympathizers, causing them to reaffirm their commitment to the denominational program. During the 1920s, though, the questioning of denominational bonds formed an important part of Southern Baptist fundamentalism.

Historians and sociologists have often overlooked the importance of premillennialism and interdenominationalism in analyzing the fundamentalist movement, focusing instead on the clash between city and countryside and concluding that fundamentalism formed part of the rural revolt against urban dominance. This explanation took root during the 1920s and has preserved its vitality over the fifty years since the decade ended. No single writer initiated this thesis; it appeared simultaneously among a number of contemporary observers. Dartmouth College sociologist John M. Mecklin and French political scientist André Siegfried set the pattern for social scientists by interpreting fundamentalism as the offspring of rural resentment. Students of American religion agreed with this view; Stewart Cole, a doctoral candidate at the University of Chicago, pointed out the lingering "ecclesiastical" control of society in the South and rural North, and H. Richard Niebuhr of Yale Divinity School argued that "in the social sources from which it drew its strength fundamentalism was closely related to the conflict between rural and urban cultures in

---

[63]*Messenger*, 11 May 1921, p. 8.

America."[64] These early studies laid the basis for an enduring attitude toward fundamentalism. Other views of the movement have been advanced, notably Ernest Sandeen's attempt to direct scholars to an examination of fundamentalist theology, but the rural-urban thesis has become entrenched in the scholarly and popular mind. During the past twenty years studies of the fundamentalist controversy, works on antievolutionism, histories of American religion, and examinations of the 1920s have produced continuing support for the rural interpretation.[65] The thesis has gained such widespread popularity that it must be reckoned with in any assessment of fundamentalism.

The Southern Baptist denomination presents a special problem in analyzing the rural influence upon fundamentalism, since most of the South's Baptists lived on farms or in small towns. Virtually all Southern Baptists cherished the rural values of an older America, but only a minority took up the cause of organized fundamentalism. Rural antagonism toward urban America, while helping to explain why the denomination remained conservative in an age of theological change, does not explain the rise of Norris's movement within the Southern Baptist Convention. Norris unquestionably directed a special appeal to the South's rural Baptists, the "boys at the forks of the creek," as he called them. Norris referred to himself as "just an ordinary, country Baptist preacher" and maintained that "the greatest hope of Christianity has ever been with the country churches." He glorified country pastors, "men who are willing to eat blackeyed peas, fat meat, cornbread and drink black coffee and sleep on a pile of cotton," as mighty witnesses for God's truth and advised young preachers to find their spiritual strength in the "wilderness" as had Moses and Paul. Many Baptists responded enthusiastically to Norris's praise, coming as it did at a time when rural America labored under the city's taunts of "hick" and "hayseed." Country dwellers

---

[64]John M. Mecklin, *The Survival Value of Christianity* (New York: Harcourt, Brace, Jovanovich, Inc., 1926), p. 7; André Siegfried, *America Comes of Age: A French Analysis* (New York: Harcourt, Brace, Jovanovich, Inc., 1927), p. 43; Stewart G. Cole, "The Psychology of the Fundamentalist Movement" (Ph.D. dissertation, University of Chicago, 1929), pp. 41-42; H. Richard Niebuhr, "Fundamentalism," in Edwin R. A. Seligman and Alvin Johnson eds., *Encyclopaedia of the Social Sciences*, 15 vols. (New York: Macmillan, 1930-1935), 6:527.

[65]For examples of this, see Ray Ginger, *Six Days or Forever? Tennessee v. John Thomas Scopes* (Boston: Beacon Press, 1958), p. 63; and Winthrop S. Hudson, *Religion in America* (New York: Charles Scribner's Sons, 1965), p. 369.

agreed with Norris's emphasis on the importance of the country church and glowed with satisfaction when a man as important as the Fort Worth pastor extolled the glories of rural religion. Many folks from the "forks of the creek" joined Norris's crusade against modernism and urged Baptists to return to the simple verities of old-time religion.[66]

Although considerable evidence can be marshalled to support the idea that rural Baptists found fundamentalism attractive, it can easily be shown that most country dwellers remained loyal to the denominational program. In the first place, the religious census of 1926 classified seventy-two per cent of the South's Baptists as rural, and only a small number of this group could be labeled as fundamentalists. Second, rural Baptists respected the men excoriated as modernists and supported the colleges and boards castigated for undermining Baptist orthodoxy. Finally, men close to rural Baptists testified to their loyalty. Clarence Poe, editor of the *Progressive Farmer*, attested to the support given Poteat by North Carolina's Baptist farmers, and John D. Mell commented that Georgia's rural Baptists understood neither modernism nor fundamentalism and wanted nothing to do with either.[67] Even in Texas, site of Norris's greatest strength, George Truett praised the loyalty of "scores and scores of village and country preachers."[68] Although some rural Baptists supported Norris, most of them remained apart from the fundamentalist movement; only in Texas did they flock to Norris's standard in significant numbers. The rural-urban thesis helps to explain Southern Baptist conservatism in the 1920s, but it fails to account for the rise of the fundamentalist movement within the denomination.

A far more important issue arose from a group of interrelated topics involving democracy, local autonomy, and spontaneity. Norris complained early in the 1920s of the concentration of power in the hands of the Texas Baptist "machine," his designation for Lee Scarborough, George Truett, Samuel Brooks, Frank Groner, and a number of other

---

[66]*Searchlight*, 11 November 1921, pp. 1-2; Norris to Thomas A. Lyle, 23 October 1931, Norris Papers, Box 24; Norris to Wilbur McDaniel, 28 January 1931, Box 28. For one example of the response to Norris's appeal see J. H. O'Neall to Norris, 2 February 1931, Norris Papers, Box 31.

[67]Clarence Poe, *My First 80 Years* (Chapel Hill: University of North Carolina Press, 1963), p. 124; William Poteat to Charles L. Snider, 8 September 1928, W. L. Poteat Papers.

[68]Truett to J. M. Harder, 9 November 1923, Truett Papers.

leaders, charging that they had pursued a "closed Denominational policy" that had concealed the workings of the state convention from average Baptists.[69] Later in the decade Norris extended his attack to include leaders and boards of the Southern Baptist Convention, centering his most trenchant criticism on the Sunday School Board, which he accused of practicing a "centralized tyranny . . . that would make Tammany Hall blush." Of this fight, Norris commented:

> I dared to stand against the ecclesiastical dictatorship of a small bunch of tyrants in masquerade in the delivery [sic] of heaven, tyrants who had oppressed the hearts of hundreds of pastors with a relentlessness that would make Pharaoh's oppression of the children of Israel pale into insignificance.[70]

Other fundamentalists saw the same tyranny. Victor Masters charged that the Convention's executive committee threatened Baptist democracy;[71] a New Orleans Baptist perceived an attempt "to make an autocracy out of our democracy;"[72] and a Texan railed against the denomination's "half-baked, run-down[,] fizzle-threaded aristocracy."[73] This centralization of power had reached the point where the Southern Baptist Convention had begun to resemble the Papacy, some fundamentalists charged.[74] Finally, fundamentalists believed that this powerful coterie had surrendered to modernism by promoting modernist education, destroying missions work, and favoring heretical pastors. Southern Baptist leaders had usurped authority and had delivered the Convention into the clutches of modernism; if they did not "dethrone" the tyrants the fight would be lost, fundamentalists concluded.[75]

Fundamentalists countered by glorifying localism, freedom, and spontaneity. They abhorred the bureaucratization that had occurred among Southern Baptists in the twentieth century, a development most

---

[69]*Searchlight*, 6 October 1922, p. 1.

[70]Norris to M. H. Dodson, 20 August 1930, Norris Papers, Box 10.

[71]*Fundamentalist*, 6 September 1929, p. 5.

[72]P. E. Briley to Frank Norris, 28 May 1930, Norris Papers, Box 2.

[73]A. C. Maxwell to Norris, 30 March 1931, Norris Papers, Box 27.

[74]R. S. Harris, untitled essay in the Norris Papers, Box 37.

[75]Charles Alexander to Frank Norris, 28 December 1929, Norris Papers, Box 1; Reverend Taylor to Norris, ca. 1928, Box 19, Mordecai Ham to Norris, 14 February 1930, Box 18.

easily observed in the Seventy-Five Million Campaign. Fundamentalists harked back to an earlier, less complex era when the spontaneity and freedom of frontier evangelism had characterized the South's Baptists; like many Americans they found it difficult to come to terms with the twentieth century. In response, J. Frank Norris urged Baptists to decentralize, to return to the local church with its program of constant evangelism.[76] Fundamentalists complained that spiritual vitality had been supplanted by institutionalism, and that this stifling of individual initiative had weakened Baptist evangelism. As Mordecai Ham contended: "The Gospel is the good news to be realized in the next world and when you institutionalize the Lord's work it[']s 'Judaized.' "[77]

Fundamentalists wished to restore Baptist democracy which, they charged, had been subverted by an elite group of leaders. In contrast to this elitism, fundamentalists advocated an egalitarianism that stressed the importance of the "common masses," prompting Norris to remark: "On the question of big men and little men, to me there are no such distinctions."[78] Baptist fundamentalists strove to maintain the local church as a citadel of democracy and a haven for the common man. When Norris accepted the pastorate of Fort Worth's First Baptist Church in 1909 he inherited the pulpit of an urban, middle-class church dominated by a few men of wealth. For two years Norris left the congregation undisturbed, until, irritated by the complacency of his ministry, he expanded his appeal. One event symbolized his new departure.

> I went down in the poor section near the Trinity River and got a whole crowd of people with their children, and got them all up at the church one night and gave them free entertainment—ice cream was served, as well as some other things, and they got it all over that fine heavy carpet.

---

[76]Norris to Isaac Gates, 12 July 1929, Norris Papers, Box 16.

[77]Ham to Norris, 1 January 1930, Norris Papers, Box 18.

[78]Charles Alexander to Frank Norris, 25 September 1929, Norris Papers, Box 1; Norris to Joe H. Hankins, 27 December 1928, Box 17. There is a connection here between Norris's appeal and the nineteenth century movement known as Landmarkism, of which James R. Graves was the most prominent leader. Among other things, the Landmarkers protested the organizational structure of the Southern Baptist Convention. See "Landmarkism," *Encyclopaedia of Southern Baptists*, 2:757.

The next day when the diamond bedecked sisters of the
Ladies Aid came and saw how their very rich, highly colored
carpet was ruined—"It is terrible—It is terrible—It is
terrible"—"He is going to ruin our church, going to make a
regular Salvation Army out of it."[79]

Thereafter Norris combined sensationalism with a warm folksiness that
endeared him to thousands of poor and marginally poor Baptists.

A. C. Dixon, who also believed strongly in extending his ministry to
the masses, employed less dramatic measures. Upon assuming the pastorate of Baltimore's University Baptist Church, a congregation of wealth
and education, Dixon insisted that poor people be invited to join the
church, warning that "an atmosphere which keeps away the 'common
people' who heard Christ gladly . . . is, in the long run, fatal to the
prosperity of any church."[80] Fundamentalists wanted churches in which
the lowliest Baptist could mix with college graduates and not feel resented, where the congregation comprised "one big family" with "sweet
and beautiful" fellowship.[81]

Southern Baptists outside the fundamentalist circle refused to allow
Norris a monopoly on democracy and the masses. The Southern Baptist
Convention, through its boards and committees, sounded the democratic
theme throughout the 1920s, and the Convention's presidents concurred.[82] At the outset of the decade, James Gambrell praised political and
religious democracy, asserting that "all the people have more sense than
some of the people," and E. Y. Mullins advocated spiritual democracy
because all men "are equidistant from God." Two other Convention
presidents, George McDaniel and George Truett, expressed similar opinions, McDaniel viewing the common people as a bulwark against heresy,
and Truett proclaiming that "the day of the reign of the common people
is everywhere coming like the rising tides of the ocean."[83] Although not a
president of the Convention in the 1920s, Lee Scarborough wielded as

---

[79]Norris, *Inside History*, pp. 41-43, 105ff.

[80]Dixon to Joshua Levering, 29 September 1921, Dixon Papers, Box 30.

[81]L. S. Cole to Frank Norris, 27 May 1930, Norris Papers, Box 5; Norris to Mrs.
Herman Baker, 18 September 1930, Box 2.

[82]SBC, *Annual*, 1919, p. 70; 1920, p. 57; 1928, pp. 32, 389; 1929, p. 88.

[83]Ibid., 1919, p. 22; *Herald*, 5 July 1928, pp. 5, 8; George W. McDaniel, *The Supernatural Jesus* (Nashville: Sunday School Board, 1924), p. 168; *Herald*, 8 July 1920, p. 6.

much influence as any Southern Baptist; he, too, in numerous books published after World War I, honored the common folk and extolled democracy.[84] This commitment appeared also among the denomination's leading educators, learned and scholarly men who conceivably might have been tinged with elitism. For example, Southwestern Seminary's W. T. Conner offered a theological justification for democratic church organization; and W. O. Carver proudly identified himself with men of all classes.[85] In short, non-fundamentalists asserted their belief in democracy and their love of the masses as eagerly as did the fundamentalists.

How, in light of this, could fundamentalists rail against "ecclesiastical tyranny" and "machine rule"? Some Baptists dismissed such charges as nothing more than the false accusations of chronically discontented men intent on wrecking the Southern Baptist Convention. A Texan labeled Norris and his followers "a typical Jim Ferguson bunch,"[86] a reference to the controversial Texas governor who had ridden a wave of rural dissatisfaction into office in 1914, only to be impeached in 1917. A similar image sprang to the mind of a North Carolinian who, upon learning of fundamentalist depredations in South Carolina, wrote to William McGlothlin: "I suppose it has been a little case of Bleasism and primitive Tillmanism overflowing into Baptist life."[87] Opponents of fundamentalism contended that Norris's charges stemmed from the inferiority and resentment he felt in the presence of denominational scholars and statesmen.[88] Scarborough added that Norris's accusations demonstrated the embittered jealousy of one excluded from the highest councils of Baptist life.[89]

As much as some Baptists wanted to write off Norris's crusade as a false issue, the matter resisted such simplification. Norris had in fact raised a legitimate question. When he spoke of machine rule, centraliza-

---

[84]For a typical statement by Scarborough see *Christ's Militant Kingdom*, p. 38.

[85]Walter T. Conner, *Gospel Doctrines* (Nashville: Sunday School Board, 1925), pp. 123-25; W. O. Carver, *Out of His Treasure: Unfinished Memoirs* (Nashville: Broadman Press, 1956), p. 51.

[86]R. E. Bell to Samuel Brooks, 3 October 1927, Brooks Papers, File Di-Faculty.

[87]R. L. Bolton to McGlothlin, 18 December 1930, William J. McGlothlin Papers, Dargan-Carver Library (microfilm), Reel 1.

[88]Mr. and Mrs. R. T. Smith to Samuel Brooks, 26 October 1924, Brooks Papers, File Di-Faculty.

[89]Scarborough to J. D. Sandifer, 1 November 1921, Scarborough Papers.

tion, and loss of democracy he articulated anxieties that nagged many Baptists outside the fundamentalist circle. These men realized that the individualism and local autonomy of the nineteenth-century church had been weakened by the quest for efficiency, organization, and central control, and that the large masses had been neglected in the haste to train experts in everything from Sunday School management to fund raising. As the denomination had grown and broadened its vision to include the entire world, it had begun to place greater emphasis on boards and committees. By the 1920s a non-fundamentalist such as A. T. Jamison, president of the South Carolina convention, could lament that "the menace that is apparent at present is the loss of the democratic spirit."[90] Other non-fundamentalists viewed the trend with equal alarm. Robert E. Smith, Texas author of a biting critique of his denomination, asserted that "our *theory* of Baptist democracy is as beautiful as God's stars, but our *practice* falls pathetically short."[91] Smith buttressed his argument by citing the control of Baptist periodicals by small cliques, the rise of powerful deacons, and the proliferation of denominational bureaucracy.

Such criticism from a Texan could always be attributed to one who had fallen under the sway of J. Frank Norris, but nothing could blunt the words of Robert Pitt, one of the most influential Southern Baptist moderates of the 1920s. Writing in 1920, he advised Southern Baptists:

> As we work together for more effective organization of our Baptist forces in our States and in our Southern Convention let us be careful lest in our natural reaction from a loose-jointed, free-and-easy democracy we go into something closely akin to autocracy or at any rate to oligarchy or bureaucracy. . . . Freedom is the native air of the sound and instructed Baptist; any other air stifles and suffocates him.[92]

Pitt vigorously promoted democracy, urging Virginians to rely less on organization and more on the people, and did his personal part by "turning more and more to the simplicities, simplicities of the gospel and the simplicities of practical organization for its promotion."[93] During the

---

[90]South Carolina, *Minutes*, 1924, pp. 9, 11.

[91]Robert E. Smith, *Little Foxes in the Baptist Vineyard* (Waco: Hill Printing, 1923), pp. 18-19, 22, 27, 82; emphasis in the original.

[92]*Herald*, 24 March 1920, p. 3.

[93]Pitt to George Truett, 6 May 1930, Truett Papers.

postwar decade the warnings of Pitt and a few others validated fundamentalist charges. Norris and Pitt perceived the same truth: the denomination could not become a well-financed missionary organization,
centralized for efficiency and staffed with experts, without damaging its
standing as the champion of democracy and the masses.

In the soul-searching that accompanied the Depression of the 1930s
this became easier to see, but in the heady days of the 1920s, when world
evangelization seemed imminent, Baptists outside of Norris's alienated
flock found it a difficult proposition to accept. They failed to see the
kernel of truth in Norris's cries of machine rule. In reality, the Southern
Baptist Convention and its state counterparts did constitute "machines"
dedicated to saving lost sinners. The leaders of the denomination, opera-
tors of these machines, brooked no opposition to their aim of world
evangelization. At times, as Norris charged, the methods of enforcing
conformity bordered on the repressive. Norris's ouster from the Baptist
General Convention of Texas showed the lengths to which Baptists
would go to be rid of troublemakers. Early in 1924 Pitt, who had criticized
T. T. Martin for meddling in Baptist affairs outside his own state,
suggested to George Truett that "surely the time has long past [sic] when
Texas Baptist people ought to clear their skirts entirely of this fellow
[Norris]."[94] In the fall of 1924, with the annual meeting of Texas Baptists
set for 20 to 22 November, Samuel Brooks began a campaign to persuade
his fellow Baptists "to clear their skirts" of Norris. In letters to colleagues
he spelled out what he had in mind: through parliamentary maneuver-
ing, to prevent Norris from turning the convention into a platform from
which to expound his ideas. Baptists responded by voting Norris out of
the convention in 1924, and in 1925, when he tried to reenter, they
"squelched" him by raising a question of consideration, thereby shutting
off discussion and bringing to an immediate vote the First Baptist
Church's request for reinstatement.[95] Norris caused Texas Baptists
untold difficulties, but in cleansing themselves of him they employed
methods more suitable to politics than religion.

Fundamentalists found numerous reasons to believe that denominational leaders were trying to silence them. Rumors spread that the

---

[94]Pitt to Truett, 22 April 1924, Truett Papers.

[95]Brooks to A. A. Duncan, 6 November 1924; Brooks to Wallace Bassett, 8 October
1924; Brooks to William McGlothlin, 11 May 1926, Brooks Papers, File Di-Faculty.

Sunday School Board meant to punish Norris for refusing to use its
literature and that the denominational press, an adjunct of the board,
would not publish books written by fundamentalists. Richard Vann
threatened A. C. Dixon that if he continued to attack William Poteat the
biologist's friends would broadcast the fact that Dixon had once been
pastor of a church that practiced infant baptism. In the 1926 meeting of
the Southern Baptist Convention Kentucky fundamentalist George
Ragland attempted to present a memorial accusing E. Y. Mullins, A. T.
Robertson, and John R. Sampey of heresy. Before he could finish, L. E.
Barton called a question of consideration, preventing Ragland from
reading the paper.[96] Finally, two Baptist editors, Eugene C. Routh of the
Texas *Baptist Standard* and Clarence Stealey, editor of the Oklahoma
Baptist Messenger, experienced the power of the "machine" firsthand.
Routh proved to be too sympathetic to fundamentalism for Texas Baptist
leaders, especially Brooks, who accused Routh of promoting Norris's
cause in the *Standard*. According to Routh, his refusal to attack Norris led
to his ouster as editor.[97] Oklahoma Baptist leaders fired Stealey because of
his "obsession" with antievolutionism and his threatening gestures at
denominational solidarity. Stealey's dismissal prompted a number of
Oklahoma Baptists, who wanted the editor's fate decided by the local
churches, to charge their leaders with "reject[ing] the doctrine of soul
liberty" and "spurn[ing] the doctrine of New Testament democracy."[98]
As these cases demonstrate, state and southwide leaders, reluctant to
tolerate militant right-wing dissenters, sometimes attempted to silence
fundamentalists and their sympathizers.

The task of separating fundamentalists from their fellow Baptists is
not an easy one. To some degree, fundamentalists can be distinguished by
their outspoken opposition to modernism; they generally formed the
vanguard of the attack on Darwinism and higher criticism. But the lines
blur when one uses this to define fundamentalism, for virtually all

---

[96]J. J. Taylor to Lee Scarborough, 5 May 1922, Scarborough Papers; Charles Alexander
to Norris, 16 December 1929, Norris Papers, Box 1; Vann to Dixon, 27 January 1923,
Dixon Papers, Box 11; *Herald*, 10 June 1926, p. 8.

[97]Samuel Brooks to I. J. Van Ness, 25 November 1924, Brooks Papers, File Di-Faculty;
Eugene C. Routh, *Adventures in Christian Journalism* (Nashville: Broadman Press,
1951), pp. 39-40.

[98]James W. Bruner, *Life and Works of James W. Bruner* (Dallas: pub. by the author,
1950), pp. 76-77; *Messenger*, 7 March 1928, p. 7.

Southern Baptists rejected modernism. A more satisfactory method lies in singling out Baptists who turned their discontent over modernism inward upon their own denomination, accusing their leaders of selling out to modernism. This test presents problems as well; one did not have to be a fundamentalist to express displeasure over the teaching of evolution in Wake Forest College and Baylor University. The best means of understanding Southern Baptist fundamentalism lies in formulating a definition that combines intense, at times irrational, opposition to modernism with a group of issues that includes Frank Norris's personal influence, dispensationalism, interdenominationalism, and an emphasis on democratic church polity. Only by using such characteristics can one identify Southern Baptist fundamentalists and bring some clarity to a confusing situation.

CHAPTER 9

Urban America, Roman Catholicism and the Election of 1928

The presidential election of 1928 highlighted two more problems that plagued Southern Baptists from 1919 to 1931. The Democratic Party's nomination of Alfred E. Smith, Roman Catholic grandson of immigrants who had settled on New York City's East Side, affronted the sensibilities of rural, Old Stock, Southern Baptists. For at least a year, from the fall of 1927 until the November elections of 1928, Al Smith's assault on the verities of Southern civilization dominated their thoughts. But Smith's candidacy was only one episode in the ongoing Baptist struggle against urbanism and Roman Catholicism. The antagonism toward Catholicism, reaching back to the Protestant Reformation, had been kept alive by centuries of hostility between Protestants and Catholics. This antipathy had been stirred anew in nineteenth-century America—in the 1840s by the influx of Irish Catholics and from 1880 until World War I by a wave of Roman Catholics from Southern and Eastern Europe. These immigrants exacerbated Protestant anxieties by settling in urban areas, thereby linking Catholicism and immigration with rural America's fear of the city. The addition of strange tongues and alien religions to the urban scene convinced country dwellers of the truthfulness of a tenet they had cherished since the earliest days of the Republic. They believed with Thomas Jefferson that cities, with their crowded masses engaged in manufactures, were a blight upon the land, and that "those who labor in the earth are the chosen people of God."[1] This long-standing antiurbanism, combined with an even older antipathy toward Roman Catholicism, formed the background for the election of 1928.

Al Smith's urban origins especially disturbed Southern Baptists, who belonged to one of the most solidly rural groups in the United States. In 1926 seventy-two per cent of those affiliated with the Southern Baptist Convention lived in the open country or in towns of less than 2,500 people; ten years later sixty-two per cent of the denomination's membership still resided in rural areas.[2] More important, the 986,000 Baptists who lived in Southern cities often differed little from their rural brethren. Many of them had only recently forsaken the farm for the city, and once in the city they joined churches that maintained the warmth and folksiness of country congregations. Urban pastors such as Sparks W. Melton of Norfolk, Virginia, and William W. Weeks of Richmond admonished their flocks in sermons replete with the imagery of plowing, planting, and harvesting, and George Truett of Dallas, Texas, presided over a large urban congregation with the "reverent informality" of a country church.[3]

This rustic cast resulted from the "rural lag" in Southern cities. Recent migrants clung to their upbringing, preserving the traditions of provincial America in the heart of the South's largest cities. This was especially noticeable in the 1920s, because Southern urbanization did not begin on a significant scale until World War I.[4] The South's cities differed from those of the North, justifying Edd Winfield Parks's 1934 statement that "at present they remain a group apart, . . . stamped with the

---

[1]Thomas Jefferson, *Notes on the State of Virginia* (New York: Harper and Row, 1964), pp. 157-58.

[2]U.S. Bureau of Census, *Religious Bodies* (1926) 2:103; (1936) 2:1:114.

[3]Sparks W. Melton, *Will He Find Faith?* (Nashville: Broadman Press, 1934), pp. 40-41; William W. Weeks, *The Face of Christ* (Nashville: Sunday School Board, 1927), pp. 43-44; Powhatan W. James, *George W. Truett: A Biography* (New York: Macmillan Co., 1939), p. 162.

[4]T. Lynn Smith, "The Emergence of Cities," in Rupert B. Vance and Nicholas J. Demerath eds., *The Urban South* (Chapel Hill: University of North Carolina Press, 1954), pp. 24-37; Gerald M. Capers, "The Rural Lag on Southern Cities," *Mississippi Quarterly* 21 (Fall 1968): 253-61.

atmosphere of an old South."[5] The transformation of country "hicks" into urbanites proceeded slowly in this environment.

As heirs of rural cultural traditions, Southern Baptists shared the fear and distrust of cities that typified rustic America. They often talked about the pitfalls of the city and endlessly listed its faults. Immorality and worldliness plagued the entire nation, but they thrived best in "cesspools of iniquity and sin" found in "metropolitan centers." "Commercialized vice" flourished in dance halls, movie houses, and gambling dens that pulsed with activity even on Sunday.[6] These instruments of the devil thrived on the city's worship of money, for urbanites measured everything by its material worth. New York City illustrated this: the "stress and strain" of its "commercial life" had destroyed spirituality; "mammon," as a North Carolinian pointed out, had "done its dirty work in that American Babylon." Along with everything else, politicians had their price, and the "stench of American municipal government" attested to the existence of widespread corruption.[7]

The flagrant bribery of politicians, judges, and policemen contributed to another urban defect: daily disregard of the law accompanied by rising crime rates. The pitifully weak enforcement of Prohibition best demonstrated the breakdown of law and order, Baptists contended, but it also appeared in such heinous crimes as the hammer bludgeoning of a young Chicago boy. Horrified by such occurrences, Southern Baptists agreed with A. T. Robertson that "there are schools of crime in the large cities."[8]

---

[5]Edd Winfield Parks, "Southern Towns and Cities," in William T. Couch, ed., *Culture in the South* (Chapel Hill: University of North Carolina Press, 1934), p. 518. Blaine A. Brownell has recently argued against this idea in *The Urban Ethos in the South, 1920-1930* (Baton Rouge: Louisiana State University Press, 1975). Brownell presents his case well, but limits his study to Atlanta, Birmingham, Memphis, Nashville, and New Orleans. Moreover, too much evidence exists to the contrary to accept in total his thesis that Southern cities in the 1920s did not differ appreciably from those elsewhere in the nation. Brownell's greatest contribution has been to open a debate that other urban historians need to join.

[6]Alabama, *Annual*, 1931, p. 22; SBC, *Annual*, 1922, pp. 75-76; *Herald*, 9 January 1929, p. 9.

[7]R. L. Bolton to William Poteat, 30 December 1931, W. L. Poteat Papers; *Herald*, 9 January 1929, p. 9; Victor I. Masters, *The Call of the South* (Atlanta: Home Mission Board, 1920), p. 213; SBC, *Annual*, 1920, pp. 75-76.

[8]SBC, *Annual*, 1922, p. 76; *Messenger*, 22 December 1926, p. 2; Archibald T. Robertson, *Paul and the Intellectuals: The Epistle to the Colossians* (Garden City: Doubleday, Doran, 1928), p. 176.

Criminality ran rampant in part because the city cheapened human life by encouraging impersonality and disregard of others. It demanded selfish attention to one's own interests and unconcern for the nameless masses that thronged urban areas. "Human sympathy tends to become atrophied" in such surroundings, Victor Masters wrote.[9] Urban man, trying to survive by his animal instincts, had no time to help others.

Baptists recognized another dangerous tendency in the city's weakening of family ties. Domesticity flourished only in the country, where families remained free of the disintegrating influences of city life. Urbanization had removed the home as the focal point, had separated parents from children, and had brought divorces and broken homes.[10] Finally, Southern Baptists believed that urbanization had created an environment hostile to evangelical Protestantism. The city's worldliness, materialism, corruption, lawlessness, and impersonality had dampened the evangelical spirit, leaving a lifeless Protestantism that downgraded doctrinal distinctiveness and practiced the ritualistic "churchianity" of Lutheranism and Episcopalianism. Roman Catholicism, Judaism, modernism, and Oriental cults thrived in this atmosphere.[11] There could be no mistake, Baptists concluded; America's cities were havens of evil and the enemies of everything cherished by rural Americans.

Although the defects of urban civilization stood exposed for all to see, thousands of Baptists, particularly the young, failed to heed the warnings and continued to migrate to cities during the 1920s. Bored with rural routine and drabness, and lured by the "spell of urban life," Baptist youth looked longingly at the "delights of the city."[12] Victor Masters understood this, writing in 1916 that:

> The beauty of plate glass, attractive shop windows, and bright eyes in the hurrying throngs, makes the blood of the country boy or girl course more quickly through the veins. The

---

[9]*Herald*, 12 March 1925, p. 9; Victor I. Masters, *Country Church in the South* (Atlanta: Home Mission Board, 1916), pp. 40-42; *Herald*, 12 March 1925, p. 9.

[10]John W. Jent, *The Challenge of the Country Church* (Nashville: Sunday School Board, 1924), p. 18; Masters, *Country Church in the South*, pp. 44-45.

[11]*Herald*, 12 March 1925, pp. 13-14; John E. White to George Truett, 16 December 1930, Truett Papers; A. C. Dixon to M. G. Kyle, 20 March 1923, Dixon Papers, Box 10; SBC, *Annual*, 1922, pp. 75-76.

[12]Jent, *The Challenge of the Country Church*, p. 18; Virginia, *Minutes*, 1930, pp. 139-40.

city is to them an enchantress, a challenge to adventure. Men
like to be where big things happen. They like to take big risks
and explore the unexplored. In the city, powerful currents of
life are forever crossing and recrossing.[13]

The lure of the city created an unsettling tension among Baptists,
who knew that it contained traps for the unwary, but who also realized
that their children would readily exchange rolling hills and green mea-
dows for glittering lights and "hurrying throngs." The city's seductive-
ness and its threat to American civilization convinced Southern Baptists
that they could no longer handle the problem with rhetorical denunciations. Something concrete had to be done. The Home Mission Board
warned in 1919 that "the struggling constituencies in these urban centers
must have reinforcement if they are to hold the gates against the tides of
sin and all that is false in civilization."[14] It dawned on some Baptists that
America's future would be decided in her cities; not even the South would
remain rural forever. Baptists should not despair, they counseled, but
should interpret this as an opportunity to spread the gospel into mission
fields that lay as close as the nearest metropolis. Jesus had wept over
Jerusalem and had died for it, and the Apostle Paul, believing that if he
won the city the country would follow, had carried his message to
population centers rimming the Mediterranean Sea.[15] The South's Baptists must follow this example, a writer advised in the Oklahoma *Baptist
Messenger*, and "see" the city, "sorrow over it," and "save it." "The crying
need of the hour in every city," he concluded, "is for men who are set for
the salvation of their fellows and the honor of God."[16]

Southern Baptists did not know exactly how to cope with the city, but
they felt that they had to combat urban wickedness and reach the
unchurched masses. Some Baptists sought a solution in the training of
specialists in Sunday School and youth work who could attack the problem by winning young people to Christ.[17] A second approach lay in the
Baptist city councils that had begun in Richmond, Virginia, in 1904 and

---

[13]Masters, *Country Church in the South*, pp. 39-40.

[14]SBC, *Annual*, 1919, p. 78.

[15]*Herald*, 14 August 1930, pp. 14-15; SBC, *Annual*, 1922, p. 76.

[16]*Messenger*, 20 August 1919. p. 6.

[17]Virginia, *Minutes*, 1921, p. 50.

had spread to other Southern cities. These councils established outposts where dedicated men and women witnessed for Christ.[18] A third means, best exemplified by Baptist work in New Orleans, called for spreading the gospel from Baptist institutions located in metropolitan areas. The New Orleans Baptist Bible Institute, founded in 1919, served as a base for assaults on urban sinfulness. By 1926 the school's trustees claimed that the Institute had played a vital role in increasing New Orleans' Baptist population from 1200 to 4500. Equally important, the establishment of a Baptist hospital had won favor for the denomination and had brought thousands under Baptist influence.[19] Institutions in other cities— Southern Seminary in Louisville, Southwestern Seminary in Fort Worth, and the Sunday School Board in Nashville—carried on similar efforts to spread the truth in their areas.

The greatest Baptist effort in the South's cities went into evangelism, the straightforward preaching of the gospel to win the lost to Christ. This offered the fastest and most dramatic means of grappling with urban sin. The author of an Alabama report on evangelism spoke for many of his fellow churchmen in 1931: "We need a living, breathing, sizzling, searching evangelism to cope with the situation within the hospitable gates of our mighty cities and larger towns."[20] The Home Mission Board followed this policy throughout the 1920s, holding major evangelistic campaigns in most of the South's important cities. The success of these meetings convinced Southern Baptists that "this is the very best way to reach the hurrying throngs in these centers of population."[21]

Southern Baptists remained loyal to their principles in relying on evangelism. For the trouble lay in men and not in the structural weaknesses of society, they contended; win enough souls to Christ and the root problem of the city would be solved. The simplicity of this solution encouraged some Baptists to argue that the denomination's program for urban salvation "is the brightest and most hopeful aspect of Baptist work in the nation today."[22] But the situation did not produce optimism among

---

[18]*Herald*, 3 February, 1921, pp. 8-9.

[19]SBC, *Annual*, 1926, pp. 38, 62-63.

[20]Alabama, *Annual*, 1931, pp. 22-23.

[21]SBC, *Annual*, 1920, pp. 417-18.

[22]Eugene P. Alldredge, *The New Challenge of Home Mission* (Nashville: Sunday School Board, 1927), p. 75.

all Baptists. A more realistic assessment came from a representative of the Baptist city councils who addressed the Southern Baptist Convention at its 1922 session in Jacksonville, Florida "Our Baptist City Councils stagger under this load of responsibility," he said, "and in despair cry out 'What is the use; ours is an impossible task; who even dares to hope or pray for a Christian City?' "[23] Baptists fluctuated between these two poles in the 1920s. They recognized the innumerable and seemingly incorrectable flaws in urban civilization and the menace they posed to America and the South, but at the same time, Baptists could not help but believe that the city could be mastered if enough urbanites received the message of redemption. Whatever their attitude, Baptists could not get the subject off their minds during the twenties. The city served as a constant reminder of the wickedness of man, thus spurring the denomination to evangelize the unsaved.

If the city called up images of immorality, lawlessness, and corruption, the country induced visions of "clean sweet air," "mellow and fragrant soil," and a land with "its crops so heavy, its hay so high, its apples so red, its grapes so blue and its honey so sweet, that it is truly a marvel to everyone who beholds it."[24] Baptist idealization of the rural setting partook of a time-honored American tradition of veneration of the countryside and its inhabitants. Behind this lay a religious rationale. God had meant for man to live in pastoral surroundings, Baptists said, for he had housed Adam and Eve in idyllic splendor in the Garden of Eden. The human race had originated amidst trees, flowers, birds, and animals; not until sin had robbed mankind of its innocence had cities sprung up.[25] The Garden of Eden continued to serve as the image of the perfect environment, part of the heritage man had forfeited in his fall from grace. The rural South was not Eden, but it approximated the ideal more closely than the cities that dominated America. Although the perfection of Eden no longer existed, one could at least thankfully say: "How delightful is a country home; remote from the bustle of towns and cities, with a spring near by."[26]

---

[23]SBC, *Annual*, 1922, p. 76.

[24]William L. Poteat, "Thanksgiving Prayer," ca. 1930, copy in the W. L. Poteat Papers; Carl F. McCool to E. E. Lee, 9 May 1925, Edgar E. Lee Papers, Dargan-Carver Library, Box 6.

[25]Weeks, *The Face of Christ*, p. 110.

[26]*Herald*, 18 December 1919, p. 3.

Life in the country offered numerous advantages, Baptists declared. It produced liberty-loving men of strong character, and "health, happiness, and usefulness" awaited those who geared their lives to the rhythms of the natural world.[27] John Jent, professor of sociology at Oklahoma Baptist University, listed the many benefits of country life in a book published in 1924. They included proximity to nature, freedom from urban social ills, "independence and individual initiative," economic opportunity, "fraternal sentiment and sympathy," and an agreeable setting in which to raise a family.[28] Victor Masters, propagandist for provincial America in the 1920s, penned his most important appreciation of rural life in his 1916 book *Country Church in the South*. Labeling agriculture "the most fundamental and permanent of human pursuits," Masters contended that the countryman had provided the bedrock of all civilizations, and that "the self-reliance, the physical stamina, and the stalwart moral force" of rural dwellers undergirded the American Republic.[29]

The most important advantage of country living came from its conduciveness to evangelical religion, Southern Baptists said, for "the nearer one keeps to nature, the easier it is for him to keep in touch with nature's Creator."[30] Country people displayed a "zeal for God" and a reverence for "the sacred things of life" that made them more religious than their urban brethren. In the unhurried atmosphere of the country, men had time to contemplate spiritual matters, while the isolation of rural life made them eager to attend church.[31] As a preacher remarked of the residents of Pittsylvania County, Virginia: "They are very appreciative and come [to church] in great numbers."[32] Above all, Baptists asserted, the spiritual strength of rural Americans demonstrated the

---

[27]Benjamin F. Proctor to Wiliam McGlothin, 13 February 1930, Truett Papers; Thomas L. Sydnor ed., *Living Epistles: the Old Guard* (Danville, Virginia: pub. by author 1924), p. 34.

[28]Jent, *The Challenge of the Country Church*, pp. 19-21.

[29]Masters, *Country Church in the South*, pp. 37-38, 45.

[30]Sydnor, *Living Epistles*, p. 33.

[31]George D. Faulkner, "The Efficient Country Church" (Th.D. thesis, Southern Baptist Theological Seminary, 1925), p. 91; George W. Gray, "Out of the Mountains Came This Great Preacher of the Plains," *American Magazine* 100 (November 1925): 147; SBC, *Annual*, 1920, p. 418.

[32]Joseph T. Watts to A. T. Robertson, 21 February 1921, Robertson Papers, Folder 1921B.

superiority of country life.

The country church formed the bedrock of the rural life praised by Southern Baptists. Baptists venerated the weathered old churches that dotted the countryside and commended their congregations for the blessings they had brought the denomination. In the first place, Baptists believed that rural and small-town congregations had preserved their doctrinal purity in an age of heresy and compromise.[33] While urban churches flirted with new ideas, country churches stuck by the old views, serving as "the stabilizing center" of Baptist "doctrinal integrity." Their evangelistic fervor and unceasing loyalty to Baptist principles had enabled them to hold on to their members while urban churches were losing theirs.[34]

A second important feature of the country church stemmed from its function as a source of pastors and members for city churches. Baptists noted that most of their urban pastors had been reared on farms or in small towns. Powhatan James, George Truett's son-in-law and biographer, remarked that "the Lord seems to specialize in country-bred fellows . . . when he is looking for preachers,"[35] and John Jent observed that "nearly all the great city pastors in the South were reared in the country."[36] The migration of rural Southerners to the city brought thousands of new members who, because of their fervor and doctrinal soundness, often became mainstays of city congregations. In addition, scores of Baptist leaders, missionaries, and denominational workers had come from unpretentious country churches.[37]

Third, Southern Baptists recognized the church's value to the rural community. It formed the focal point of people's lives, nurturing them in childhood, consecrating their marriages, and reassuring them in death. Annual revivals provided recreation and spiritual rejuvenation, and weekly services brought people together for conversation and fellowship. As sociologists pointed out, the church was often the most important

---

[33]William J. McGlothlin, "Our Rural Churches—What Have They Done?," unpaged typescript, ca. October 1931, McGlothlin Papers, Reel 2.

[34]John W. Jent, *Rural Church Development: A Manual of Methods* (Shawnee, OK: Oklahoma Baptist University Press, 1928), p. 2; *Record*, 12 June 1930, p. 2.

[35]James, *George W. Truett*, p. 67.

[36]Jent, *The Challenge of the Country Church*, p. 149.

[37]*Herald*, 21 October 1920, pp. 4-5; McGlothlin, "Our Rural Churches."

institution in the rural South. Although most Baptists failed to grasp the full sociological significance of the rural church, they sensed its importance for country life.[38]

But the much-praised country church labored under grave difficulties. As Jefferson Ray of Southwestern Seminary wrote:

> A careful and sympathetic study of the country church situation produces mingled feelings of joy and sadness, pride and shame, hope and despair. Viewed from one standpoint the situation seems good, conditions improving and the outlook hopeful, but viewed from another set of phenomena the picture is dark and the atmosphere depressing.[39]

John Jent, aware of the same distressing situation, considered it the number one issue facing Southern Baptists,[40] and the executive board of the Arkansas Baptist State Convention noted in 1919 the "desolate conditions surrounding many of our country churches."[41]

In admitting the existence of a rural church problem, Southern Baptists contributed to a body of literature that had been growing steadily since the first decade of the twentieth century. In 1908 President Theodore Roosevelt had appointed a Country Life Commission to investigate rural America's deficiencies and to suggest ways of improving country life. Although Congress had refused to appropriate funds to publish the commission's report, rural America had received new attention. As part of this interest, books analyzing the rural church had begun to appear. Works such as Warren H. Wilson's *The Church of the Open Country* (1911) and Charles O. Gill and Gifford Pinchot's *The Country Church* (1914) had examined the difficulties faced by rural congregations. Southern Baptists had joined the movement in 1916 with the publication of Victor Masters's *Country Church in the South*, and though distracted by

---

[38]*Herald*, 4 December 1930, p. 8; Edwin McNeill Poteat, Jr., "Religion in the South," in William T. Couch ed., *Culture in the South* (Chapel Hill: University of North Carolina Press, 1934), p. 518; Newell L. Sims, *Elements of Rural Sociology* (New York: Thomas Y. Crowell Co., 1928), p. 349.

[39]Jefferson D. Ray, *The Country Preacher* (Nashville: Sunday School Board, 1925), p. 43.

[40]Jent, *The Challenge of the Country Church*, p. 84.

[41]Arkansas, *Proceedings*, 1919, p. 71.

the war, they returned to the discussion in the 1920s.

The Baptist country church faced a variety of difficulties in the 1920s. The minister furnished the most pressing problem. Too few preachers existed to fill the pulpits; almost one-fifth of the denomination's country churches lacked pastors in 1922. Those churches fortunate enough to find a preacher usually had a poorly educated man who cared nothing for such programs as the Sunday School and the Baptist Young People's Union, choosing instead to devote himself to emotional sermons recounting the glories of personal redemption.[42]

Regardless of the pastor's qualifications he had little to work with. His salary was meager, the church building was often ramshackle, and his members contributed little to the church program.[43] Added to these burdens, the rural pastor and his flock often felt the sting of discrimination from some urban Baptists anxious to bury their rural pasts. "Dr. Big Reputation, pastor of Society Avenue church, in Wealthtown," sometimes scorned the humble folk of the rural South.[44]

A final problem, one often overlooked by country people, reached beyond the internal deficiencies of the church to the social and economic environment in which it existed. Leading Baptist analysts noted that the rural church had failed to keep step with the sweeping changes that had overtaken provincial America. Masters pointed out in 1916 that power machinery, automobiles, telephones, and other material benefits had transformed rural America. But the church had gone about its business as if it still ministered to a pioneer age. No longer could the rural church assume that its sole function lay in promulgating fervent evangelism; it must recognize these changes in country life and adjust itself accordingly, Masters concluded.[45] John Jent, remarking that "a pioneer church in the midst of the Twentieth Century life is a misfit, an unstable, doomed institution," contended that rural Baptists must blur the lines between the sacred and the secular. To this end, the church should take an interest

---

[42]Eugene P. Alldredge ed., *Southern Baptist Handbook 1923* (Nashville: Sunday School Board, 1924), pp. 62, 68; Edmund deS. Brunner, *Church Life in the Rural South: A Study of the Opportunity of Protestantism Based Upon Data from Seventy Counties* (New York: George H. Doran Co., 1923), p. 74; Eugene P. Alldredge, *The New Challenge of Home Missions*, pp. 140-41.

[43]Alldredge (ed.), *Handbook 1923*, pp. 71, 135-39.

[44]*Herald*, 15 May 1919, pp. 6-7.

[45]Masters, *Country Church in the South*, pp. 19, 38.

in improved roads, scientific agriculture, better schools, and the social life of rural youngsters. The country church could further help rural America adjust to the modern world by rejecting the idea that "mere emotionalism" formed the end-all of religion, Jent said.[46]

Neither Masters nor Jent advocated a rural Social Gospel that would turn the church from saving souls to reforming society, but they realized that the church could not allow itself to stagnate while the twentieth century rushed past. The church should continue to preach the gospel, but it must also become part of community life, attuned to the "secular" problems of its members.

Goaded by such men as Masters and Jent, Southern Baptists came to realize that the country church's shortcomings had to be corrected. They took seriously the warning that "to neglect our country churches and let them die is to commit *denominational suicide*."[47] For if Baptists shirked their responsibility the slack would be taken up by rural sociologists who looked upon the church as simply another institution that had to be reformed in the most efficient manner, regardless of denominational principles. Above all, the country church must be revitalized because it formed a crucial part of the scheme for world evangelization.[48] But the job would not be easy, Jent warned: "The business of Baptists in the country is not a task for a day, or a year, or a decade, but for a century—an endless task."[49]

Jent and other Baptists interested in the country church spent the 1920s conceiving and promoting solutions to its problems. They advocated consolidation of scattered churches into efficient units, urged pastors to get more education, and insisted that church finance be conducted more rationally. Organizations such as the Baptist Young People's Union and the Woman's Missionary Union should be supported by rural churches. The regular functioning of these agencies would impress rural Baptists with the need to extend religious activity beyond revivalism. These organizations would draw rural churches closer to the denomination, giving them a sense of participating in a larger body of believers.

---

[46]Jent, *Rural Church Development*, pp. 32-33, 176-78; Jent, *The Challenge of the Country Church*, p. 109.

[47]Jent, *The Challenge of the Country Church*, p. 184.

[48]Ray, *The Country Preacher*, pp. 91-92.

[49]Jent, *Rural Church Development*, p. 25.

This would erase invidious distinctions between rural and urban brethren and alleviate rural Baptists' feelings of neglect. Country church experts felt that these suggestions would strengthen the rural Baptist church and restore its preeminence within the denomination.[50]

Baptist organizations on every level sought to transform these suggestions into action. State mission boards concentrated on rural areas, colleges held country church conferences, and special training institutes produced rural Sunday School workers. Annual meetings of the Southern Baptist Convention welcomed country pastors to address the delegates on the problems of the rural church.[51] Perhaps most important, the Southern Baptist Convention sponsored a thorough study of the problem. The results, published in the 1923 edition of the *Southern Baptist Handbook*, constituted the most complete statistical survey of rural Baptist churches available in the 1920s. It provided the starting point for most of the denomination's efforts at rural church reform.

This concern over the country church produced mixed results. Baptists undoubtedly became more aware of the problem. They admitted that the country church had been neglected and realized that it would take much time and energy to solve its problems. This realization led the denomination to increase its efforts to correct the deficiencies of churches outside the cities. Although much was accomplished, too often the denomination settled for rhetorical solutions, a problem attested to by a Virginian who, after observing the Southern Baptist Convention's handling of the matter at its 1925 meeting, remarked: "But other than the fact that 'something must be done,' nothing constructive was effected."[52]

The denomination should not be judged too harshly for its failure to solve the problems of the country church, for these ills formed part of a larger pattern of rural decline. The 1920s saw the rural South in flux. Migration to the cities drained off many of the most adventurous and vigorous residents. The incursion of mechanization and technology in the form of radios, automobiles, and other appurtenances of the twentieth century disrupted the rhythm of rural life and distracted people's

---

[50]Jent, *Rural Church Development*, pp. 21-23, 181; *Herald*, 18 June 1931, p. 3; Jent, *The Challenge of the Country Church*, pp. 151, 163.

[51]Arkansas, *Proceedings*, 1923, p. 18; *Messenger*, 14 January 1920, p. 1; Virginia, *Minutes*, 1923, p. 58; *Herald*, 21 May 1925, p. 14.

[52]*Herald*, 21 May 1925, p. 14.

attention from the church. Finally, the agricultural depression of the 1920s made it more difficult for rural Baptists to support their churches. The Southern Baptist denomination stood helpless in the face of these economic and social forces. In many cases the pronouncement that "something must be done" was all that could be done. This produced anxiety and frustration among Southern Baptists, for they believed that world evangelization must be rooted in a strong rural South. Urbanization and rural decline were thus more than sociological and economic problems to Southern Baptists; they involved the denomination's ability to fulfill its destiny as God's instrument for the conversion of mankind.

Along with fears of urban dominance, Al Smith's bid for the White House raised the specter of Roman Catholicism. Baptists linked the urban and Catholic threats, for they believed that Catholicism flourished best in cities. J. Frank Norris, for example, warned that New York City had been conquered by Rome's emissaries who had turned the city into a "modern Babylon."[53] Chicago had also fallen to the enemy, a former Virginia pastor reported; the city's Catholic churches packed in tens of thousands for weekly mass, while Protestantism withered.[54] Other Baptists announced that "Roman Catholics are gaining an influence in the Capitol City which is nothing less than alarming;" through philanthropy and education, the latter centered in Georgetown and Catholic universities, the papacy had gained the upper hand in Washington, D.C. Even the South's cities had not escaped the Catholic onslaught. Baptists pointed out that the papacy had more power in New Orleans than in Rome and had attained great strength in such cities as Charleston, Mobile, and El Paso.[55]

Roman Catholic influence in America's cities stemmed largely from the presence of foreigners, some Southern Baptists maintained. Baptists of this mind equated "immigrant" with "Catholic," and found little difficulty in agreeing with evangelist Baxter McLendon's contention that three-fourths of the recent arrivals were "a foreign brood of vultures with the smell of steerage on their carcasses that say that we want the world to yield allegiance to Rome."[56] These "vultures" had flocked to America's

---

[53]*Searchlight*, 5 February 1926, p. 1.

[54]*Herald*, 12 March 1925, p. 13.

[55]SBC, *Annual*, 1921, pp. 24, 50-51; 1923, p. 300; *Searchlight*, 5 February 1926, pp. 1, 6.

[56]Baxter F. McLendon, *The Story of My Life and Other Sermons* (Bennettsville, South

cities, turning Chicago into a city dominated by the foreign-born and New York into a place where "one hears hardly any English spoken."[57] Anglo-Saxon Protestants still dominated the South's cities, but how long could they hold out? With Negroes going north, leaving opportunities for foreigners in the South, with Southern industry attracting immigrants, and with the Gulf Coast already being inundated by foreigners, the situation looked ominous.[58]

In the eyes of Southern Baptists these newcomers menaced the political, economic, moral, and religious life of the United States. They "constituted a hotbed for heresies, bad thinking, bad morals and false ideals," and were "anti-American, anti-home, anti-church, and anti-Almighty God."[59] There remained only one thing for Baptists to do; they must Americanize and Christianize these foreign hordes before they subverted Protestant, Anglo-Saxon civilization. Alabama Baptists spelled out the situation clearly in 1920:

> Immigrants from European and Oriental countries are swarming thither bringing age-old customs and traditions. ... . Thus a dilemma is before us: if conditions remain as they are and threaten—if peoples are to come to us with customs foreign to our usages and to preserve these customs among us, if we are unable to absorb these people and instill within them the ideals so precious to us, then the Old South is "not to be," and its people will be absorbed by a whirlpool the depths of which no man can now fathom.[60]

The only hope for America and the South lay in instilling Americanism and Protestantism in these immigrants.

Despite the close connections among Catholics, cities, and immigrants, the Catholic problem went beyond these associations. Baptists found a multitude of reasons, some of them unique to the 1920s, others

---

Carolina: pub. privately, 1923), p. 57.

[57]*Herald*, 12 March 1925, p. 9; Inman Johnson to A. T. Robertson, 8 September 1923, Robertson Papers, Folder 1923C.

[58]SBC, *Annual*, 1923, p. 65; Alldredge, *The New Challenge of Home Missions*, pp. 150, 283.

[59]Kentucky, *Proceedings*, 1921, p. 37; Virginia, *Minutes*, 1919, p. 88.

[60]Alabama, *Annual*, 1920, pp. 77-78.

reaching into the past, for distrusting and fearing Roman Catholicism. To begin with, World War I influenced Baptist attitudes toward Catholicism. Baptists complained that the United States government had given Catholics an unfair advantage in working with American troops both here and abroad. Federal officials had divided wartime religious work among Catholics, Jews, and Protestants, forcing Protestants to bury their differences and work together under the banner of the Young Men's Christian Association. The Knights of Columbus had been given three million dollars in government funds to carry out their camp work, Baptists charged. Worst of all, Catholics had used their favored position to ingratiate themselves with young Protestants, many of them Baptists, and to convert them to the Catholic religion. Baptists found it easy to believe the alleged boast of the hierarchy that over one hundred thousand young men had accepted Catholicism because of the diligence of Catholic workers.[61]

World War I also highlighted the contrast between Baptist democracy and Roman Catholic autocracy. Southern Baptists had taken Woodrow Wilson's call for a crusade to "make the world safe for democracy" seriously, interpreting it religiously as well as politically. They had helped to vanquish German autocracy, only to discover that the Roman Catholic Church remained an unrelenting foe of democracy and individualism. There could be no compromise between these conflicting principles, for Roman Catholicism struck Baptists as "a ghastly tyranny in the realm of the soul."[62] World War I had ended, but the religious conflict initiated by Martin Luther's ninety-five theses would rage "until every country is freed from the autocratic church of Rome." Not until their principles had triumphed would the world truly be safe for democracy, Southern Baptists concluded.[63]

A recurring theme in Baptist history has been the struggle for religious liberty. As a minority group advocating unpopular ideas, Baptists have frequently been persecuted. For this reason, they have

---

[61]SBC, *Annual*, 1919, p. 19; Alabama, *Annual*, 1919, p. 56; George W. McDaniel, *The People Called Baptists* (Nashville: Sunday School Board, 1919), pp. 129-30; Thomas T. Martin, *Viewing Life's Sunset from Pikes Peak: Life Story of T. T. Martin*; ed. A. D. Muse (Louisville: pub. by editor, n. d.), p. 160.

[62]*Herald*, 20 February 1919, p. 11; 5 July 1920, p. 5.

[63]*Record*, 9 January 1919, p. 2; James B. Gambrell, *Baptists and Their Business* (Nashville: Sunday School Board, 1919), pp. 35-36.

demanded full religious liberty and have interpreted their mission as "proclaiming, exemplifying and extending this Liberty throughout the earth."[64] The struggle against Germany reminded Southern Baptists once again that autocracy thrived on the suppression of dissent. With Germany defeated, Roman Catholicism became the villain, for, according to Baptists, it claimed to be the repository of all religious truth and advocated the persecution of dissenters. The history of the papacy attested to this, Baptists argued, for throughout its existence it had employed church courts and civil powers to stamp out heresy.[65]

Current Catholic activities convinced Baptists that little had changed. Catholic authorities in Latin America and Europe actively persecuted evangelical Protestants, with Mexico providing the best example, Baptists observed. At various times during the 1920s Mexican Catholics beat and killed Baptist pastors and laymen, dynamited churches, and destroyed the homes of church members. A Baptist missionary at Irapuato reported that a Catholic mob had "destroyed ten houses where the members of our church live, wounded six of the members, left one of them for dead and killed one of the faithful women after having tortured her in a horrible way."[66] Similar reports from Spain, Italy, and Eastern Europe confirmed suspicions that Roman Catholics had dedicated themselves to exterminating evangelical Protestants.[67]

Another reason for Baptist uneasiness arose from the prejudices, half-truths, and misunderstandings that formed the Southern Baptist conception of Roman Catholicism. Southern Baptists believed that Catholicism flourished only in an atmosphere of superstition and ignorance, because no intelligent person could accept the dogmas dictated by the pope. To ensure the ignorance of its votaries the Church forbade people to read the Bible or to pursue truth on their own.[68] Equally

---

[64]E. Y. Mullins, "Why I Am a Baptist," *Forum* 75 (May 1926): 729; Josiah W. Bailey, "Historical Testimonies to the Baptists' Contributions of Religious Liberty," ca. 1928 typescript, W. L. Poteat Papers.

[65]SBC, *Annual*, 1929, p. 257; *Herald*, 4 June 1931, p. 11; Rufus W. Weaver, "The Baptist Opportunity in a Scientific Age," p. 2, typescript dated 5 February 1932, Weaver Papers, Box 11.

[66]SBC, *Annual*, 1927, p. 254.

[67]SBC, *Annual*, 1920, p. 316; 1923, p. 114; 1925, p. 269; 1926, p. 232.

[68]*Herald*, 22 July 1926, p. 5; Jefferson Ray to F. M. McConnell, 16 January 1931, Jefferson D. Ray Papers, Southwestern Baptist Theological Seminary.

abhorrent to Baptists was the worship of idols and images which appeared in the reverence accorded the crucifix and in the worship of "gruesome" stone and wooden images of Christ. The greatest idolatry of all occurred in the mass, where participants ate the "body" of Christ.[69] The Catholic adoration of martyrs, saints, and the Virgin Mary disgusted Southern Baptists, who believed that Catholics looked to these figures for answers to their prayers. Baptists also found the asceticism of monks and nuns incomprehensible and blanched at the self-mutilation practiced by the Penitentes of New Mexico.[70] The Church's ceremonialism furnished another source of suspicion and distrust, for robed ecclesiastics, magnificent cathedrals, candlelight processions, and the ritualism of the mass contrasted sharply with the stark simplicity of the Baptist worship service.[71] And last of all, Catholicism carried strong connotations of immorality, as seen in the Baptist practice of referring to the Roman Catholic Church as a "scarlet-robed woman" with "a golden cup in her hand full of abomination and filthiness of her fornication."[72] When put together, these ideas created a powerful image of Roman Catholic wickedness and evil.

The final and most important reason for Southern Baptist fear of Roman Catholicism stemmed from the conviction that the papacy hungered for temporal power. In the words of Victor Masters: "It is a religio-political autocracy seeking to become dominant in a country whose most sacred traditions and ideals are those of democracy."[73] Not satisfied with its dominance of such benighted lands as Spain and Italy, the papacy had turned its sights on America. It intended, as the *Searchlight* showed in an editorial cartoon, to snuff out the torch of freedom held by the Statue of Liberty.[74] The Roman Catholic question thus transcended the bounds of religious disagreement for Baptists; it involved their very existence, for they believed that they would be the first to suffer should Catholics seize power in the United States.

---

[69]SBC, *Annual*, 1922, p. 241; *Herald*, 22 July 1926, pp. 4-6.

[70]SBC, *Annual*, 1919, pp. 229-30; 1922, p. 241; Robertson, *Paul and the Intellectuals*, p. 140; J. C. Owen to William McGlothlin, 30 June 1930, McGlothlin Papers, Reel 1.

[71]*Record*, 23 January 1919, p. 5.

[72]*Searchlight* 18 July 1924, p. 1; 25 July 1924, p. 1.

[73]Masters, *The Call of the South*, pp. 165-66.

[74]*Searchlight*, 24 September 1926, p. 1.

Southern Baptists offered "evidence" to substantiate these fears. First, they accused Catholics of undermining the public school system, the training ground of democracy, by sending their children to parochial schools where priests and nuns filled their minds with un-American ideas.[75] Catholics also attempted to weasel their way into the public system to destroy it from within, a movement J. Frank Norris discerned in Forth Worth, where members of the Knights of Columbus vied for election to the school board.[76] Second, Baptists saw Catholic schemes at work in the mass media. The hierarchy brought pressure to bear on American newspapers so that few items unfavorable to Catholicism reached the public. Not content with this, the Church forced the press to give free publicity to Catholic activities. In the city of Nashville, for example, where Methodists outnumbered Catholics three to one, the city's newspapers gave more coverage to Catholic affairs than to those of Methodists, Baptists noted. Catholics had also moved into the religious publishing business, establishing the journal *Commonweal* as a papal "mouthpiece," supporting 106 other periodicals, and pouring out books espousing Catholic doctrine. Finally, Baptists charged that "agents of the hierarchy" had infiltrated the burgeoning motion picture industry to ensure favorable portrayal of priests and nuns.[77]

A third feature of the Catholic conspiracy struck Southern Baptists as especially insidious. Baptists charged that the Roman Catholic Church had mounted a concerted drive to convert Southern Negroes. Catholics had good reason to turn southward optimistically, for as Eugene Alldredge pointed out in 1927, the Church held a "three-fold appeal" for blacks. This appeal started with the Catholic promise to build "schools and still more schools" for blacks; went on to the Church's practice of allowing blacks to worship side-by-side with whites; and culminated in the ritual and ceremony that attracted Negroes who enjoyed the superstitious cant, gaudy priestly garments, and elaborate services offered by Rome.[78] Armed with this appeal, Catholics would convert blacks and

---

[75]Masters, *The Call of the South* pp. 165-66.

[76]*Searchlight*, 5 May 1922, p. 1.

[77]*Herald*, 25 August 1921, p. 11; Eugene P. Alldredge ed., *Southern Baptist Handbook 1924* (Nashville: Sunday School Board, 1925), p. 57; SBC, *Annual*, 1929, pp. 100-101; Masters, *The Call of the South*, pp. 165-66.

[78]Alldredge, *The New Challenge of Home Missions*, pp. 73, 177, 179, 181-82.

create social and religious chaos in the South by turning them against white Protestants.

A final piece of "evidence" lay in the Roman Church's success in electing its lackeys to political office. Most of the large Northern cities—New York, Chicago, and Boston, for example—had already fallen into Catholic hands. Given the ethnic composition of the North this was unavoidable, but what really disturbed Southern Baptists were signs of waxing Catholic influence in their own region. Texas presented a particularly good example. Persecution by the Mexican government had driven thousands of Mexicans, many of them priests and nuns, into Texas where they had taken over whole towns and counties. Catholic voters in Waco had elected one of their own as mayor and had immediately cabled the good news to the pope, an irate Baptist asserted. Another Baptist complained that a Catholic had obtained a federal judgeship in Texas, that Beaumont had a Catholic postmaster, and that Houston had elected a Catholic mayor.[79] These developments impressed Baptists as more than isolated incidents; rather, they formed part of a larger Catholic design to control the United States. By gaining appointive and elective office Catholics obtained footholds for furthering the papacy's aims.

Some Baptists unleashed their imaginations when contemplating the fragmented pieces of evidence that, in their minds, formed a gigantic conspiracy. J. Frank Norris, seeing the hand of Rome everywhere and painting its presence in the most lurid hues, typified this tendency. Incensed over the efforts of a Catholic to win a district attorneyship in Fort Worth in 1922, he warned that if Catholics gained control of Fort Worth: "They would behead every Protestant preacher and disembow[e]l every Protestant mother." Two years later he implied that the Knights of St. John planned to mount a nationwide campaign of terror against Protestants. Norris also discerned less bloody plots afoot, charging Catholics, for example, with undermining morality by fighting Prohibition. On one of his witch hunting forays within his own denomination, Norris exposed an attempt by the College Avenue Baptist Church of Fort Worth to allow a member of the Knights of Columbus to participate in the church's Boy Scout program. A year later, in 1927, he accused Baylor

---

[79]Ibid., pp. 284-85; J. M. Provence to Pat M. Neff, 1 August 1922, Neff Papers, Governor Correspondence 1922; J. N. Davis to J. Frank Norris, ca. 1929, Norris Papers, Box 9.

University of corrupting young Baptists by employing a Roman Catholic in its medical school.[80]

Norris's attitude comes as no surprise; he routinely took extremist stances on issues that came before the denomination after World War I. Less understandable was the readiness of more moderate Baptists, ably represented by Robert Pitt, to add to the furor over a papal conspiracy. Pitt conducted his campaign against Catholics on a higher plane than Norris, but he feared the same quest for temporal power that distressed the Fort Worth pastor. Pitt questioned America's entry into the League of Nations because a majority of the member nations would be Roman Catholic. On the domestic scene, he wondered how many participants in the Boston police strike of 1919 were Catholics and what role the Church had played in the strike. Reporting the arrival of the papal legate in New York City in 1926, Pitt noted that both Mayor James Walker and Governor Al Smith had genuflected and kissed the cardinal's ring, signifying their obeisance to him. Besides his own strictures on Catholic activities, Pitt printed anti-Catholic articles by other Baptists in the *Religious Herald*. In 1919, for example, the paper published remarks critical of President Wilson's visit with the pope, and in 1926 Richmond pastor George McDaniel suggested in the *Herald's* pages that "the blackshirted followers of Fascism and the Knights of Columbus are one and the same in some American cities."[81] Although Pitt never stooped to the level of invective employed by Norris, he encouraged Baptists to ferret out Catholic designs, and through his participation lent respectability to his denomination's anti-Catholicism.

Not all Baptists accepted the idea of a papal conspiracy to wrest control of the United States away from Protestants. R. E. Bell, pastor of the First Baptist Church of Decatur, Texas, refused to heed the belief. To Eugene C. Routh, editor of the Texas *Baptist Standard*, he wrote:

> I think you exag[g]erate the Catholic menace. I understand that, officially, the Catholic church claims the right of civil rule for the pope, but in Italy where the Catholics are in control they deny the exercise of this pretended right to him. If they

[80]*Searchlight*, 14 July 1922, p. 1; 25 July 1924, p. 1; 7 May 1926, p. 3; *Funadmentalist*, 12 June 1931, p. 6; Frank Norris to Samuel Brooks, 4 June 1927, Norris Papers, Box 5.

[81]*Herald*, 3 July 1919, p. 10; 25 September 1919, p. 3; 24 June 1926, p. 10; 20 February 1919, p. 11; 22 July 1926, p. 6.

deny him this right in Italy is it likely that they would give him this right in America if they were in controll [sic] here? I hardly think so.[82]

A fellow Texan voiced similar sentiments, suggesting that Protestants who had failed to attract attention by other means had turned to Catholic-baiting to gain a following.[83] But such statements were scarce in the 1920s; most Baptists looked upon the papal menace with apprehension and eagerly joined the crusade against Catholicism. This assured that the Presidential candidacy of Al Smith would whip Baptist anti-Catholicism to a frenzy.

The Democratic Party realized the worst fears of Southern Baptists at its 1928 convention in Houston, Texas, when it nominated Al Smith. Smith, grandson of immigrants, product of New York City, Roman Catholic, and opponent of Prohibition, antagonized the South's Baptists as no one else could have. As early as June of 1927, a year before the Democratic convention, J. Frank Norris wrote to Samuel Brooks that "this nation at this present time is facing the greatest crisis of its existence."[84] Tension continued to mount through 1927 and into 1928, an Oklahoman remarking in March of 1928 that never in his life had America been faced with greater peril.[85] After Smith's nomination the contest between him and Herbert Hoover pushed other concerns aside; the urban, Catholic, immigrant challenge to rural, Old Stock, Protestant America had come to a focus in the person of Al Smith. Believing that "if Al Smith should be elected it would be the beginning of the end of our civilization,"[86] Baptists girded to fight for God, America, and the South.

Scholars have spent considerable time arguing the influence of various issues in the election of 1928.[87] Some point to Prohibition as most

---

[82]Bell to Routh, 10 October 1924, Brooks Papers, File Di-Faculty.

[83]J. T. Jordan to Samuel Brooks, 16 September 1927, Brooks Papers, File Di-Faculty.

[84]Norris to Brooks, 4 June 1927, Norris Papers, Box 5.

[85]Mordecai Ham to Norris, 5 March 1928, Norris Papers, Box 18.

[86]Norris to James Cranfill, 23 August 1928, Box 9.

[87]Good discussions of the election may be found in Edmund A. Moore, *A Catholic Runs for President: The Campaign of 1928* (New York: Ronald Press, 1956); Ruth C. Silva, *Rum, Religion, and Votes: 1928 Re-examined* (University Park, PA: Pennsylvania State University Press, 1962); and Lawrence H. Fuchs, "Election of 1928," in Arthur M. Schlesinger, Jr., ed., *History of American Presidential Elections, 1789-1968* (New York: 1971), III, 2585-609.

important; other investigators single out the urban and immigrant threats as crucial; while still others contend that religion superseded all else. Elections seldom serve as referenda on a single issue; more often, they offer confused testimony to the electorate's mixed feelings about an array of subjects. The election of 1928 varied little from this pattern. The safest way to analyze the Southern Baptist attitude toward the election, then, lies in recognizing the pressures exerted by a number of issues.

The contrast between Al Smith's opposition to Prohibition and Herbert Hoover's support of the Eighteenth Amendment certainly captured the electorate's attention. Robert Moats Miller has contended that the liquor question alone motivated millions of Americans to vote against the Democratic candidate.[88] Views expressed by a number of Southern Baptists support this thesis. William Poteat, one-time president of the North Carolina Anti-Saloon League, remarked that "it is the Governor's avowed opposition to the Eighteenth Amendment which is so universally offensive in the South and West."[89] Even J. Frank Norris, the leading Baptist anti-Catholic in the 1920s, admitted that one could dismiss Smith's other faults and still oppose him for his support of "the greatest curse of all time, namely, the liquor traffic."[90] Baptists have traditionally been wary of involving their denomination in politics because of their commitment to the separation of church and state. But this did not stop the Baptist Convention of Georgia from openly opposing any candidate in favor of ending Prohibition,[91] nor did it prevent the Missouri Baptist General Association, in a thinly disguised reference to the liquor question, from advising its constituents "to vote for such men who will advance the moral welfare of our country."[92] Given such statements, Virginian George Braxton Taylor's comment that "to my mind the election was a referendum on 'prohibition' " contains a good deal of truth.[93]

---

[88]Robert M. Miller, *American Protestantism and Social Issues, 1919-1939* (Chapel Hill: University of North Carolina Press, 1958), p. 51.

[89]Poteat to Royal Copeland, 7 January 1928, W. L. Poteat Papers.

[90]*Fundamentalist*, 18 November 1927, 4-5.

[91]Georgia, *Minutes*, 1927, p. 23.

[92]Missouri, *Minutes*, 1928, p. 89.

[93]George Braxton Taylor Diary, 6 November 1928, Virginia Baptist Historical Society, Richmond, Virginia.

Smith's urban background and his identification with immigrants guaranteed that Prohibition would not monopolize Baptists' attention, for his bid for the White House brought to a focus Baptists' fears of urban wickedness, godlessness, and un-Americanism. Moreover, Smith's urban ties exacerbated Baptist anxieties over the waning influence of rural America and the decline of the country church. In 1928 Baptists translated these fears and anxieties into concern over Smith's urban and immigrant support. Robert Pitt admitted that the Democratic candidate's reliance upon such unsavory backing troubled him. If the nation elected Smith, Pitt said, it would be because her cities, led by the "essentially foreign" metropolis of New York, had provided the margin of victory.[94] E. Y. Mullins indicated his intention to vote Republican partly because the Democratic party had "changed hands," passing from Thomas Jefferson's noble tillers of the soil to the "boss-ridden city masses."[95] In an anti-Smith campaign speech delivered in Jackson, Tennessee, John Jeter Hurt, later president of that city's Union University, denounced Smith's home city.

> New York is not an American city, only a city in America. They speak 63 different languages, 13 in one block. I have here a list of the city officials and will give a five dollar bill to anyone who can pronounce them correctly.[96]

Southern Baptists had long been troubled by the city and its foreign masses, and now, to their horror, these urbanites threatened to boost one of their own into the White House.

The third major issue in the election of 1928, Smith's religion, probably disturbed Southern Baptists the most. They could, with little difficulty, subsume the urban-immigrant problem under the general heading of Catholicism. Smith's identification with urban America and its immigrants thus automatically aroused apprehension over Catholicism. It is probably impossible to prove that Catholicism outweighed Prohibition in Baptist minds. Suffice it to say that religious liberty and the separation of church and state, issues closely identified with Baptist antagonism toward the Roman Catholic Church, did, and still do, take

---

[94]*Herald*, 20 September 1928, p. 10.

[95]*Herald*, 26 July 1928, p. 3.

[96]John Jeter Hurt, *This Is My Story* (Atlanta: pub. by author, 1957), p. 199.

precedence over the liquor question. Both before and after Southern Baptists turned their attention to Prohibition, the quest for religious liberty provided one of the denomination's central concerns.[97] Baptists saw Al Smith's opposition to the Eighteenth Amendment as an affront to morality, but even if he should be elected and oversee the repeal of Prohibition the Baptist denomination would survive. But Smith's supposed subjection to papal directives caused Baptists to shudder. It took little prompting to believe that the election of a Catholic president would be the first step toward the persecution of the Baptist people and the silencing of their witness for God.

Although Smith's religion alienated Baptists more than any other issue, it must be recognized that not all Southern Baptists lapsed into wild bigotry. Some Baptists, employing a moderate, intelligent approach, raised honest questions about the temporal power of the Roman Catholic Church. In 1960 many Americans rightfully maintained that religion should be of no consideration in determining John F. Kennedy's fitness for the Presidency. But 1960 was not 1928. In 1928 Baptists drew upon prejudices and misconceptions they had been collecting for centuries. They felt threatened by immigration and urbanization, both of which they associated with Roman Catholicism. The other problems of the decade—interdenominationalism, social Christianity, and modernism—added to their frustration. Finally, as James H. Smylie has pointed out, the Roman Catholic hierarchy did not always allay Protestant suspicions.[98] Considering the circumstances, it is a minor wonder that Baptists did not fall prey to mass hysteria.

Despite the urge to lash out indiscriminately, a few Baptists limited their discussion to the church's quest for temporal power. "Roman Catholicism, as a personal religion, is not involved," a Virginian wrote, "but the political pretensions of Romanism are involved."[99] Baptists discussed the secular influence of the hierarchy in Latin America, Spain, and Italy, and cited the papacy's decrees as the basis for this violation of civil boundaries. An Oklahoman listed Pope Boniface VIII's 1302 claim of

---

[97]Beryl F. McClerren, "Southern Baptists and Roman Catholics: Religious Issues during the Presidential Campaigns of 1928 and 1960," *The Quarterly Review* 34 (April-June 1974): 80-81.

[98]James H. Smylie, "The Roman Catholic Church, the State, and Al Smith," *Church History* 29 (September 1960): 321-43.

[99]*Herald*, 20 January 1927, p. 9.

secular power and Gregory XVI's 1831 justification of church-state union as ample reason for Baptists to suspect the papacy's motives.[100] A Florida Baptist church, concerned with the "political pretensions of Romanism," exemplified the intelligent approach at its best, holding special classes for analysis of scholarly books and inviting Professor William Warren Sweet of the University of Chicago to address the congregation.[101] Ideally, Al Smith's religion should not have been mentioned, but the conjuncture of various problems made it inevitable that Southern Baptists would raise the issue.

Too few Baptists pursued the moderate course, choosing instead to rely on slanderous attacks. J. Frank Norris wielded this weapon as effectively as anyone. Contending that Roman Catholic ascendancy would lead to another Saint Bartholomew's Day massacre, he aroused the darkest emotions among Baptists. He allied himself with the notorious Catholic-baiter Senator Thomas Heflin of Alabama, encouraged circulation of the spurious "Jesuit's oath," and published a fanciful article by a former Catholic priest entitled "The Vatican Scheme to Move the Papacy to Washington." Norris reached the depths of scurrilousness in advertising anti-Catholic books and pamphlets in the *Fundamentalist*. He promoted the sale of a book exposing an alleged papal scheme to take over the American government by force; advertised *The Devil's Prayer Book*, an exposé of priests' use of the confessional for sexual purposes; and recommended "92 red hot books telling the inside truth of Roman Catholicism," including such gems as *Jesuit Murders in the British Empire*, *Traffic in Nuns*, *Priest and Women*, *Crimes of Priests*, and *The Anti-Catholic Joke Book*.[102]

Many Southern Baptists readily accepted Norris's propaganda, for it reinforced what they already believed. For example, a North Carolinian,

---

[100]*Messenger*, 22 February 1928, p. 9.

[101]Copy of a handbill printed by the Morgan Park Baptist Church, in Michael Williams, *The Shadow of the Pope* (New York: McGraw-Hill, 1932), p. 263.

[102]*Fundamentalist*, 17 February 1928, p. 3; Norris to Heflin, 14 April 1928, Norris Papers, Box 19; Norris to W. W. Anderson, 8 October 1928, Box 1; *Fundamentalist*, 2 November 1928, p. 2; 13 April 1928, p. 2; 6 July 1928, p. 2; 9 March 1928, p. 6. As such actions and attitudes might suggest, many Southern Baptists found the Ku Klux Klan's approach to Catholicism appealing. But at least on an official level, Southern Baptists did not say a great deal about the Klan. See Ira V. Birdwhistell, "Southern Baptist Perceptions of and Responses to Roman Catholicism, 1917-1972" (Ph.D. dissertation, Southern Baptist Theological Seminary, 1975), pp. 50-54.

calling the Knights of Columbus "the most vicious organization today on the earth," warned of widespread persecution if Smith reached the White House, and another Baptist attributed the assassinations of Presidents Lincoln, Garfield, and McKinley to Catholic plots.[103] A poem sent to J. Frank Norris by one of his followers expressed the attitudes of such Baptists. Entitled "Alcohol Smith's Platform," it read in part:

> I'll rule the people and the Pope will rule me,
> And the people's rights you will never see,
> And the Protestant heretics who vote for me,
> I'll reduce to abject slavery.

> I'll take down the flag from the public schools,
> And put up the cross for the ignorant fools,
> The Bibles in the schools shall not be read,
> But instead we'll say masses for the dead.

> And the flag you love shall be put down,
> And put up instead the Papal crown;
> Then the Pope of Rome shall rule the homes,
> And bring back the glory that once was Rome's.[104]

To stave off their reduction to "abject slavery," Norris and like-minded Baptists stooped to the lowest levels in attacking Roman Catholicism.

Few Southern Baptists openly challenged either the moderate or scurrilous brands of anti-Catholicism in 1928. Still, a handful, braving the disapproval of their fellow churchmen, defended Smith. North Carolinian Josiah W. Bailey, an active Baptist layman elected to the United States Senate in 1930, backed Smith in 1928 and through his stand won the support of a number of North Carolina Baptists.[105] John Moncure of Maryland, though admitting that Smith's religion raised a legitimate issue, sought to allay the apprehension of Southern Baptists. Writing in the *Religious Herald*, Moncure contended that if elected Smith would do nothing to justify Protestant fears, for he would not risk the public outcry that would greet blatantly pro-Catholic actions. Moreover, Moncure said, many American Catholics were ardent democrats, loyal supporters of

---

[103]B. H. Tyson to William Poteat, 9 May 1928, W. L. Poteat Papers; H. Beauchamp, "Roman Catholic Politics," ca. 1928 typescript, Norris Papers, Box 3.

[104]Dorothy Cowan to Norris, 12 September 1928, Norris Papers, Box 5.

[105]William Poteat to Josiah Bailey, 30 January 1929, W. L. Poteat Papers.

American institutions who, if elected to public office, "would not allow
any sectarian influences" to sway their decisions. "I have no reason to
suppose that Smith is not among this number," Moncure concluded.[106]
Not many Southern Baptists spoke so forthrightly, but a few did, enough
to show that not all Baptists allowed Smith's religion to determine their
vote.[107]

In the broader view, whether Al Smith's religion troubled Southern
Baptists more than his identification with the cities, his immigrant ties,
or his opposition to Prohibition is irrelevant. The importance of the
election of 1928 lies in its dramatization of the urban and Catholic
threats. From 1919 to 1931 Southern Baptists worried about the decline
of rural America, the dominance of America's cities, and the growing
strength of Roman Catholicism. This had two effects on Baptists. It
inspired the denomination to action, persuading Baptists that they must
revitalize rural religion, evangelize the cities, and contest Roman
Catholic efforts to control the United States. At the same time, it
undermined Baptists' optimism, diverted attention better given to other
matters, added to the problems that swept the denomination in the
1920s, and undercut Baptists' will and ability to evangelize the world.

---

[106]*Herald*, 5 April 1928, p. 11.

[107]The actual number of Southern Baptists who voted either for or against Smith on
the basis of his religion cannot, of course, be determined. But it is significant to note that
Smith carried Alabama, Arkansas, Georgia, Louisiana, Mississippi, and South Carolina,
all states heavily populated by Southern Baptists. Despite Baptists' aversion to Smith's
religion, as well as to drinking, immigrants, and cities, many of them no doubt voted for
him.

CHAPTER 10

The Great Depression

In late October of 1929 the New York stock market collapsed. The market's crash, in combination with economic weaknesses obscured by the prosperity of the 1920s, plunged the United States into the Great Depression. Southern Baptists, like millions of their countrymen, soon felt the sting of privation. But the onset of the Depression meant more than breadlines, unemployment, and shrinking incomes to the South's Baptists. The financial woes of the 1930s marked the end of the brief era of hope and opportunity born in the exuberant aftermath of World War I. By the end of 1931, after two years of worsening economic conditions, Baptists realized that conquest of the world for Christ would have to be postponed while they grappled with declining receipts and faltering programs. The events of 1930 and 1931, following upon the controversies of the previous decade, dealt the final blow to the optimism and sense of destiny that had captured Baptists' imaginations in 1919.

The Depression did not suddenly plunge Southern Baptists into poverty, for they had been experiencing financial difficulties since the early 1920s. Their tribulations had begun with the Seventy-Five Million Campaign. Launched amidst postwar fervor, the campaign had been an immediate success. Baptists had oversubscribed the intended goal, pledging to give $92,630,923 to missions and education over a five-year period. By the end of 1919 solicitors had collected over twelve million dollars of this amount. Reasoning from the campaign's glorious beginning, the

South's Baptists had foreseen nothing but triumph for the years ahead.

But expectations far exceeded reality; the payment of pledges began to lag in 1920 as the excitement of 1919 waned and people began to weigh their commitments in hard cash. As the flow of money slackened, the importance of attaining the goal loomed larger in the eyes of many Baptists. In the fall of 1920 Lee Scarborough, director of the campaign, warned that "DENOMINATIONAL HONOR" and "ALL THE INTERESTS WHICH WE HOLD DEAR" depended on the venture's success. A year later, with conditions even worse, another Texan, declaring that the campaign superseded all other Baptist enterprises, sadly contemplated the damage its failure would wreak. Southern Baptist Convention President E. Y. Mullins advised the 1923 gathering of Baptists in Kansas City, Missouri, that defeat would undermine the denomination's "faith and courage" and discredit Baptist democracy. In January of 1924, with certain failure only months away, Scarborough refused to lower his expectations. Designating 1924 the "Southern Baptist conscience year," he told Baptists that only two alternatives existed: victory for Christ's cause or a defeat that would weaken efforts to spread the gospel. Despite Scarborough's exhortations, Baptists redeemed only $58,000,000 of the 92.6 million dollars they had pledged in 1919. They had even failed to reach the initial goal of $75,000,000, falling seventeen million dollars short of that coveted amount.[1]

Weaknesses in the American economy, postwar psychology, errors committed by the campaign's managers, and other denominational problems accounted for Baptists' inability to bring the Seventy-Five Million Campaign to a successful conclusion. The wartime economic boom in which Baptists had launched their endeavor came to an abrupt end in the fall of 1920, producing what economic historian George Soule has called "one of the most violent crashes of prices that the nation has ever experienced."[2] Baptist businessmen suffered disastrous setbacks, and Baptist farmers, lured into overexpansion by wartime demands, saw the price of cotton plummet from forty cents to ten cents a pound. Low prices and mounting debts created an inhospitable atmosphere in which to nag

---

[1]*Herald*, 23 September 1920, p. 1; 24 May 1923, pp. 8-9; 10 January 1924, p. 14; R. O. Huff to George Truett, 21 December 1921, Truett Papers; SBC, *Annual*, 1925, p. 23.

[2]George Soule, *Prosperity Decade: From War to Depression, 1917-1929* (New York: Harper, 1968, original publication, 1947), p. 96.

church members about their obligations, and in the face of these conditions the redemption of pledges slackened.[3] The importance of this recession cannot be overemphasized because Southern Baptists never really recovered from it during the rest of the decade. It was the main reason for the failure of the Seventy-Five Million Campaign, and it launched Baptists on a course of economic instability that culminated in the Depression of the thirties.

Even without the deflationary spiral of 1920 to 1922 the Seventy-Five Million Campaign would have suffered from the waning of wartime fervor. Baptist leaders had relied heavily on Woodrow Wilson's crusade to inspire their own "war" to conquer mankind for Christ. This blend of religious and patriotic zeal undergirded the Seventy-Five Million Campaign and accounted for the enthusiasm Baptists showed for the program. But the fever pitch of 1918 and 1919 could not be sustained indefinitely; by the early 1920s the emotional fervor necessary for gathering large sums of money had begun to cool. This psychological damage proved to be almost as harmful to Baptist plans as the economic recession.[4]

A growing disillusionment with the internal workings of the campaign also contributed to its downfall. Critics offered conflicting assessments of the program's shortcomings. Many Baptists especially disliked the five-year pledges which, by setting up a timetable for payments, formalized the act of contributing to God's work and took the pleasure out of it. Baptists bridled at the centralization that accompanied the campaign. Fundamentalists in particular railed against the "despots" who headed the drive, but one did not have to be a disciple of J. Frank Norris to decry the establishment of a central committee empowered to set quotas for individual churches.[5] In direct contrast, some Baptists complained that the collection of funds had lagged because the tight organization that had secured pledges in 1919 had been allowed to disintegrate.[6] Although Baptists differed on the exact nature of the

---

[3]SBC, *Annual*, 1921, pp. 401-402; *Herald*, 13 January 1921, p. 2.

[4]*Herald*, 9 May 1929, p. 13.

[5]Rufus W. Weaver, "The Spiritual Values of the 75 Million Campaign," pp. 6-7, undated typescript, Weaver Papers, Box 7; *Record*, 8 November 1923, pp. 4-5.

[6]Harvey E. Dana, *Lee Rutland Scarborough: A Life of Service* (Nashville: Broadman Press, 1942), p. 105.

campaign's internal weaknesses, they agreed that it had been carried out with something less than perfection.

A number of denominational problems hindered the Seventy-Five Million Campaign. Controversies over modernism and fundamentalism broke out at the same time that economic recession struck and religious fervor began to wane. In 1920 T. T. Martin launched his attack on William Poteat, and the following year J. Frank Norris began his crusade against Baylor University. These events, in conjunction with agitation over interdenominationalism and social Christianity, created unrest and distracted people from church finances. Practical problems also undercut the fund drive. State conventions initiated programs which diverted money from the Southern Baptist Convention's treasury, and individual churches instituted costly building projects. Pastorless churches, especially in rural areas, lacked the stimulus to inspire sacrificial giving. Finally, many Baptists who had pledged in 1919 either died or moved during the five-year period, in both cases complicating the collection of funds.[7]

Although Baptists did not attain their goal, they benefited from the attempt. It broadened their outlook by offering a vision of a world converted to Christ, and it strengthened their resolve to preach the gospel to all mankind. Second, the fund-raising drive afforded a measure of unity in a period of dissension. The pledges and quotas produced a third beneficial result: they prepared the way for adoption of a budget system of finance. The Seventy-Five Million Campaign provided the transition between the high-pressure canvassing and impulse giving of the past, and the systematic funding of denominational programs that came to characterize Southern Baptists. Fourth, even though Baptists fell short of their goal they raised an enormous sum for missions and education. In this respect the program failed only in a relative sense, for the $58,000,000 aided Baptist work immeasurably. Finally, the South's Baptists reaped spiritual blessings from their labor. As Arkansas Baptists exclaimed in 1924: "The past five years have marked the greatest spiritual strides in Arkansas and in the South that Baptists or any other religious group have made in the history of Christianity." These Arkansans exaggerated a bit, but nevertheless, especially in its first two years

---

[7]Dana, *Scarborough*, pp. 106-107; SBC, *Annual*, 1923, pp. 22-23.

the campaign stirred the spirtual vitality of Southern Baptists.[8]

Although the long-range effects of the Seventy-Five Million Campaign benefited Southern Baptists, the immediate impact proved to be harmful. Inspired by ninety-two million dollars in pledges and twelve million in cash, Baptists increased their work and expanded their facilities. State and southwide conventions stepped up their activity, colleges erected new buildings, hospitals and orphanages expanded, and churches constructed larger worship halls, only to find that the harvest of Baptist wealth yielded less than expected. Indebtedness grew as Baptists borrowed money to pay for new programs.[9] The denomination never escaped this burden during the 1920s; declining receipts kept it saddled with debt and left Baptists ill-prepared to cope with the setbacks of the 1930s. The campaign's failure caused even greater psychological damage. It marred Baptists' optimism, undermined their sense of destiny, and weakened their resolve to carry out the Lord's work. They had counted on the Seventy-Five Million Campaign to open the way for the assault on wickedness; instead it gave them blessings mixed with sorrows and triumph intertwined with defeat. The conclusion of the fund-raising drive left Baptists shaken and unsure of the future.

Financial difficulties continued to plague Southern Baptists in the years immediately following the conclusion of the Seventy-Five Million Campaign. In the fall of 1925 North Carolina Baptists noted a continuing decline in contributions, and a year later Alabama's state board of missions reported that insufficient funds had forced it to reject "many heart-breaking appeals." Virginia Baptists commented that similar shortages had brought them to a "critical" period in their history; Georgians complained that a severe drought in the summer of 1925 and the migration of thousands of their number to Florida had left their churches in fiscal disarray; and Kentuckians warned that they must act swiftly to save their colleges.[10] Few Baptists encountered more difficulty than those in Arkansas. Many of the state's Baptists had quit supporting denomina-

---

[8]Dana, *Scarborough*, p. 107; SBC, *Annual*, 1923, pp. 23-24; *Herald*, 9 May 1929, p. 13; Arkansas, *Proceedings*, 1924, pp. 74-75.

[9]Jesse L. Boyd, *A Popular History of the Baptists in Mississippi* (Jackson: Baptist Press, 1930), pp. 232-33; Leslie L. Gwaltney, *Forty of the Twentieth or the First Forty Years of the Twentieth Century* (Birmingham: pub. by author, 1940), p. 142.

[10]North Carolina, *Annual*, 1925, p. 65; Alabama, *Annual*, 1926, p. 25; Virginia, *Minutes*, 1926, p. 53; Georgia, *Minutes*, 1925, p. 57; Kentucky, *Proceedings*, 1926, p. 46.

tional programs by mid-decade, and those who remained faithful had their patience tried by devastating cyclones and widespread flooding. In 1927 the state's executive board pleaded for Arkansans to stop neglecting the convention's plight and to "seek God and the straight road of obedience."[11]

The Southern Baptist Convention fared as poorly as its state counterparts. J. W. Gillon of Winchester, Kentucky, noting in 1925 that southwide causes had sunk to a deplorable level, prophetically remarked that the Convention would plunge deeper into debt in the years ahead. Eugene Alldredge verified Gillon's foresight a year later, disclosing in the *Southern Baptist Handbook* that since 1925 the Convention's indebtedness had increased by over one million dollars. Southern Baptists had come face-to-face with the "most crucial and precarious situation" since the post-Civil War era, Alldredge said. Part of the problem lay in the shakiness of the Southern economy, but equally important, as Alldredge made clear, Baptists had responded halfheartedly to the Cooperative Program, the fiscal plan that had replaced the Seventy-Five Million Campaign. Those who felt that local causes had been slighted during the first five years of the decade decided to balance matters at the expense of the new program. Some churches refused to contribute any money to southwide causes, and many that cooperated rejected quotas and gave only a small percentage of their collections to the Southern Baptist Convention.[12] This intense localism brought distress to broader efforts. The Foreign Mission Board, fearful of a general "indifference to foreign missions," warned that without more money it would have to close down. The Home Mission Board, laboring under similar circumstances, abandoned its department of evangelism in 1925. The Education Board, a "dispensable enterprise" in the *Religious Herald's* opinion, also struggled with indebtedness, and finally collapsed in 1928. The situation reached such grave proportions that Convention President George McDaniel inserted a special plea into his 1927 address to the messengers in Louisville, Kentucky. Advising that "heroic measures must be adopted to avoid bankruptcy," he asked that property be sold, salaries cut, and local interests slighted to save the

---

[11]Arkansas, *Proceedings*, 1925, p. 23; 1927, pp. 9-10.

[12]Gillon to Lee Scarborough, 20 October 1925, Scarborough Papers; Eugene P. Alldredge ed., *Southern Baptist Handbook 1926* (Nashville: Sunday School Board, 1926), pp. 17-20.

programs of the Southern Baptist Convention.[13] McDaniel's address left no doubt that Baptist financial problems had not ended with the disappointing returns from the Seventy-Five Million Campaign.

To add to their woes, Southern Baptists experienced a series of defalcations in the second half of the 1920s. Employees at both Baylor and Furman universities embezzled substantial amounts, but these cases were mild compared to the scandals that shook the mission boards of the Southern Baptist Convention. Late in 1926 it came to light that the treasurer of the Foreign Mission Board had siphoned off over $100,000 of the board's receipts.[14] The shock of this had scarcely died out when in August of 1928 the denomination learned that Clinton S. Carnes, treasurer of the Home Mission Board since 1919, had embezzled $909,461. The discovery left the board unable to pay its employees and forced Secretary B. D. Gray to suspend the board's work to prevent its collapse.[15] Baptists gasped at the enormity of Carnes's theft, calling it "the hardest blow and greatest calamity that has even befallen our great denomination." The disclosure that Carnes had previously served time in prison led to widespread criticism of the board for not checking into his background. Incensed by such carelessness, some Baptists argued that the Home Board should be abolished and its work turned over the state conventions.[16] In this atmosphere of discontent and recrimination the idea took root that further revelations of Carnes's activities had been suppressed by the Home Mission Board. From an undercurrent of suspicion this ballooned into J. Frank Norris's charge that several officials of the Home Board had protected Carnes because they had been speculating on the New York Stock Exchange with funds supplied by the treasurer.[17] This view gained credence among some who sought an explanation for a perplexing event. But all Baptists, whether conspiratorially minded or

---

[13]T. B. Ray to McNeill Poteat, 25 June 1925, Edwin McNeill Poteat, Jr., Papers; SBC, *Annual*, 1926, p. 159; 1925, pp. 312-13; *Herald*, 27 October 1927, p. 11; 12 May 1927, pp. 8-9.

[14]*Herald*, 24 February 1927, p. 11; 13 January 1927, p. 22; John White to William McGlothlin, 4 October 1930, McGlothlin Papers, Reel 1.

[15]*Herald*, 13 September 1928, pp. 6-7; SBC, *Annual*, 1929, p. 269.

[16]Appomattox, *Minutes*, 1929, p. 16; *Herald*, 13 September 1928, pp. 6-7, 10; 20 December 1928, p. 10.

[17]*Record*, 21 February 1929, p. 2; Norris to Senator Carter Glass, 10 October 1929, Norris Papers, Box 17.

not, found Carnes's defalcation hard to bear. Not only did the loss of funds hurt, but realization that over $900,000 had been spirited away dealt a blow to their morale.

A growing conviction during the twenties that rich lodes of Baptist wealth lay unmined increased frustration over the denomination's financial plight. A number of Baptists believed that their fellow churchmen could lift the denomination out of debt if they would contribute a fair share of their resources to God's work. The commission established to design a program to follow the Seventy-Five Million Campaign reported in 1925 that if the number of regular contributors could be increased from 500,000 to 1,000,000 Baptists' financial problems would be solved. Three hundred thousand church members giving a weekly tithe of their income would also free Baptists from indebtedness, the commission added. But the task of awakening Baptists to their duty seemed overwhelming, for sixty-two and one-half percent of the South's Baptists were not supporting southwide enterprises. Eugene Alldredge seconded the commission's complaints in the 1929 edition of the *Southern Baptist Handbook*, where he denounced the "lavish spending and profligate wasting of the growing wealth which has come to our people."[18] Such observations heightened the frustration of those trying to keep the denomination's missions, educational and medical work alive, and produced pangs of guilt in a people burdened with financial and spiritual troubles.

Additional frustration came from the feeling of powerlessness in the face of great opportunity. Financial instability had forced the denomination to cut back its programs, but world conditions would not wait for it to regain its equilibrium. Baptists continued to maintain, as they first had immediately after World War I, that the postwar era offered a unique occasion for preaching the gospel. The times seemed especially auspicious for foreign missions. As William McGlothlin, president of the Southern Baptist Convention, commented in 1930: "The world is open to us for Christian service and the spread of the kingdom, perhaps, as never before." Home missions commanded equal attention, for Baptists believed that the spiritual cast of the South for generations to come would be determined in their day. The South, with its industrialization, urban growth, and influx of "aliens," presented a fruitful mission field, and, of

---

[18]SBC, *Annual*, 1925, p. 28; Eugene P. Alldredge ed., *Southern Baptist Handbook 1929* (Nashville: Sunday School Board, 1929), p. 61.

course, the rest of America lay waiting to be converted to the true faith.[19] Yet Baptists felt helpless as they contemplated these opportunities. They had been chosen by God for a special work, but financial weakness prevented them from fulfilling their destiny.

The discouragement and disappointment induced by financial difficulty left Baptists vulnerable to the "American religious depression" of 1925 to 1935 that Robert T. Handy has so perceptively analyzed.[20] Although signs of this "depression" appeared before 1925, it began in earnest among Southern Baptists around mid-decade. For example, Kentucky Baptists observed in 1925 that the church's "spiritual health" had faltered, as evidenced by the small number of Baptists still attempting to win souls for Christ. By 1926 warnings of a religious depression had become commonplace among Southern Baptists. South Carolinians reported "gloom and despondency" in their state; Alabamians complained of irreverence among Baptist youth; and a Virginian asserted that Southern Baptists "are spiritually bankrupt."[21] Conditions remained grim as the decade dragged to a close. In 1928 the president of South Carolina's state convention pleaded for a spiritual renewal, and the following year a Mississippian contended that the denomination was mired in the "worst period of depression and gloom that has come upon us for forty years." "Perplexity and unrest" continued to weaken Baptist morale in 1929, and "spiritual inertia" gripped the denomination on the eve of the nationwide economic collapse.[22]

On top of the problems that had been piling up during the 1920s, Southern Baptists came face-to-face in 1929 with the worst economic crisis that America has experienced. By 1930 the financial problems of the previous decade had paled in comparison to current difficulties.

---

[19]McGlothlin to Members of the First Baptist Church, Columbus, Mississippi, 6 October 1930, McGlothlin Papers, Reel 1; Richard H. Edmonds, *Home Missions and Its Relation to World Missions* (Atlanta: Home Mission Board, ca. mid-1920s), p. 2; SBC, *Annual*, 1929, p. 278.

[20]Robert T. Handy, "The American Religious Depression, 1925-1935," *Church History* 24 (March 1960): 3-16.

[21]Kentucky, *Proceedings*, 1925, pp. 79-80; South Carolina, *Minutes*, 1926, p. 30; Alabama, *Annual*, 1926, p. 50; *Herald*, 23 December 1926, p. 4.

[22]South Carolina, *Minutes*, 1928, pp. 9-11; *Record*, 26 April 1928, p. 6; *Messenger*, 11 April 1929; p. 1; John L. Rosser, *A History of Florida Baptists* (Nashville: Broadman Press, 1949), p. 103.

Denominational programs were in "dire distress," and people wondered if the boards and institutions of the Southern Baptist Convention would survive.[23] The Cooperative Program faltered and almost collapsed. Local churches, dissatisfied with both state and southwide conventions, retained money for their own needs instead of forwarding it to higher administrative bodies. A number of states, especially in the Southwest, spoke openly of withdrawing from the Cooperative Program. Louisiana and Arkansas cut their contributions to a trickle and applied their collections to state matters. Faced with rebellion by the states, such institutions as Southwestern Seminary and the New Orleans Bible Institute forsook the normal means for obtaining funds and organized *ad hoc* campaigns without the permission of the Southern Baptist Convention. As John Sampey remarked in 1930: "The affairs of our Baptist democracy are demoralized in the matter of co-operative giving."[24]

The boards of the Southern Baptist Convention entered the 1930s burdened with debt and unable to render needed services. In December of 1930 Corresponding Secretary I. J. Van Ness curtailed the activities of the Sunday School Board's field workers to reduce expenses. J. B. Lawrence, executive secretary-treasurer of the Home Mission Board, complained in June of 1931 of "crushing debts" that prevented the board from sending men and women into fields begging for Baptist workers.[25] By the fall of 1931 the Foreign Mission Board had amassed a debt of over one million dollars, but declining receipts forced it to continue borrowing to support its workers. Missionaries looked anxiously to the homeland, wondering if they would be abandoned, and at least one complained that Baptist leaders had refused to sacrifice to maintain foreign missions.[26] Encum-

---

[23]William McGlothlin to Milton G. Evans, 12 June 1930, McGlothlin Papers, Reel 1; John R. Sampey, *Memoirs of John R. Sampey* (Nashville: Broadman Press, 1947), p. 216.

[24]*Herald*, 30 October 1930, p. 4; J. B. Ray to William McGlothlin, 19 September 1930, McGlothlin Papers, Reel 1; John White to McGlothlin, 19 May 1930, Reel 1; John Sampey to Members of the Promotion and Enlistment Committee, 24 June 1930, McGlothlin Papers, Reel 1.

[25]Van Ness to E. E. Lee, 2 December 1930, Lee Papers, Box 8; Lawrence to George Truett, 8 June 1931, Truett Papers; Lawrence to William McGlothlin, 4 December 1931, McGlothlin Papers, Reel 2.

[26]Joshua Levering to William McGlothlin, 9 October 1931, McGlothlin Papers, Reel 2; SBC, *Annual*, 1931, p. 168; J. R. Saunders to Jefferson Ray, 27 November 1931, Ray Papers.

bered with heavy debts and faced with a sharp decrease in income, the boards of the Southern Baptist Convention abandoned all pretense of meeting the challenges of a needy world. They turned their full attention to staying alive.

"Not only are the Convention institutions in distress," William McGlothlin wrote to Lee Scarborough in January of 1931, "but in many of the States the State institutions are equally hard pressed."[27] Proof of McGlothlin's statement lay readily at hand. Virginians, complaining of "well-nigh crushing debts," closed the evangelistic department of the state missions board in 1930; that same year the North Carolina convention defaulted on its debt. The executive secretary-treasurer of the Florida state convention wrote in 1931 that "we have only humiliation and defeat to record when we come to a study of the amount of money given to missionary and benevolent causes the past year." No Southern Baptist Convention state suffered more than Arkansas which, laboring under a $1,200,000 deficit, defaulted on its debts and withdrew from the Cooperative Program in 1931.[28] State organizations, following the example of the Southern Baptist Convention, combated the Depression by paring away superfluities and trying to save as many of their programs as possible.

Rufus Weaver, former president of Mercer University, toured seven Southern states in early 1930 and found the educational situation depressing. He saw that the denomination could no longer provide adequate financial support for its schools and that these institutions would have to look beyond the Baptist people for aid. Weaver continued to worry over the plight of Baptist schools, and a year and a half later he documented his concern in a letter to William McGlothlin. According to Weaver, from 1922 to 1931 Baptists had lost 58 of their 140 seminaries, colleges, and lower-level schools; fourteen more had recently been cut off; a number of others faced imminent extinction; and the remaining institutions possessed a combined indebtedness of over ten million dollars. But McGlothlin needed no reminder of the seriousness of the situation, for in mid-1930 he had observed that many Baptist schools had

---

[27]McGlothlin to Scarborough, 14 January 1931, McGlothlin Papers, Reel 1.

[28]Dover, *Minutes*, 1931, p. 28; Virginia, *Minutes*, 1931, p. 59; Charles E. Maddry, *An Autobiography* (Nashville: Broadman Press, 1955), p. 67; C. M. Brittain to William McGlothlin, 18 April 1931, McGlothlin Papers, Reel 1; John R. Buchanan to McGlothlin, 22 September 1930, Reel 1; Arkansas, *Proceedings*, 1931, p. 44.

reached "the point of collapse."[29] Neither Weaver nor McGlothlin exaggerated; along with state and southwide boards, Baptist schools curtailed expenditures, cut back programs, and tried to ride out the storm.

Baptists continued to anguish over the deepening religious depression that had first appeared in the 1920s. Charles Maddry, general secretary of the North Carolina convention, suggested that financial troubles had accelerated the decline of spiritual fervor, and the religious depression had in turn darkened the economic outlook. Other Southern Baptists joined Maddry in his gloomy assessment. Virginians referred to "spiritual drowsiness" and "religious famine," while North Carolinian Richard Vann sadly noted a "spritual declension" throughout the land. The corresponding secretary of the Mississippi convention reported spiritual vitality "at a low ebb," and an Arkansas Baptist bewailed the poor spiritual conditions in his area. Finally, a Texan observed in 1931: "The average pastor of the average fashionable church seems to have formed an alliance with the world [,] the flesh and the Devil. The real soul arousing gospel is not preached nowadays by the average preacher."[30] Southern Baptists maintained their witness for Christ through the darkest days of the Depression, but they could not preserve the fervor of an earlier period. Spiritual decline had united with economic instability to cast a pall over the denomination.

The hardships of the early 1930s prompted Baptists to probe for the deeper meaning of their travail. Through the centuries both in Europe and in America, Baptists had suffered for their beliefs, so their twentieth-century heirs knew that trials and persecution accompanied God's witnesses. As George McDaniel's widow wrote in 1930: "The Christian believes that sorrow and pain are not intruders from without, but companions of the spirit on its journey to God."[31] The best examination of

---

[29]Weaver to John C. Dawson, 22 April 1930, Weaver Papers, Box 5; Weaver to McGlothlin, 2 November 1931, McGlothlin Papers, Reel 2; McGlothlin to Joshua Levering, 23 June 1930, Reel 1.

[30]Maddry to William McGlothlin, 18 April 1931, McGlothlin Papers, Reel 1; *Herald*, 6 November 1930, p. 5; 19 February 1931, pp. 4-5; Richard T. Vann, *The Things Not Seen* (Nashville: Sunday School Board, 1931), p. 166; R. B. Gunter to William McGlothlin, 17 April 1931, McGlothlin Papers, Reel 1; R. L. Bridges to McGlothlin, 21 April 1931, Reel 1; W. E. Tumlin to Frank Norris, 1 April 1931, Norris Papers, Box 39.

[31]Douglass S. McDaniel, *Stewardship of Sorrow* (Nashville: Sunday School Board, 1930), p. 53.

this problem came from Jefferson Ray in 1929 in a thin volume entitled *Trouble*. In an attempt to explain the existence of adversity, Ray singled out various reasons why God afflicts his followers. "Trouble," as Ray referred to the trials of the righteous, warned man of God's displeasure with his sinfulness, cleansed him of evil, and helped him to avoid future transgressions. It also developed character in the sufferer and made him more fruitful in the eyes of God. Then, it helped one to sympathize with the world's unfortunates, those who had tasted life's bitterness. God made His presence felt through tribulation, for in the hour of breavement one drew closer to the Lord. Finally, Ray concluded, by suffering nobly one glorified God.[32]

The words of Jefferson Ray and likeminded Baptists did not go unheeded, for Southern Baptists quickly decided that God had intentionally visited the tribulations of the Depression upon his people. In typical fashion, the Oklahoma *Baptist Messenger* maintained that the Depression demonstrated, as similar instances had throughout history, God's displeasure with His wayward children. Conditions would worsen, the editor predicted, until Americans, Baptists especially, repented their sins and restored God to preeminence. Americans had become too caught up in the pursuit of temporal affairs, too busy chasing after prosperity to acknowledge God's lordship, Baptists said. The atmosphere of the 1920s had encouraged men to rely on material possessions, to place their faith in the goods of this world rather than in the treasures that awaited the righteous in heaven. Perhaps, a Virginian suggested, "a little pinch of poverty will restore us to sanity." After an examination of God's role in the Depression, C. P. Orr of Texas concluded that God had intervened in order to demonstrate His anger toward an America that had plummeted to the same depths of wickedness that had led Him to chastise ancient Israel. But even though Baptists believed that God's wrath had been vented upon them, they clung to a comforting thought: God had afflicted them out of love, much as a parent punishes an unruly child for his own good.[33]

---

[32]Jefferson D. Ray, *Trouble* (Philadelphia: Judson Press, 1929), pp. 17-31.

[33]*Messenger*, 21 August 1930, p. 3; *Herald*, 19 February 1931, pp. 4-5; 23 October 1930, p. 7; 18 September 1930, p. 5; C. P. Orr, "Is God Controlling This Depression?," ca. 1931 typescript, Norris Papers, Box 32; Walter M. Gilmore to William McGlothlin, 29 January 1931, McGlothlin Papers, Reel 1.

In addition to viewing the Depression as a punishment for wrongdoing, some Baptists asserted that God had brought difficulty upon his people to test their mettle, to probe the foundations of their faith. They reasoned that since God had selected them to bear his message he had to be certain they would persevere under trying circumstances. He had to make sure that Baptists would not falter when tormented by affliction.[34] Baptists uttered no complaints at God's severity, praying instead that they would pass the test and emerge better Christians, ready to face the world with renewed vigor. "Surely they will stand the test," Austin Crouch of the Sunday School Board wrote. "If they do, they will come out of the fire with spirit refined and enriched and with a new sense of power and solidarity."[35]

Southern Baptists thus saw the Depression as a direct act of God. The Lord had used it to punish America and the Baptist denomination for their sins and to recall them to righteousness. He had also instigated the Depression to test Baptists, to cement their loyalty to Him, and to steel them for future battles with evil. If one actually believed this, and certainly many Baptists did, the Depression became a profound spiritual event. This did not ease physical hardship, nor did it make hunger and cold and financial instability pleasant. But it raised Baptists' suffering to a higher plane, giving them something to cling to through the long night of trouble.

Although Southern Baptists accepted the Depression as a divine occurrence, they rejected the idea of passive suffering. Believing in the adage that God helps those who help themselves, they sought to shake off the spiritual lassitude that had brought God's judgment upon them. "As I see it," William McGlothlin wrote in 1930, "what we need most of all is a profuse and vital revival among Christian people."[36] Many Southern Baptists offered this as a cure-all for the Depression. Hostile to the Social Gospel and committed to an individualistic religion, Southern Baptists advanced spiritual cures for temporal ills. The Riverside Baptist Church in Tampa, Florida, called upon Baptists to seek spiritual renewal and

---

[34]George Truett to Jefferson Ray, 6 April 1931, Ray Papers; *Herald*, 14 August 1930, p. 10.

[35]Austin Crouch, "The Critical Situation of the Baptist Bible Institute," ca. 1931 typescript, McGlothlin Papers, Reel 2.

[36]McGlothlin to D. F. Stamps, 20 August 1930, McGlothlin Papers, Reel 1.

advised the denomination's pastors to preach "sin, righteousness, and the judgment to come." The Mississippi *Baptist Record* noted approvingly the constant pleas for revival emanating from pulpit and religious press, and Victor Masters spoke of the need for a "deep spiritual quickening." Texas, as usual, furnished some of the most colorful exhortations. Ben H. Kelly of San Antonio, for example, advised pastors to awaken their congregations by preaching more "hell." J. Frank Norris took Kelly's words to heart, holding an "Old Fashioned Heaven-Sent Fire-Baptized Holy Ghost Sin-Convicting Mourners-Bench Shouting Revival" in Amarillo to exorcise the devils of the Depression.[37]

This emphasis on spiritual renewal may seem naive and inhumane in light of the privation that blanketed America and the South in the 1930s. But perhaps Baptists did not miss the point after all. The image of a mighty America brought to its knees through economic weakness had ravaged Americans' sense of well-being, weakening their will to combat the Depression and struggle back to normality. By urging men to turn inward, to rejuvenate their spirits, and to rekindle their religious fervor, Baptists helped their people regain this lost sense of well-being. Religion may well be at times the "opiate" of the masses, as Marxists contend, but it may also furnish the inner tenacity that enables men to overcome life's trials. Southern Baptists thus hit upon a vital truth in offering spiritual revival as an antidote to the Depression.

Because of their faith in God and their willingness to seek spiritual revival, Southern Baptists glimpsed a ray of hope amidst the distressing conditions of the Depression. No matter how bad conditions might be, they believed that God would watch over His chosen people and would shepherd them through the 1930s. An era ended on this note, for by the end of 1931 the period born in the optimistic aftermath of World War I had died. Baptists had entered this era filled with enthusiasm, convinced of their ability to spread the gospel to a sinful world. Their optimism had been muted by the trials of the 1920s and brought to the breaking point by the hard times of the early thirties. Southern Baptists had been forced to set aside plans for quick conquest of the world. But their goals had remained the same; in 1931, as in 1919, Southern Baptists spoke of the

---

[37]Florida, *Annual*, 1931, p. 12; *Record*, 24 September 1931, p. 4; Victor Masters to William McGlothlin, 9 December 1931, McGlothlin Papers, Reel 2; Ben H. Kelly, "What Is the Matter with the World?," pp. 8-9, typescript of an address delivered 26 July 1931, Norris Papers, Box 22; *Fundamentalist*, 21 November 1930, p. 1.

need to preach the gospel to all mankind. They saw that their task would be more difficult than they had anticipated, but they were better for it. The glib, often mindless, optimism of 1919 had been burned away, leaving a more realistic perception of the world and the Baptist place in it. Those who amidst the discouragement and pessimism of 1931 took the long view could see that Southern Baptists would survive the vicissitudes of the past dozen years, just as they had struggled successfully through centuries of trials and difficulties. Even if the situation looked bleak in 1931 they knew that Baptists would shake off their spiritual malaise, regain financial stability, and continue to witness for Christ.

Epilogue

Most Southern Baptists would gladly have closed the books on the period 1919 to 1931 and never have reopened them. Worry over outside foes, internal conflict, financial instability, and declining spiritual vitality had disrupted well-laid plans, turning a period of promise into an era of unfulfilled dreams. But as much as Baptists wanted to forget the twenties, they could not. The issues lingered on, forcing Southern Baptists to confront them again and again. But if the issues remained, the response to them became less intense, less charged with anxiety. After passing through the turmoil of the 1920s many Southern Baptists were ready to deal more calmly with the religious problems of the twentieth century. The story of Southern Baptists from 1931 to the present involves the coming of age of the denomination, a restoration of its vitality and self-confidence, and a marked improvement in its ability to cope with the trials of the world.

In their relations with other churches Southern Baptists have toned down their militant denominationalism. They still shun ecumenism, refusing to join the National Council of Churches or its international counterpart, the World Council. But as members of America's largest Protestant denomination they no longer feel compelled to scrap with other churches or to warn of interdenominational conspiracies. This self-assurance has enabled Southern Baptists to develop fraternal ties with men of other faiths and has permitted such evangelists as Billy

Graham to preach the gospel with little reference to church affiliation. The insularity of the 1920s has given way to a friendlier attitude toward other Protestants, and concern over the ecumenical movement has lessened.[1]

The debate over the church's obligation to promote social reform has continued to bother Southern Baptists. Their belief in individual sin and personal salvation has kept them adamantly opposed to the Social Gospel, but as the denomination has become more sophisticated and urban, Baptists have begun to realize that Christians cannot ignore society's defects. McNeill Poteat tried to convince his brethren of this in the 1930s when he proposed that a research agency be established to study such problems as poverty, racism, and the plight of industrial workers. But Poteat was ahead of his time; the Southern Baptist Convention rejected his idea in 1936. By the end of World War II Baptists were more receptive to such suggestions. In 1946 the Social Service Commission asked the Southern Baptist Convention to appoint a committee to study race relations. The Convention complied, and the committee's report, presented a year later, started Baptists on their way toward facing the South's number one social problem. In the same year the Convention granted the Social Service Commission a full-time staff headed by Hugh Brimm, who only three years earlier, in a doctoral thesis written at Southern Seminary, had pointed out Baptist shortcomings in dealing with blacks, farm tenants, migrant workers, and mill hands. Brimm's appointment marked the beginning of increased efforts to convince Baptists of their duty to minister to their fellow man. Southern Baptists, indeed all Southern Protestants, may lag behind their Northern brethren in trying to rectify society's shortcomings. Yet many of the South's Baptists, particularly the young, no longer believe that an evangelical theology precludes sensitivity to society's ills.[2]

Since the 1920s Southern Baptists have avoided major internal conflicts over theological liberalism. Fundamentalists gained a wide hearing

---

[1]William R. Estep, *Baptists and Christian Unity* (Nashville: Broadman Press, 1966), p. 158; Bob W. Brown, "A Southern Baptist Talks about Southern Baptist Hang-ups," *Christian Herald* 94 (April 1971): 18.

[2]*Encyclopaedia of Southern Baptists* 2 vols. (Nashville: Broadman Press, 1958), 1:260; Hugh A. Brimm, "The Social Consciousness of Southern Baptists in Relation to Some Regional Problems, 1910-1935" (Th.D. thesis, Southern Baptist Theological Seminary, 1944); Brown, "Southern Baptist Hang-Ups," p. 24. An excellent study of

in the 1920s through their defense of the Bible and their leadership of the fight against Darwinism, but they failed to win control of the denomination. Although Norris continued to snipe at the Southern Baptist Convention until his death in 1952, he had lost most of his influence by the mid-1930s. Norris's failure did not mean that liberalism had triumphed, for the denomination remained conservative, with a sprinkling of moderates and liberals. But most Southern Baptists, regardless of their own views on the millennium, rejected Norris's attempt to make dispensationalism the test of orthodoxy.

Despite the lessening of theological strife after the 1920s, conservatives have remained on guard against the encroachments of liberalism. For this reason, controversies over the Bible have continued to surface. Early in 1969 Broadman Press, the Southern Baptist publishing house in Nashville, issued a book by Convention President Wallie A. Criswell entitled *Why I Preach That the Bible Is Literally True*. Criswell, pastor of the church in Dallas once served by George Truett, reaffirmed the validity of the Genesis account of creation and urged that literalism alone was the proper means of studying the Bible. The Association of Baptist Professors of Religion criticized the book and warned of the danger of "harassment, biblicism, and witch hunting." In June of 1969, at the annual meeting of the Southern Baptist Convention, dissenters from Criswell's literalism nominated Dr. William C. Smith, Jr., assistant professor of religion at the University of Richmond, for the Convention presidency. Conservatives united behind Criswell and easily beat back the challenge. But liberal discontent continued to mount, and in April 1970, Smith and another teacher at the University of Richmond withdrew from the denomination. Two months later, at the Convention's meeting in Denver, conservatives lashed out at the liberals, demanding that Broadman Press withdraw a commentary on Genesis and Exodus that presented both liberal and conservative positions.[3] Despite this renewal of theological warfare one may safely assume that Southern Baptists will not repeat the internecine warfare of the 1920s. Moderating influences have progressed too far to be stopped, and besides, W. A. Criswell is no J. Frank Norris. Southern Baptists remain wary of liberalism, but the

---

social involvement among Southern Protestants may be found in Samuel S. Hill, Jr., *Southern Churches in Crisis* (New York: Holt, Rinehart, and Winston, 1966).

[3]"Southern Baptists and the Bible," *Christianity Today* 13 (25 April 1969): 34; *Washington Post*, 7 April 1970, p. B6; 4 June 1970, p. A26.

frantic acrimony of the twenties has been left behind.

Southern Baptists have also calmed down over the issues raised by the Presidential election of 1928. The mention of Roman Catholicism no longer creates images of sexually depraved priests and bloodthirsty inquisitors. Baptists still eye their Catholic countrymen uneasily at times, but the venomous anti-Catholicism of the 1920s seldom reappears. The casual attitude of many Catholics toward the separation of church and state still troubles Baptists, but John F. Kennedy showed that the Republic would not topple with a Roman Catholic in the White House.[4] In addition, the immigrant threat, so closely allied with Baptists' fear of Catholicism in the 1920s, has waned. Restrictions on immigration and the Americanization of newcomers and their children have allayed the fears of Protestant Anglo-Saxons.

Finally, urbanization no longer gnaws at the Baptist sense of well-being as it did in the twenties. The average Baptist would still probably complain that the nation's cities foster crime, vice, and irreligion, but he does not fear them as he once did. For one thing, the South has urbanized rapidly since World War I. Atlanta, New Orleans, Houston, and Dallas rank among the nation's leading cities, while Little Rock, Memphis, Birmingham, Louisville, Richmond, and dozens of smaller cities have made urbanization a reality in the South. In 1920 only one Southern Convention state—Maryland—had an urban majority; in 1960 nine states had passed the fifty per cent mark, with Texas and Florida listing three-fourths of their population as urban.[5] And Baptists have made peace with these cities. The towering headquarters of the Sunday School Board in Nashville, the seminaries in Louisville, New Orleans, and Fort Worth, and the impressive churches in such places as Richmond and Dallas demonstrate that Southern Baptists no longer see themselves as innocent rustics fighting to preserve rural purity.

The final problem encountered by Baptists from 1919 to 1931—spiritual and economic depression—has also been altered by the passage of time. From the spiritual and financial depths of the early 1930s the

---

[4]For recent Southern Baptist attitudes toward Roman Catholicism, see Ira V. Birdwhistell, "Southern Baptist Perceptions of and Responses to Roman Catholicism (Ph.D. dissertation, Southern Baptist Theological Seminary, 1975).

[5]U.S. Bureau of the Census, *Statistical Abstract of the United States: 1920* (Washington, D. C., 1921), p. 49, chart 30; *Statistical Abstract of the United States: 1970* (Washington, D.C., 1970), p. 17, chart 16.

denomination has progressed to its present state. The Southern Baptist Convention has become the largest Protestant denomination in the United States, with almost fourteen million members in 35,831 churches. Migration to the North and West, combined with Baptist evangelism, has led to growth outside the South. State organizations (there are now 34 state conventions) affiliated with the Southern Baptist Convention have been established in many non-Southern states, including Alaska and Hawaii. Southern Baptists annually contribute more than two billion dollars to finance an impressive array of missionary, educational, and publishing endeavors. Southern Baptists publish some 150 periodicals, and devotional and scholarly books pour from the presses in Nashville. The Home Mission Board, mired in debt in the 1920s and 1930s, employs over 2,900 missionaries in the U.S. and territories. The Foreign Mission Board has over 3,000 missionaries, and operates missions schools, universities, and seminaries; hospitals, clinics, and dispensaries; vast agricultural projects, and many other programs and projects, in addition to the regular evangelistic programs, in 100 countries around the world. The state conventions of the Southern Baptist Convention operate dozens of schools, colleges, and universities; and the convention itself operates six of the most vigorous theological seminaries in the world. By every standard the Southern Baptist Convention constitutes one of the most aggressive and successful denominations in America.[6]

Given the unity, prosperity, and vitality now typical of Southern Baptists, memories of the tumultuous years from 1919 to 1931 have no doubt grown dim. The issues of the period have either disappeared or been sharply transmuted by the passage of years. Small wonder that few Southern Baptists today realize that less than fifty years ago these issues produced fear and anxiety, split the denomination into warring factions, and prevented Baptists from channeling their full energies into preaching the gospel to a sinful world.

---

[6]The above statistics are for 1980, as reported in the *Annual of the Southern Baptist Convention*, 1981. For a recent general survey of the SBC, see Robert A. Baker, *The Southern Baptist Convention and Its People, 1607-1972* (Nashville: Broadman Press, 1974).

Bibliographical Note

The footnotes reveal the sources from which I have drawn this study. A lengthy bibliography which lists every item I consulted would be of limited value. However, it does seem appropriate to comment further on some of the materials I used.

Primary Sources. The scholar who delves into the history of Southern Baptists in the 1920s finds a staggering number of books and articles written by Southern Baptists. Works of all kinds abound: memoirs and autobiographies, inspirational works, collections of sermons, biblical studies, theological treatises, denominational histories, histories of Baptists within individual states, and works on Baptist endeavors in education and home and foreign missions. The books and articles of several men were especially helpful; among these are T. T. Martin, Victor I. Masters, E. Y. Mullins, William L. Poteat, A. T. Robertson, and Lee R. Scarborough.

The records of the annual Southern Baptist Convention meetings, as well as similar records for the yearly gatherings of state Baptist conventions, furnish a superb source for following the official activities of Southern Baptists in the 1920s. All the controversies that plagued the denomination in this period show up—if only indirectly at times—in these records.

Baptist periodicals published within each state provide a rich source of information. These periodicals focused on state activities, but they also contain articles, sermons, and polemical essays. Although the editorials reflect the idiosyncrasies of the individual editors, they serve as an excellent means of tracing developments in Baptist thinking. I read every issue of three of these periodicals—the Mississippi *Baptist Record*, the Oklahoma *Baptist Messenger*, and the Virginia *Religious Herald*—for the years 1919 to 1931. I chose these three in order to gauge Baptist opinion in three areas of the South: the Southeast, the deep South, and the Southwest. I also read all the issues of J. Frank Norris's *Searchlight* (renamed the *Fundamentalist* in April 1927) for these same years. Norris's paper is the best place to look for the most extreme views among Southern Baptists during the 1920s.

An abundance of manuscript collections exists for studying Baptists in the 1920s. Wake Forest University, Baylor University, Southern Seminary in Louisville, Southwestern Seminary in Fort Worth, and the Dargan-Carver Library of the Sunday School Board in Nashville hold the papers of a number of prominent Southern Baptists. I worked my way through the letters and documents in twenty-three of these collections, but I found most helpful the papers of J. Frank Norris, Samuel P. Brooks, E. Y. Mullins, William L. Poteat, A. T. Robertson, Lee. R. Scarborough, and George W. Truett.

Secondary Works. As with the primary sources, my footnotes show the scholarly books and articles of which I made direct use. Beyond these studies which I have cited, I consulted hundreds of books, articles, and dissertations. Again, it seems pointless to list all of these works. I would, however, like to mention a number of books that I heavily relied upon for information or as interpretative aids in clarifying my ideas. Mentioning these also allows me to record my debt to some of the scholars who made my own work easier.

One of the most important issues for Southern Baptists in the 1920s involved the debate over the degree to which the church should participate in social reform. For the broader Protestant debate on this matter I used Paul A. Carter's *The Decline and Revival of the Social Gospel: Social and Political Liberalism in American Protestant Churches, 1920-1940* (Ithaca: Cornell University Press, 1956). In examining this matter among Southern Baptists I drew upon two studies. Rufus B. Spain's *At Ease in Zion: Social History of Southern Baptists, 1865-1900* (Nashville: Vanderbilt University Press, 1967) helped me to understand the background of the period I studied, and John L. Eighmy's doctoral dissertation, "The Social Conscience of Southern Baptists from 1900 to the Present as Reflected in Their Organized Life" (University of Missouri, 1959), guided me through Baptist social attitudes in the twentieth century. Eighmy's excellent study was published in 1972 by the University of Tennessee Press under the title *Churches in Cultural Captivity: A History of the Social Attitudes of Southern Baptists.*

A key part of my book involves Southern Baptists' participation in the controversy between fundamentalists and modernists. Since the decade of the 1920s ended, this controversy has furnished a fruitful ground for scholarly study. Dozens of books and articles have examined the struggle between modernists and fundamentalists from every imaginable angle. I consulted most of this material, but I found several books to be of particular help. William R. Hutchison's *The Modernist Impulse in American Protestantism* (Cambridge, Massachusetts: Harvard University Press, 1976) defined for me the amorphous term "modernism." Norman F. Furniss, *The Fundamentalist Controversy, 1918-1931* (New Haven: Yale University Press, 1954); Stewart G. Cole, *The History of Fundamentalism* (New York: Richard Smith, 1931); and Maynard Shipley, *The War on Modern Science: A Short History of Fundamentalist Attacks on Evolution and Modernism* (New York: Knopf, 1927) provided much basic information on the controversy. C. Allyn Russell's *Voices of American Fundamentalism: Seven Biographical Studies* (Philadelphia: Westminster, 1976) offered insight into the workings of fundamentalism outside of the South. My greatest debt in this matter of fundamentalism is to Ernest R. Sandeen's *The Roots of Fundamentalism: British and American Millenarianism, 1800-1930* (Chicago: University of Chicago Press, 1970). Sandeen clarified many ideas that I had fitfully been trying to put together. George M. Marsden's *Fundamentalism and American Culture: The Shaping of Twentieth Century Evangelicalism, 1870-1925* (New York: 1980), possibly the best book to date on fundamentalism, unfortunately appeared too late to have much impact on my own interpretation of Southern Baptist fundamentalism.

The Presidential election of 1928 proved of immense importance for Southern Baptists because the issues it raised made it a focal point for Baptist discontent in the 1920s. Edmund A. Moore's *A Catholic Runs for President: The Campaign of 1928* (New York: Ronald Press, 1956) helped me to understand much about this event.

Index of Subjects

(A number of terms that appear with considerable frequency throughout the book have not been indexed. These include: catholicism, conservatism, Darwinism, evangelism, evolution, fundamentalism, higher criticism, interdenominationalism, liberalism, modernism, premillennialism, social Christianity, and Social Gospel. Entire chapters or parts of chapters are devoted to most of these topics; in addition, some of these subjects can be found under the names of persons listed in the Index of Persons.)

Index of Persons